# ABC's of Cultural Understanding and Communication

## National and International Adaptations

*a volume in*
Literacy, Language, and Learning

*Series Editor:*
Patricia Ruggiano Schmidt,
*Le Moyne College*

# Literacy, Language, and Learning

Patricia Ruggiano Schmidt, Series Editor

*Preparing Educators to Communicate and Connect with
Families and Communities* (2005)
edited by Patricia Ruggiano Schmidt

*Reading and Writing Ourselves Into Being:
The Literacy of Certain Nineteenth-Century Young Women* (2004)
by Claire White Putala

*Reconceptualizing Literacy in the New Age of
Multiculturalism and Pluralism* (2001)
edited by Patricia Ruggiano Schmidt and Peter B. Mosenthal

# ABC's of Cultural Understanding and Communication

## National and International Adaptations

*edited by*

**Patricia Ruggiano Schmidt**
*Le Moyne College,*
*Syracuse, New York*

and

**Claudia Finkbeiner**
*Universität Kassel,*
*Kassel, Germany*

INFORMATION AGE
PUBLISHING

Greenwich, Connecticut • www.infoagepub.com

**Library of Congress Cataloging-in-Publication Data**

ABC's of cultural understanding and communication : national and
   international adaptations / edited by Patricia Ruggiano Schmidt and
   Claudia Finkbeiner.
      p. cm. — (Language, literacy, and learning)
   Includes bibliographical references and index.
   ISBN 1-59311-464-8 (hardcover : alk. paper); 1-59311-463-X (paperback)
1. Multicultural education.    I. Schmidt, Patricia Ruggiano,
1944-
II. Finkbeiner, Claudia. III. Series.
   LC1099.A1235 2006
   370.117—dc22

                                                 2006000199


ISBN 13: 978-1-59311-463-3 (pbk.)
           978-1-59311-464-0 (hardcover)
ISBN 10: 1-59311-463-X (pbk.)
           1-59311-464-8 (hardcover)

Printed in the United States of America

# CONTENTS

# ACKNOWLEDGMENTS

We are grateful to present and future teachers, students, teacher educators, researchers, and colleagues who made this volume possible. Their cultural understanding, communication, and appreciation of similarities and differences have helped us realize that true unity comes with a celebration of diversity. They have taught us as we were teaching them. Our hope is that this grand transatlantic collaboration grows and develops as we adapt the *ABC's of Cultural Understanding and Communication*, both locally and globally.

# FOREWORD

**Patricia A. Edwards**

In 1993, I first heard Patricia Ruggiano Schmidt talk about the "ABC's Model" she had designed to help present and future teachers develop comfort levels and communication skills when attempting to understand students and families from diverse racial, ethnic, and social-class groups. She also linked the resulting powerful understandings and relationships to literacy development. It was immediately apparent that this model would be an invaluable source of information for all educators, researchers, and teacher educators. Well, my prediction was correct. Schmidt's collaboration with Claudia Finkbeiner has created a text that is a compilation of fascinating adaptations of the ABC's Model in a variety of settings in the United States and Europe.

For years, teacher educators have passionately presented the case explaining why teachers needed to learn how to work with culturally different students, families, and communities. Schmidt's and Finkbeiner's edited text is a powerful response to this passionate plea. This book promises to make a significant contribution. It should be read by all teacher educators as well as preservice and in-service teachers. In the new millennium teachers must redefine their responsibilities to ensure that *ALL* students have the opportunity to succeed. *ABC's of Cultural Understanding and Communication: National and International Adaptations* is a perfect place to start.

# CHAPTER 1

# WHAT IS THE ABC'S OF CULTURAL UNDERSTANDING AND COMMUNICATION?

### Patricia Ruggiano Schmidt and Claudia Finkbeiner

## INTRODUCTION

The *ABC's of Cultural Understanding and Communication* is an intercultural model that includes (a) autobiography, (b) biography, (c) cross-cultural analysis, (d) cultural self-analysis of differences, and (e) communication plans for connecting home, school and community for literacy learning. This book deals with applications and adaptations of the model on a global scale.

The purpose of this introductory chapter is to explain the theoretical orientation of the *ABC's Model*, the literature to support the design of the model, the rationale for including the model in teacher preparation programs, and the organization of the book chapters. But first, an explanation is in order for how the idea for this book originated.

## HOW THIS BOOK BEGAN: TWO PERSPECTIVES

### Dr. Schmidt's Perspective

Claudia Finkbeiner and I, teacher educators, met at the 1998 World Congress in Reading, Jamaica, and immediately began to discuss the sim-

*ABC's of Cultural Understanding and Communication:*
*National and International Adaptations,* 1–18
Copyright © 2006 by Information Age Publishing
All rights of reproduction in any form reserved.

ilarities and differences in our research. Claudia Finkbeiner teaches inter-cultural communication and foreign language research at the University of Kassel, in Kassel, Germany; I teach multicultural literacy courses at Le Moyne College, Syracuse, New York. We soon realized that collaboratively we might make a significant difference in the preparation of present and future teachers. Therefore, we began collecting, analyzing, and present-ing data gathered from teachers and researchers in the United States and Europe who have implemented my model known as the *ABC's of Cultural Understanding and Communication* (1998). For her intercultural studies classes, Dr. Finkbeiner designed adaptations of the *ABC's Model* and from that work, derived her own intercultural model (Finkbeiner, in this book, 2005; Finkbeiner & Koplin, 2001, 2002). Thus, the idea for this book took shape as we began to see and hear about successful adaptations and appli-cations of the *ABC's Model* from researchers, teachers, and students who have experienced the process. Many of their life changing insights, recorded here, demonstrate how the ABC's affected their teaching, learn-ing, and appreciation of differences.

## Dr. Finkbeiner's Perspective

I have worked with Patricia Ruggiano Schmidt for many years. Right from the beginning, we developed and shared a very inspiring and syner-gistic international research partnership. Early on, it was clear that we fol-lowed comparable principles and goals in intercultural communication. We not only shared respect and interest for each other's work, but we were convinced that the real challenge of our intercultural learning experi-ences was to bring together multiple perspectives from differing parts of the world: views and experiences collected in the Old World with views and experiences gathered in the New World.

## Our Perspective

We started our international team by sharing and comparing our research outcomes during international conferences, such as the annual National Reading Conferences (NRC) and the biannually held World Congress of the International Reading Association. We continued by implementing ideas we learned from each other in new settings and by recruiting young and dynamic researchers and teachers on both sides of the Atlantic, who were willing to break new ground for intercultural learn-ing and research. This group grew annually as we developed this interest-ing and challenging joint venture. Although, this book contains only a few examples of the research gathered from the ABC's Model and intercul-tural learning, we hope these will stimulate implementation and adaptation in teacher education programs worldwide. This is why we have included the voices of authors from different ethnic, cultural, and linguistic backgrounds who bring successful examples to the teacher educator and to present and future teachers for their research, classes, and in-service programs.

## THEORETICAL ORIENTATION

### Sociocultural Perspective

This book is situated in the sociocultural perspective, a social constructivist approach for understanding literacy learning (Heath, 1983; Purcell-Gates, L'Allier, & Smith, 1995; Rogoff, 1990; Trueba, Jacobs, & Kirton, 1990; Vygotsky, 1978). In classrooms embracing this perspective, children construct meaning through social interactions across and within cultural settings. They become literate within the cultures of home, school, and community as they construct the classroom culture (Dyson, 1989; Finkbeiner & Koplin, 2001, 2002; Heath, 1983; Moll, 1992; Schiefflin & Cochran-Smith, 1984; Taylor, 1983; Taylor & Dorsey-Gaines, 1988; Wells, 1986). Therefore, the sociocultural perspective is created by students and teachers who elect to bring the home cultures into social interactions and contribute to the definitions of language and literacy (Bloome & Green, 1982; Kantor, Miller, & Fernie, 1992). This book, based on sociocultural research, focuses upon the complexity of developing literacy within cultures of home, school, and community as well as the structural aspects of language (Cummins, 1986; Purcell-Gates et al., 1995; Vygotsky, 1978). With this theoretical perspective in mind, critical literacy logically follows.

### Critical Literacy

This book embraces critical literacy, a theoretical concept that sees literacy teaching and learning as "never neutral" (Powell, Cantrell, & Adams, 2001). Critical literacy is a powerful concept that confronts dominance and equity issues. It deals with democratic principles and promotes strong democratic values (Edelsky, 1991). Students are encouraged to be critical of all reading writing, speaking, listening and viewing that they encounter (Rogers, 1999). The aim of critical literacy is to strengthen and alter student literacy learning, so that they will be moved to the action needed to transform societal injustices (Banks, 1994).

Critical literacy and the sociocultural perspective serve as the foundation for the *ABC's of Cultural Understanding and Communication*. Present and future teachers who become involved in the process begin to critically discuss and evaluate their experiences. They begin to look inward and outward simultaneously, and describe a discomfort, disequilibrium, or anxiety often associated with learning new information that conflicts with old ideas and norms. What frequently occurs in many classes, soon after the discomfort, is an "Ahah! Phase," one in which students actually echo the old saw, "Know thyself and understand others."

## KNOW THYSELF AND UNDERSTAND OTHERS: THE ABC'S MODEL

The key to the *ABC's Model* is "Know thyself, understand others." Teacher education programs that use reading, writing, listening, and speaking to create consciousness-raising experiences, help teachers gain a knowledge of self and others through autobiographies, biographies, reflection on diversity issues, and cross-cultural analysis (Cochran-Smith, 1995; Florio-Ruane, 1994; Noordhoff & Kleinfield, 1993; Spindler & Spindler, 1987; Tatum, 1992; Willis & Meacham, 1997). However, those programs have not linked self-knowledge to teachers' implementation of home, school, and community connections for literacy instruction. Therefore, the ABC's of Cultural Understanding and Communication (Schmidt, 1998b) is a model designed to fill this gap in teacher education. K-12, present and future teachers who experience the model's process often begin to successfully connect home, school, and community for literacy learning (Finkbeiner & Koplin, 2001, 2002; Leftwich, 2001; Nagel, 2002; Schmidt, 1998c, 1999, 2000, 2001; Xu, 2000a,b). The following paragraphs briefly explain the five-step process.

*Autobiography.*   First, each present or future teacher writes an autobiography that includes key life events related to education, family, religious tradition, recreation, victories, defeats, et al. This helps to build awareness of personal beliefs and attitudes that form the traditions and values of cultural autobiographies (Banks, 1994). Since it is well documented that writing is linked to knowledge of self within a social context (Emig, 1971; Yinger, 1985), writing one's life story seems to construct connections with universal human tenets and serves to lessen negative notions about different groups of people (Progoff, 1975). Also, the autobiographies are confidential, only the teacher educator sees them. Quality is determined by the details written, but no evaluation is given, only encouragement to write more, if possible. (This seems to promote more candid responses.) This autobiography experience sets the stage for the second step, learning about the lives of culturally different people (Banks, 1994; Sjoberg & Kuhn, 1989).

*Biography.*   After several in depth, audiotaped, unstructured or semi-structured interviews (Bogdan & Biklen, 1994; Spradley, 1979) of a person who is culturally different, each present or future teacher constructs a biography from key events in that selected person's life. Teachers are encouraged to choose a student's parent or guardian. They may begin the interview with asking the parent to tell what he or she would want the child to learn this year. This is a way of allowing parents to voice their ideas and begin developing a comfort level with the teacher. During the interview, the teacher shares some personal, relevant, life events. This allows for a give and take that create a more democratic interview setting. Also, it is recommended that the interviews occur in a place that the parent requests … possibly neutral ground, such as a park, coffee shop, or recreation center. (School may be considered hostile or intimidating for some family members or parents who fear educational settings.) When teachers meet with family members and learn about their lives, they begin to learn the cultural sensitivity necessary to analyze similarities and differences between life stories (Schmidt, 1998b,c, 2000; Spindler & Spindler, 1987).

*Cross-cultural analysis.* For the third step in the process, each present or future teacher studies the autobiography and biography and charts a list of similarities and differences. This may be accomplished in a list or Venn diagram. The Venn Diagram is two intersecting circles clearly showing differences and similarities. This leads to the fourth step, or self-analysis of differences, a key component of the process (Cummins, 1986; Derman-Sparks, 1992; Finkbeiner, 2005; Finkbeiner & Koplin 2001, 2002; McCaleb, 1994; Osetek, in this book; Paley, 1989; Spindler & Spindler, 1987; Trueba et al., 1990).

*Appreciation of differences.* The present or future teacher then carefully examines the diagram that lists similarities and differences and writes an in depth self-analysis of cultural differences. She or he explains how the differences make he or she feel, i.e., "Why am I feeling uncomfortable about this difference? Why do I admire this difference?" Present and future teachers write about these feelings in specific detail. Through this process, teachers begin to acquire insights about others and sense their own ethnocentricity (Spindler & Spindler, 1987).

*Home/school/community connection plans for literacy development.* After experiencing the previous steps, K-12 teachers (Kindergarten to grade 12 teachers) design year-long plans for connecting home, school, and community for children's reading, writing, listening, and speaking, based on numerous modifications of the *ABC's Model*. They see ways to design culturally relevant lessons. For example, a math teacher studies ethnomathematics and uses indigenous people's designs to teach geometry, a biology teacher explains DNA through human cell characteristics and their adaptations to environments, and a first grade teacher celebrates an appreciation of differences through, multicultural crayon, self-portraits. The myriad of examples are inspiring when teachers actually learn to take notice and see that true unity comes with an appreciation of differences (Ruggiano Schmidt, in this book). And European teachers find similar understandings as they pursue adaptations of the ABC's and other intercultural models.

## The ABC's Model: European Adaptation

The *ABC's Model* has been adapted by Finkbeiner and colleagues (Finkbeiner & Koplin, 2001, 2002) within the European context in order to take into account the special sociocultural characteristics in a continuously changing Europe. These are,

1.  The geographic closeness of the European countries.
2.  The linguistic and cultural multi-perspectives, the European dimension (Finkbeiner, 1995) as expressed in the Maastricht treaty.
3.  The permanent change that has taken place in Europe since 1989.
4.  The challenges that can be seen in the continuous expansion and growth of the European Union.

The European adaptations of the ABC's enables situational and intercultural communication and allows participants' cognitive and affective processes to be taken seriously (Finkbeiner & Koplin, 2001, 2002). This cooperative, collaborative approach fosters intercultural learning goals together with cooperative values that can contribute to the development of responsible citizens (Finkbeiner, 2002, 2003, 2004). It is believed that cooperative practice promotes student achievement and facilitates democratic and social processes.

In the university setting, face-to-face contact with people from different cultures and exposure to their life stories can make students (and, in an adapted version, students in secondary schools) prepared for a lifelong intercultural learning process (Finkbeiner & Koplin, 2001, p. 120). The following outlines the adaptations of Schmidt's *ABC's Model*.

## FINKBEINER'S AND KOPLIN' S ADAPTATION OF SCHMIDT'S MODEL

*   Writing an autobiography to explore self-image and cultural self-concepts.
*   Eliciting thinking about cultural concepts through dialogue with a partner.
*   Conducting reciprocal or triangular narrative interviews focusing on relevant aspects of each partner's life story.
*   Writing reciprocal or triangular biographies.
*   Analyzing self-image and image of the partner by relating and comparing images.

- Conducting reciprocal interviews to validate the biographies, clarify, resolve misunderstandings, and make comparisons.
- Creating a metacognitive reflection of the learning process through an intercultural diary.
- Raising awareness with intercultural communication strategies.

To date, university students have been offered rich opportunities for exploration through the *ABC's Model* within their courses. Students have found partners from different cultures with whom to work on the ABC's and on intercultural learning. They commit to being both a researcher and a research subject (Finkbeiner, 2001, 2003, 2004) which requires a willingness to be interviewed as part of a partner's research. This encourages a highly cooperative approach that brings an invigorating spirit to the classroom.

After preparing their autobiographies, conducting interviews, and writing biographies of their partners, participants discover that their perspectives are bound to their cultural knowledge. A cross-cultural analysis follows, in which the future teachers reflect on differences and similarities between biographies. While transcribing their conversations, participants reflect on their learning processes, in detail. In addition, they are asked to look for communication strategies that the transcriptions reveal: What do you do when you have to talk about misunderstandings, differences, or similarities with someone from a different cultural background? And, finally, an intercultural diary is written to reflect on the learning process as a whole. In an elementary or secondary school setting, this model is less complex. However, the writing of an autobiography, the interview, the writing of a biography, a discussion, and a diary entry are all necessary components. In addition, in schools, international visitors are invited to class for this process, and students are informed and prepared to participate in the experience. Before the visitor arrives, students discuss preconceived notions that they may have about a particular culture. This allows students to dispel any fears or stereotypes and to reflect on their image of the visitor during and after an interview.

## The Language Issue in the European Adaptation

The *ABC's Model* is used in English as a foreign language class (Finkbeiner, 2004). At the beginning of the ABC's implementation, autobiographies and biographies are written in English, the common *lingua franca*. However, it was discovered that it was difficult to share life stories, since there were varying English proficiencies. Also, there were 10 to 15 native languages represented in classes. Even for those who spoke English exceptionally well, it was difficult (and, for some, off putting) to express life stories in a language different from the one in which the life stories themselves are situated. Schemata and scripts often differ considerably, and values as well as attributions are not comparable. This means that the events described in the stories do not always translate easily from the native tongue into English. Very often the words were just not there (Finkbeiner & Koplin, 2002). For example, in Turkish or Chinese, there are different words for *brother-in-law*, depending on whether one is referring to the man's or woman's family. In those cultures, the male and female family categories are more distinct and culturally more important. Such cultural issues explain the importance of biographical validation.

When the biography was read aloud by the author, the person whose life story was being related was encouraged to clarify, reject, or intervene if misinterpretations resulted from language or cultural differences. The validation was only effective, if it was considered a cooperative act between researcher and subject (Finkbeiner, 2001, 2003, 2004).

The language issue had to be carefully considered even more in the secondary school setting. Proficiency levels in English as a second, foreign, or other language are generally lower among these students than among those in the university setting, and the challenges even greater. Issues related to cultural differences in schemata and scripts and the implications for second and foreign language teaching methodology or intercultural education were necessary research concentrations. However, despite the challenges, the advantages in asking students to write about their lives in a nonnative language are evident. This literacy activity seemed to create a distance that allowed students to reflect on their lives and write more easily, particularly when the life story had been tragic, or traumatic (Finkbeiner & Koplin, 2002).

After several years of research on the language issue, a possible solution has emerged (Finkbeiner, 2005): the autobiography ought to be written in the mother tongue, as personal life stories are best described in one's own language. The biography is written in English as lingua franca, so that discourse is possible in multilingual settings. If there is another second or third shared language that can function as a lingua franca among the participants, such as Spanish; German, French etc. that language should be chosen for the biography. Again, this research appears to emphasize the necessity for cultural understanding in successful language learning and meaningful communication.

## The Research Rationale for Cultural Understanding and Communication

Research and practice demonstrate that strong home, school, and community connections not only help students make sense of the school curriculum, but also promote literacy development (Au, 1993; Edwards, 1995, 1996; Faltis, 1993; Finkbeiner, 2005; Goldenberg, 1987; Heath, 1983; Leftwich, 2001; McCaleb, 1994; Moll, 1992; Reyhner & Gracia, 1989; Schmidt, 2000; Xu, 2000b). However, for several reasons, in recent years, home, school, and community connections have become a significant challenge. First, as school populations on either side of the Atlantic have become increasingly diverse, both culturally and ethnically, teaching populations have remained homogeneous. Teachers, however, are usually from European and American, suburban, cultural experiences. Typically, educators in the United States describe themselves as white and middle class and often add, during discussions about diversity, "I'm an American; I don't have a culture," (Florio-Ruane, 1994; McIntosh, 1990; Paley, 1989; Schmidt, 1999; Snyder, Hoffman, C. M., & Geddes, 1997). Second, despite the fact that both the United States and many European countries, such as Germany, England, France and the Netherlands, have turned into multicultural societies, most present and future teachers have not had sustained relationships with people from different ethnic, cultural, and lower socioeconomic backgrounds. As a result, much of their knowledge about diversity has been influenced by media stereotypes (Pattnaik, 1997; Tatum, 1997). Third, school curriculum, methods, and materials usually reflect only European, European American or white culture and ignore the backgrounds and experiences of students and families from lower socioeconomic levels and differing ethnic and cultural backgrounds (Boykin, 1978, 1984; Delpit, 1995; Foster, 1994; Howard, 2001; Ladson-Billings, 1994, 1995; Moll, 1992; Nieto, 1996; Purcell-Gates, 1993; Sleeter & Grant, 1991; Walker-Dalhouse & Dalhouse, 2001). Fourth, many teacher education programs do not adequately prepare educators for "culturally relevant pedagogy" (Ladson-Billings, 1995) a term that directly relates to making strong home, school, and community connections (Gay & Howard, 2000; Lalik & Hinchman, 2001; Sleeter, 2001; Wallace, 2000). Consequently, this disconnect has become an international, national problem whose influence has been linked to poor literacy development and extremely high dropout rates among students from urban poverty areas (Au, 1993; Banks, 1994; Cummins, 1986; Edwards, Pleasants, & Franklin, 1999; Goldenberg, 1987; Heath, 1983; Nieto, 1999; Schmidt, 1998c; Trueba et al., 1990). This has also proven true in Germany, where the results of the second wave of the PISA Study (Program for International Student Assessment) directly revealed the huge educational disadvantage children from low income families and families with a migration background have to face. Obviously, this information concerning teacher education programs makes the promotion of cultural understanding and communication an urgent set of issues, but the ABC's Model and its adaptations provide opportunities for teachers to learn how to make home/school/community connections and create culturally relevant literacy lessons.

## Home/School/Community Connections and Culturally Relevant Pedagogy

Teachers who reach out to families and create connections to the curriculum are actually implementing culturally relevant pedagogy. Culturally relevant pedagogy or teaching connects the curriculum to the knowledge and experiences of the diverse cultures in the classrooms by validating student family backgrounds and experiences, and using the literacies found in the students' cultures. And when families from diverse ethnic and cultural backgrounds and lower socioeconomic levels become connected with the school, as resources for learning, there is often a narrowing of the student academic gap and an increase in positive attitudes toward school (Edwards et al., 1999; Faltis, 1993; Goldenberg, 1987; Moll, 1992).

A comprehensive study by Reyhner and Garcia (1989) showed a significant decrease in cultural discontinuity between home and school when teachers from European American backgrounds and families of Polynesian, Hispanic, and Native American students in Southwestern schools gathered resources to engage the children in classroom literacy activities that reflected their cultures. Within months, literacy performance significantly improved.

Studies of African American males indicate that learning by doing rather than emulation of "White Talk" allows them to gain conceptual understandings (Gordon, 1988; Murrel Jr., 1994). Furthermore, connecting learning to African American students' community, family interests, and values produces students who are enthusiastic, engaged, and ready to learn (Boykin 1978, 1984; Howard, 2001; Lee, 1991; Levine, 1994).

However, due to many educators lack of knowledge and understanding of the literacies related to particular cultures, they are frequently unable to connect school and community literacies. For instance, Moll's (1992) "funds of knowledge" demonstrates that many Latino students have mechanical abilities involving literacy skills related to their community's needs that usually go unrecognized in schools. Similarly, African American community literacies, such as oral storytelling, recitation, song, and poetry may also be ignored (Delpit, 1995; Edwards, Dandridge, McMillon, & Pleasant, 2001; Walker-Dalhouse & Dalhouse, 2001). Additionally, cultural conflict and struggles seem to be common occurrences for children from Asian backgrounds. Ethnographic research has (Pang & Cheng, 1998; Schmidt, 1998a; Trueba et al., 1990) demonstrated that family knowledge and traditions are typically ignored by teachers from European American backgrounds.

To counteract the insensitivity to community funds of knowledge, successful teacher education programs are attempting to prepare professionals who are responsive to diverse groups of children in their classrooms and make culturally compatible and dynamic connections between home and school (Cochran-Smith, 1995; Finkbeiner, 2004; Florio-Ruane, 1994; Noordhoff & Kleinfield, 1993; Schmidt, 1998b; Spindler & Spindler, 1987; Tatum, 1992; Willis & Meacham, 1997).

These successful teacher education or in-service programs incorporate culturally relevant pedagogy, authentic encounters with people from different backgrounds and experiences and the research related to racism, sexism, and classism (Cochran-Smith, 1995; Florio-Ruane, 1994; Noordhoff & Kleinfield, 1993; Osborne, 1996; Tatum, 1992, 1997; Willis, & Meacham, 1997; Zeichner, 1993). However, lifelong emotions and attitudes of present and future teachers regarding cultural and ethnic diversity and poverty often deter the preparation process (Florio-Ruane, 1994; Lalik & Hinchman, 2001; Schmidt, 1998a).

In light of this information, there is evidence that teacher self-knowledge may be the first and foremost consideration when attempting to help teachers understand diverse groups of students (Banks, 1994; Britzman, 1986; Osborne, 1996). This self-knowledge is promoted in the *ABC's of Cultural Understanding and Communication*, and hopefully, this book will provide the teacher educator and present and future teachers with the knowledge and examples to help them pursue intercultural understanding and appreciation of their diverse student populations.

## ORGANIZATION OF THE BOOK

This book is a valuable one for teacher educators and teacher education programs in the United States and Europe, since it is organized around numerous data sources. It contains national and international adaptations of the *ABC's of Cultural Understanding and Communication*. Authors for this book represent many languages and cultures and know, first hand, the socially constructed issues related to language, culture, and ethnicity. This first chapter of the book has served as a reader's introduction to the editors' relationships to the *ABC's Model* and the theoretical framework that supports their research.

In the second chapter, "Constructing Third Space: The Principles of Reciprocity and Cooperation," Claudia Finkbeiner presents a new perspective on the *ABC's Model*, relating it to the notion of Third Space and the principles of reciprocity and cooperation. She explains how the model is a methodological tool that allows teachers and learners to play active and self-determined roles. This is logically followed, in the third chapter, by an authentic example of the ABC's process.

In Chapter 3, "The ABC's: A Journey Toward Making a Positive Difference," Judith Osetek, English teacher from European American backgrounds, takes us on her learning journey as she experiences the model in ways she never dreamed. She spent a semester completing cross-cultural analyses of a Latino male and discovered startling information concerning herself and the human condition.

In Chapter 4, "Doing the ABC's: An Introspective Look at Process," Stacey Leftwich and Marjorie Madden, teacher educators from African American and European American backgrounds, use the *ABC's Model* to develop their own cultural sensitivity. They learn information that helps to shape their thinking about teacher preparation for diverse classroom populations.

In Chapter 5, "Investigating the Role of Awareness and Multiple Perspectives in Intercultural Education," Claudia Finkbeiner and Sylvia Fehling, explicate the interesting perspectives that emerge using adaptations of the *ABC's Model* in their intercultural communication classes. Their findings link culture and psychology.

In Chapter 6, *"Revealing and Revisitng 'Self' in Relation to the Culturally Different 'Other': Multicultural Education and the ABC's Model,"* Jyotsna Pattnaik, originally from the nation of India, makes one aware of the importance of teachers learning from families in order to successfully work with children. An adaptation of the *ABC's Model* facilitates the process.

In Chapter 7, "The Complexity and Multiplicity of Pre-service Teachers Exploring Diversity Issues," Shelley Hong Xu, Chinese American, presents data from a study demonstrating the ways in which two pre-service teachers from European American backgrounds learn about different cultures. The *ABC's* has a greater effect on one than the other.

In Chapter 8, "Successful ABC's In-Service Project: Supporting Culturally Responsive Teaching," Ruggiano Schmidt and Andrea Izzo report on an in-service project that took place over two years in an urban high poverty school. They describe and analyze significant changes in teachers' perspectives and pedagogy.

In Chapter 9, "The ABC's Online: Using Voice Chats in a Trans-National Foreign Language Exchange," by Eva Wilden, is an exciting adaptation of the *ABC's Model* for online intercultural communication and understanding. She presents ground-breaking information.

Chapter 10, "The ABC's as a Starting Point and Goal: The Online Intercultural Exchange Project," authored by Claudia Finkbeiner and Markus Knierim analyzes a wonderful intercultural communication model entitled, *ICE*, derived from the *ABC's Model* and *Cultura*, another intercultural model.

Chapter 11, "Using the ABC's Model in Management Education," written by La Verne Higgins, an African American Industrial Relations Professor, explains how this teacher education model was translated to prepare business students for global transactions. She has found that students benefit by becoming aware of their personal/professional needs, as well as concerned about the impact of intercultural understanding in the business community.

Finally, the "Afterward: The Future of the ABC's Model," summarizes the work in this book and asks significant questions concerning the future of the *ABC's*. Greta Nagel, a literacy professor of European American origins and author of *The Tao of Teaching* and numerous other provocative teacher education books and articles, takes us to the next level of national and international adaptations of the *ABC's of Cultural Understanding and Communication*. She leaves us with questions as well as powerful implications of the model.

## A FINAL WORD FROM CLAUDIA FINKBEINER AND PATRICIA RUGGIANO SCHMIDT

In recent years, global social, economic, and political actions have impacted all of the world's people. We constantly interact, face-to-face, through physical or media encounters. We come together and experience similarities and differences that powerfully affect local, national, and international situations. Therefore, effective communication is key, but we believe this can happen only when there is an understanding and appreciation of human differences.

The motivation that brings us together bridges educational gaps. Our joint endeavor for intercultural learning is in itself an expression of prosocial and proactive behaviors (Finkbeiner, 2000, see IASCE ). Together, we want to step beyond artificial and manmade borders and constructs . . . geographically, mentally, and emotionally speaking. By performing intercultural research and implementing multiple perspectives and non-dogmatic ideas in schools, we want to contribute to a better, less prejudicial future. We want to educate young children and adults in a way that they become interculturally and linguistically intelligent, critical, and competent citizens in our world community. In order to do so, every child, teenager, and adult, must be sensitized to the importance of getting this process started, that is, learning about the world . . . and the first step is learning about oneself. Thus, "Know thyself and understand others" (Schmidt, 1999) is the most important initial spring board. Knowledge of oneself is of fundamental importance when aiming at the development and growth of tolerant and empathetic citizens that can enjoy work and play, and at the same time, cooperate effectively in ethnically, culturally, linguistically, religiously, politically and socioeconomically diversified communities (Finkbeiner & Koplin, 2001, 2002).

Preparing this book was an expression of love—love of humanity for humanity. Some would think this is too lofty, an unrealistic goal for a book. But teachers/professors often believe that the main purpose for education is to promote the highest ideals, ones that guide people toward making the world a better place. We concur. We know that one book is not enough. However, we do believe that this book could be an important step on a journey toward the appreciation of differences . . . a first step toward effective communication that results in collaborative learning among diverse populations in our classrooms, schools, community, nation, and world.

## REFERENCES

Au, K. (1993). *Literacy instruction in multicultural settings.* New York: Harcourt, Brace, Javanovich College Publishers.

Banks, J.A. (1994). *An introduction to multicultural education.* Boston: Allyn & Bacon.

Bloome, D., & Green, J. (1982). The social contexts of reading: A multidisciplinary perspectives. In B. A. Hutson (Ed.), *Advances in reading language research* (Vol. 1, pp. 309-338). Greenwich, CT: JAI Press.

Bogdan, R. C., & Biklen, S. K. (1994). *Qualitative research for education: An introduction to the theory and method* (2nd ed.). Boston: Allyn & Bacon.

Boykin, A.W. (1984).Reading Achievement and the social-cultural frame of reference of Afro-American children. *Journal of Negro Education, 53*(4), 464-473.

Boykin, A.W. (1978). Psychological/behavioral verve in academic/task performance: Pre-theoretical considerations. *Journal of Negro Education, 47*(4), 343-354.

Britzman, D. (1986). Cultural myths in the making of a teacher: Biography and social structure in teacher education. *Harvard Educational Review, 56,* 442-456.

Cochran-Smith, M. (1995). Uncertain allies: Understanding the boundaries of race and teaching. *Harvard Educational Review 65*(4), 541-570.

Cummins, J. (1986). Empowering minority students: A framework for intervention. *Harvard Educational Review, 56*(1), 18-36.

Delpit, L.(1995). *Other people's children.* New York: The New Press.

Derman-Sparks, L. (1992). *Anti-bias curriculum: Tools for empowering young children.* Sacramento, CA: California State Department of Education.

Dewey J. (1969). *The school and society. Chicago*: University of Chicago Press. (Original work published 1899).

Edelski, C. (1991). *With literacy and justice for all: Rethinking the social in language and education.* Bristol, PA: Falmer Press, Taylor & Francis.

Edwards, P.A. (1995). Combining parents' and teachers' thoughts about storybook reading at home and school. In L.M. Morrow (Ed.), *Family literacy: Multiple perspectives to enhance literacy development* (pp. 56-60). Newark, DE: International Reading Association.

Edwards, P.A. (1996). Creating sharing-time conversations: Parents and teachers work together. *Language Arts, 73,* 344-349.

Edwards, P.A., Pleasants, H., & Franklin, S. (1999). *A path to follow: Learning to listen to parents.* Portsmouth, NH: Heinemann.

Edwards, P.A., Dandridge, J., McMillon, G. T., & Pleasants, H. M. (2001). Taking ownership of literacy: Who has the power? In P. R. Schmidt & P. B. Mosenthal (Eds.), *Reconceptualizing literacy in the new age of multiculturalism and pluralism.* Greenwich, CT: Information Age.

Emig, J. (1971). Writing as a mode of learning. *College Composition and Communication, 28,* 122-128.

Faltis, C.J. (1993). *Joinfostering: Adapting teaching strategies for the multilingual classroom.* New York: Maxwell Macmillan International.

Finkbeiner, C. (1995). Englischunterricht in europaeischer Dimension. *Zwischen Qualifikationserwartungen der Gesellschaft und Schuelereinstellungen und Schuelerinteressen.* Bochum: Dr. Brockmeyer.

Finkbeiner, C. (2001). One and all in Call? Learner-moderator- researcher. *Computer-assisted Language Learning, 14*(3-4), 129-151.

Finkbeiner, C. (2002). Foreign language Practice and cooperative learning. In C. Finkbeiner (Ed.)., *Wholeheartedly English: A life of learning* (pp. 109-122). Berlin: Cornelsen.

Finkbeiner, C. (2003, October). Cooperative learning and teaching in Germany. In *International Association for the Study of Cooperation in Education, 22*(3), 14-16. [Newsletter]

Finkbeiner, C. (2004). Cooperation and collaboration in a foreign language teacher training program: The LMR plus model. In E. Cohen, C. Brody, & M. Sapon-Shevin (Eds.), *Learning to teach with cooperative learning: Challenges in teacher education* (pp. 111-127). Albany: State University of New York Press.

Finkbeiner, C. (2005). Interessen und Strategien beim fremdsprachlichen Lesen. *Wie Schülerin und Schüler englische Texte lesen und verstehen.* [Interest and strategies in foreign language reading: How students read and comprehend English texts]. Tuebingen: Narr.

Finkbeiner, C., & Koplin, C. (2001). Fremdverstehensprozesse und interkulturelle Prozesse als Forschungsgegenstand. In A. Mueller-Hartmann & M. Schocker-v.-Ditfurth (Eds.), *Qualitative Forschungsansatze im Bereich Fremdsprachen lehren und lernen* (pp. 114-136). Tuebingen: Narr.

Finkbeiner, C., & Koplin, C. (2002). A cooperative approach for facilitating intercultural education. *Reading Online, 6*(3), New Literacies. http://www.readingonline.org/newliteracies/lit_index.asp?HREF=/newliteracies/finkbeiner . Newark, DE: International Reading Association.

Florio-Ruane, S. (1994). The future teachers' autobiography club: Preparing educators to support learning in culturally diverse classrooms. *English Education, 26*(1), 52-56.

Foster, M. (1994). Effective black teachers: A literature review. In E.R. Hollins, J.E. King, & W.C. Hayman (Eds.), *Teaching diverse populations: Formulating a knowledge base* (pp.225-241). Albany: SUNY Press.

Gay, G., & Howard, T.C. (2000). Multicultural teacher education for the 21stcentury. *The Teacher Educator, 36*(1), 1-16.

Goldenberg, C.N. (1987). Low-income Hispanic parents' contributions to their first- grade children's word-recognition skills. *Anthropology and Education Quarterly, 18*, 149-179.

Gordon, B. M. (1998). Implicit assumptions of the Holmes and Carnegie Reports: A view from an African American pespective. *Journal of Negro Education, 57*(2), 141-158.

Greene, M. (1995). *Releasing the Imagination.* San Francisco: Jossey-Bass.

Heath, S.B. (1983). *Ways with words: Language life and work in communities and classrooms.* Cambridge: Cambridge University Press.

Howard, T. (2001). Telling their side of the story: African American students' perceptions of culturally relevant teaching. *The Urban Review, 33*(2), 131-149.

Kantor, R., Miller, S., & Fernie, D. (1992). Diverse paths to literacy in a preschool classroom: A sociocultural perspectives. *Reading Research Quarterly, 27*(3), 185-201.

Ladson-Billings, G. (1994). *The dreamkeepers: Successful teachers of African American children.* San Francisco: Jossey-Bass.

Ladson-Billings, G. (1995). Culturally relevant teaching. *Research Journal, 32*(3), 465-491.

Lalik, R., & Hinchman, K. (2001). Critical issues: Examining constructions of race in literacy research: Beyond silence and other oppressions of white liberalism. *Journal of Literacy Research, 33*(3), 529-561.

Lee, C. D. (1991). Big picture talkers/Words walking without masters: The instructional implications of ethnic voices for an expanded literacy. *Journal of Negro Education, 60*(3), 291-304.

Leftwich, S. (2001, December). Using the *ABC's Model* to help preservice teachers involved in a community reading project. In *The ABC's of cultural understanding and communication for literacy teacher education.* Symposium conducted at the meeting of the National Reading Conference, San Antonio, TX.

Levine, D.U. (1994). Instructional approaches and interventions that can improve the academic performance of African American students. *Journal of Negro Education, 63*(1), 46-63.

Lewis, A.E. (2001). There is no "Race" in the schoolyard: Color-blind ideology in an almost all-white school. *American Educational Research Journal, 38*(4), 781-811.

McCaleb, S. P. (1994). *Building communities of learners.* New York: St. Martin's Press.

McIntosh, P. (1990). White privilege: Unpacking the invisible knapsack. *Independent School*, Wellesley College Winter Issue. Wellesley, MA.

Moll, L.C. (1992). Bilingual classroom studies and community analysis: Recent trends. *Educational Researcher, 21*(2), 20-24.

Murrell, P. C. (1994). Pedagogical and contextual issues affecting African American males in school and society. *Journal of Negro Education, 63*(4), 556-569.

Nagel, G. (2002). Building cultural understanding and communication: A modelin seven situations. *Reading Online, 6*(4). www.readingonline.org: International Reading Association.

Nieto, S. (1996). *Affirming diversity: The sociopolitical context of multicultural education.* New York: Longman.

Nieto, S. (1999). *The light in their eyes.* New York: Teachers College Press.

Noordhoff, K., & Kleinfield, J. (1993). Preparing teachers for multicultural classrooms. *Teaching and Teacher Education, 9*(1), 27-39.

Osborne, A.B. (1996). Practice into theory into practice: Culturally relevant pedagogy for students we have marginalized and normalized. *Anthropology and Education Quarterly, 27*(3), 285-314.

Pang, V. O., & Cheng, L. L. (Eds.). (1998). *Struggling to be heard: The unmet needs of Asian Pacific American children.* Albany, NY: SUNY Press.

Paley, V.G. (1989). *White teacher.* Cambridge, MA: Harvard University Press.

Pattnaik, J. (1997). Cultural stereotypes and preservice education: Moving beyond our biases. *Equity and Excellence in Education, 30*(3), 40-50.

Powell, R., Cantrell, S.C., & Adams, S. (2001). Saving Black Mountain: The promise of critical literacy in a multicultural democracy. *The Reading Teacher 54*,(8), 772-781.

Progoff, I. (1975). *At a journal workshop: The basic text and guide for using the intensive jounral.* New York: Dialogue House Library.

Purcell-Gates, V. (1993). Issues for family literacy research: Voices from the trenches. *Language Arts, 70*, 670-677.

Purcell-Gates, V., L'Allier, S., & Smith, D. (1995). Literacy at the Harts' and the Larsons: Diversity among poor inner-city families. *The Reading Teacher, 48*(7), 572-578.

Reyhner, J., & Garcia, R. L. (1989). Helping minorities read better: Problems and promises. *Reading Research and Instruction, 28*(3), 84-91.

Rogers, R. (2002). "That's what you're here for, you're suppose to tell us": Teaching and learning critical literacy. *Journal of Adolescent and Adult Literacy, 45*(8), 772-787.

Rogers, T. (1987). Exploring the socio-cognitive perspective on the interpretive processes of junior high school students. *English Quarterly, 20*(3), 218-230.

Rogoff, B. (1990). *Apprenticeship in thinking.* New York: Oxford Press.

Schiefflin, B., & Cochran-Smith, M. (1984). Learning to read culturally: Literacy before schooling. In H. Goelman, A. Oberg, & F. Smith (Eds.), *Awakening to literacy* (pp. 3-23). Portsmouth, NH: Heinemann.

Schmidt, P.R. (1998a). *Cultural conflict and Struggle: Literacy learning in a kindergarten program.* New York: Peter Lang.

Schmidt, P.R. (1998b). The ABC's of cultural understanding and communication. *Equity and Excellence in Education, 31*(2), 28-38.

Schmidt, P.R. (1998c). The *ABC's Model*: Teachers connect home and school. In T. Shanahan & F.V. Rodriguez-Brown(Eds.), *National reading conference yearbook* (Vol. 47, pp. 194-208.) Chicago: National Reading Conference.

Schmidt, P.R. (1999). Focus on Research: Know thyself and understand others. *Language Arts, 76*(4), 332-340.

Schmidt, P.R. (2000). Emphasizing differences to build cultural understandings. In V. Risko & K. Bromley, (Eds.), *Collaboration for diverse learners: Viewpoints and practices.* Newark, DE: IRA.

Schmidt, P.R. (2001). The power to empower. In P.R. Schmidt & P.B. Mosenthal (Eds.). *Reconceptualizing literacy in the new age of multiculturalism and pluralism.* Greenwich, CT: Information Age Publishing.

Sjoberg, G., & Kuhn, K. (1989). Autobiography and organizations: Theoretical and methodological issues. *The Journal of Applied Behavioral Science, 25*(4), 309-326.

Sleeter, C.E. (2001). Preparing teachers for culturally diverse schools. *Journal of Teacher Education, 52*(2), 94-106.

Sleeter, C., & Grant, C. (1991). Race, class, gender, and disability in current textbooks. In M.W. Apple & L.K. Christian-Smith (Eds.), *The politics of the textbook.* New York: Routledge and Chapel Hill.

Snyder, T.D., Hoffman, C.M., & Geddes, C.M. (1997). *Digest of education statistics.* Washington, DC: National Center of Education Statistics, Office of Educational Research and Improvement.

Spindler, G., & Spindler, L. (1987). *The interpretive ethnography of education: At home and abroad.* Hillsdale, NJ: Lawrence Erlbaum Associates.

Spradley, J. (1979). *The ethnographic interview.* New York: Holt, Rinehart & Winston.

Tatum, B. (1992). Talking about race, learning about racism: The application of racial identity theory in the classroom. *Harvard Educational Review, 62*(1), 1-24.

Tatum, B. (1997). *Why are all the black kids sitting together in the cafeteria?* New York: Basic Books.

Tatum, A. (2000). Breaking down barriers that disenfranchise African American adolescent readers in low-level tracks. *Journal of Adolescent and Adult Literacy, 44*(1), 52-64.

Taylor, D. (1983). *Family literacy: Young children learning to read and write.* Exeter, NH: Heinemann.

Taylor, D., & Dorsey-Gaines, C. (1988). *Growing up literate.* Portsmouth, NH: Heinemann.

Trueba, H.T., Jacobs, L. & Kirton, E. (1990). *Cultural conflict and adaptation: The case of the Hmong children in American society.* New York: The Falmer Press.

Vygotsky, L. S. (1978). *Mind in society: The development of higher mental process.* Cambridge, MA: Harvard University Press.

Walker-Dalhouse, D., & Dalhouse, A.D. (2001). Parent-school relations: Communicating more effectively with African American parents. *Young Children,* 75-80.

Wallace, B. (2000). A call for change in multicultural training at graduate schools of education: Educating to end oppression and for social justice. *Teachers College Record, 102*(2), 1086-1111.

Wasser, J.D., & Bresler, L. (1996). Working in the interpretive zone: Conceptualizing collaboration in qualitative research teams. *Educational Researcher, 25*(5), 5-15.

Willis, A.I., & Meacham, S.J. (1997). Break point: The challenges of teaching multicultural education courses. *Journal for the Assembly on Expanded Perspectives on Learning, 2*, 40-49.

Xu, H. (2000a). Preservice teachers integrate understandings of diversity into literacy instruction: An adaptation of the *ABC's Model. Journal of Teacher Education, 51*(2), 135-142.

Xu, H. (2000b). Preservice teachers in a literacy methods course consider issues of diversity. *Journal of Literacy Research, 32*(4), 505-531.

Zeichner, K.M. (1993). *Educating teachers for cultural diversity.* East Lansing, MI: National Center on Teacher Learning.

CHAPTER 2

# CONSTRUCTING THIRD SPACE

## The Principles of
## Reciprocity and Cooperation

**Claudia Finkbeiner**

### ABSTRACT

This chapter introduces a new perspective on the ABC's relating it to the notion of Third Space and the principles of reciprocity and cooperation. Within the framework of a multilingual and multicultural world there are a growing number of people who move back and forth between first, second and third space. Within this process cultural identity and self are important factors. Empirical data show that the sojourn to Third Spaces can be triggered and co-constructed in a cooperative and reciprocal effort. The *ABC's of Cultural Understanding and Communication* (Schmidt, 1998) is a methodological tool that allows teachers and learners to play an active and self-determined role in that process. In this chapter I will give a survey on several ABC's studies and accompanying intercultural online and face-to-face projects conducted in the school and university setting. Special emphasis is put on the dynamics of the acculturation model as well as on the multilayered model on perspective of the self and perspective of the other.

*ABC's of Cultural Understanding and Communication:*
*National and International Adaptations*, 19–42

# INTRODUCTION

Dramatis personae:

- a four-year-old boy
- the four-year-old boy's mother from Iran
- a teacher from Germany

[Scene 1: Cologne Train Station, a bench; originally the dialogue was conducted in German]

*Boy and mother sitting on the bench, talking to each other; teacher approaching them.*

**Teacher:**   Excuse me, is this seat taken?

*Mother smiles in an inviting way. Teacher sits down, takes out a book and starts reading. Boy tries to make eye-contact with the teacher.*

> **Boy:**   I am going to Saarbruecken today.
> **Teacher:**   Really?
> **Boy:**   Yes, to see my uncle, the brother of my mother.
> **Teacher:**   Oh that sounds nice . . . over the weekend?
> **Boy:**   I will stay till Sunday.
> **Teacher:**   Okay, I see.

[*pause; teacher starts reading*]

> **Boy:**   Saarbruecken is quite a large city.
> **Teacher:**   Bigger than Cologne?
> **Boy:**   I don't know, but Iran is a lot bigger than Saarbruecken.
> **Teacher:**   Really, how do you know? Are you from Iran?
> **Boy:**   No, not me, but my Mom, "Ich bin ein Koelner" [I am a Cologne man].

*Boy looks at his mother, switches into Persian, talks to her, she smiles.*

> **Teacher:**   But you speak two languages.
> **Boy:**   How do you know?
> **Teacher:**   I heard it, when you were talking to your mother.

[*The train to Saarbruecken is announced.*]

> **Boy:**   This is the train to Saarbruecken. We need to go [pulls his mother]. Ciao [smiling]
> **Teacher:**   Ciao, and have fun in Saarbruecken.

(*Traveling between Language and Culture—an International in Cologne*)

The scenario with the four-year-old "International" from Cologne station exemplifies how a cooperative and reciprocal effort is made to co-construct a new space where both participants can situate themselves in discourse. Only four years old, the boy clearly states who he is: he says he is a "Cologne man." Yet, at the same time we know that "a child lives in many worlds. Home, family, school, neighborhood, and society shape the contours of childhood and adolescence" (Edwards et al., 2001, p. 111). Furthermore, there is an often non-recognized impact of various cultural and linguistic settings a child is exposed to. These worlds sometimes overlap and influence each other. They may also have effects of mutual constraint. If things work out well, these worlds are complimentary and reinforcing, and they are a space where children and young adults can develop cognitively, emotionally, socially, and culturally.

We know that the boy from Cologne Station, just as any child of a culture, ethnicity or language different from the mainstream, might face difficulties. This might be due to language learning problems, cultural differences, or just difficulties resulting from personality. Teachers need to know who their students are and where they come from. But before they can successfully find out about this, they need to learn about themselves. This is suggested in the model of acculturation discussed within the training model by Schmidt (2001, p. 390): "Know thyself and understand others."

The dialogue at Cologne Station demonstrates the multilingual and multicultural richness which exists all over Europe and probably across the world (Banks, 1994; Finkbeiner, 1995; Hollins & Oliver, 1999; Nieto, 2000; Schmidt & Mosenthal, 2001). Taken as a situation which is prototypical for the "the age of pluralism and multiculturalism" (Schmidt, 2001, p. 389), it is most relevant to education and teaching as it mirrors the sociocultural dynamics we live in (Lantolf, 2000; van Lier, 2004).

Children are cultural and linguistic experts with parents, teachers and learners, as equal partners (Finkbeiner, 2004). Children who grow up exposed to different cultures and languages can be a model for adults as to what it means to be linguistically and culturally competent.

## FROM COLOGNE STATION TO THE ABC'S

In the boy-teacher-conversation, Cologne Station metaphorically turned into McLuhan's (1962, p. 8; 1964, p. 3) concept of the world as a "global village."[1] It represents the diversity of the worlds' peoples. The Cologne Station scenario is relevant to the *ABC's of Cultural Understanding and Communication* (Schmidt, 1998, 1999). It can serve as a model of the shortest non-anticipated Mini-ABC's (Finkbeiner & Koplin, 2002; Schmidt, 1998).

The example illustrates that many people (a) are both "locals" and "foreigners" somewhere in the world, depending on location and perspective, (b) continuously meet new people, (c) may encounter intercultural events while they are making other plans, (d) must be prepared for facing differences and similarities as they spontaneously happen in the global village.

## THE FIVE BASIC STEPS OF THE ABC'S
## (FINKBEINER & KOPLIN, 2002; SCHMIDT, 1998)

### A as in Autobiography

First, each participant must write or narrate relevant aspects and/or key events from his or her autobiography. The conversation at Cologne Station demonstrates how (within a time span of only three minutes) a boy is talking about key issues in his life. We learn that the boy speaks German and Persian fluently, that he was born in Cologne, and considers it his home. His words also imply that he has a significant influence on his mother. We learn that the mother is Iranian and that she lives in Germany but does not speak German. The boy most likely has a culturally different identity than his mother. He does not identify solely as an Iranian or as a German, but as a "Cologne man."[2]

### B as in Biography

After having written their autobiography, the participants will cooperate with a partner from a different cultural background. Therefore, the partners typically represent a different group: for instance, as to ethnicity, culture, language, religion, political viewpoint, philosophical belief, sexual orientation, age and gender. Then each of them conducts an in-depth, audio or videotaped interview (Bogdan & Biklen, 1994; Spradley, 1979) with a partner from a culture different from his or her own. The interviewer will then construct a biography describing the key events in that person's life.

The exercise in A and B above parallels how (a) the teacher and boy interacted in the train station, (b) she took notes of the conversation reconstructing the boy's biography (c) she drew conclusions from the dialogue.

### C as in Cross-Cultural Analysis and Appreciation of Differences

Here participants will study their autobiographies and compare them to the biographies they have written. They write down a list of the similarities and differences (Cummins, 1986; Derman-Sparks, 1992; Finkbeiner

& Koplin, 2000, 2001; McCaleb, 1994; Paley, 1989; Spindler & Spindler, 1987; Trueba, Jacobs, & Kirton, 1990).

The similarities between the boy and the teacher were that they spoke at least two languages, lived in Germany and used public transport. The differences were in their sociocultural background, languages and age.

## C as in Cultural Self-Analyses of Differences

Finally, the participants, using the similarities and differences, will write an in-depth self-analysis of cultural differences. Here the participants will begin to acquire insight about others and a sense of their own ethnocentricity (Spindler & Spindler, 1987). They will learn that their own view might be "biased." An important goal of C is to become aware of the "bias" that lies in the mono-perspective of one's own cultural context and setting.

## Plans for Home-School Connections

As a follow-up, participants design year-long plans to connect home and school. The focus is on children's reading, writing, listening, and speaking development. In order to facilitate this process the teachers use what they have learned about cultural sensitivity through the *ABC's Model*.

## THE ABC'S MODEL: A EUROPEAN ADAPTATION

We have implemented Schmidt's (1998, 2001) *ABC's of Cultural Understanding and Communication* in our teacher preparatory courses at the University of Kassel (Finkbeiner & Koplin, 2000, 2001, 2002) and in high school classes. The Kassel intercultural projects at a glance comprise:

- the ABC's Face to Face Projects (Finkbeiner & Koplin, 2000, 2001, 2002) at the university level;
- the ABC's Blended Learning Project (Online and face to face) at the high school level between Galway, Ireland and Wiesbaden, Germany;
- the ABC's Online Project at the teacher training in-service level (Wilden, this volume);
- the Intercultural Exchange (ICE) between the University of Kassel and the University of California Santa Barbara (Finkbeiner & Knierim, this volume);

- the European MOBIDIC Project, a European research study on *Modules of Bilingual Didactics and Methodology for Teacher Training* (Finkbeiner & Fehling, this volume);
- the Intercultural Online Project between the University of Kassel and the Monterey International Studies Institute.

All of these projects strive to develop cultural competence,[3] considering each participant an equal partner. The specific goals are: (a) learning about oneself, one's culture(s) and language(s), (b) learning about others, their culture(s) and language(s) through discourse, (c) reciprocal construction of cultural knowledge and third space, (d) cooperation and collaboration in trans-cultural contexts, (e) culture-based approach to literacy development through use of texts generated by the learners, (f) third space awareness through meta-cognition and discourse.

Due to the fact that all our teacher training classes are situated in the foreign language department at the University of Kassel, all of our ABC's classes as well as all complementary intercultural projects use English as a foreign language.[4]

## The Language Issue

Consequentially, when we first started implementing the ABC's into our classes, all autobiographies and biographies were written in English, the common *lingua franca* (Finkbeiner & Koplin, 2002). However, a variety of native languages are represented in our classes, thus, proficiency in the English language varies among our students. The lesson we learned was, that insisting on the use of English created too much of a bias due to the power of language (Fairclough, 1992, p. 7; Fehling, 2005; Hawkins, 1987; James & Garrett, 1991, p. 12):[5] Some students were more capable and comfortable than others in expressing their personal and private ideas in English, their second or foreign language. The language issue turned out to be even a greater challenge in the secondary and primary school setting. For example, in the Galway-Wiesbaden Project, some children were foreign language learners of English or German at the beginning or intermediate level but only a few had reached a high proficiency level.

We learned, that even for those who had a high proficiency in the foreign language, there was a discrepancy between what they actually wanted to say and what they said. This was due to the fact that values and attributions simply do not always translate (Finkbeiner, 2005, pp. 168-171).

We found a compromise that suited both the needs of the ABC's and our foreign language classes. The autobiography is written in the mother tongue or in the language in which the participant feels at home. The autobiography has to be seen as a mirror of the self. The self is socially constructed, thus, most closely tied to language and culture. The biography is written in English as *lingua franca*[6] or any other *lingua franca*. This allows the *lingua franca* to function as a tool for the cooperative and reciprocal effort in co-constructing the perspective of the self and the perspective of the other through discourse. Another solution is the bilingual use of the mother tongues of both partners. This is possible if each partner is learning the partner's mother tongue as a foreign language as shown in Wilden's project (in this volume).

## Cooperative Literacy Event

The ABC's have become a highly appropriate approach for the foreign language classroom, because they allow (a) for independent work with texts generated by the learners themselves (Finkbeiner, 2005, p. 425) both in the mother tongue and in the foreign language and (b) they are situated in a group-work setting that makes cooperation among the learners compulsory, as described by Matthews and Kesner (2003).

## The Validation of the Biographies

We also learned, that the validation of the biographies is very significant for the ABC's to be effective in our context. The biography portrays the perspective of the other on the self. It makes both participants become aware of the different perspectives of the self which have been expressed in the autobiography and in the biography.

The validation process is initiated by the partner reading the biography to the other partner whose life story is at focus (Finkbeiner & Koplin, 2002). The partner is encouraged to clarify, reject, or intervene if misinterpretations resulting from language or cultural differences have occurred. The validation is only effective if it is considered a cooperative act between researcher and subject (Finkbeiner, 2001, 2004).

## The Pair and Group Setting

We have also experimented with the ABC's in groups of three. The participants must still write the autobiography. The difference between the pair and group of three setting is in the grouping for the biography. For example, let us assume, Esra, Markus and Deborah cooperate in one

ABC's group. In this case, Esra interviews Markus, Markus interviews Deborah and Deborah interviews Esra. They then write the biography individually, and the validation is conducted together in the group of three.

Based on the data drawn from both settings we conclude that the ABC's in groups of three tend to attenuate and tone down the sometimes deflected "black and white" picture that might be triggered by comparing only two perspectives.

The ABC's conducted in pairs have proven to be a lot more personal. This is due to the fact that in order to tell key events of one's life it takes mutual trust and a growing relationship between partners during the process.

To sum up, the European adaptations of Schmidt's *ABC's Model* (Schmidt, 1998, 2001) include the following steps:

- Match partners either in pairs or groups of three.
- All participants compose an autobiography in their mother tongue to set free the perspective of the self and cultural self-concepts.
- Pairs or groups start discourse either in English or in any other language as *lingua franca* in order to elicit thinking about cultural concepts.
- Pairs conduct reciprocal or triangular narrative interviews focusing on relevant aspects of each partner's life story in a *lingua franca*.
- Pairs or groups reciprocally write biographies in English as *lingua franca*.
- All participants analyze the perspectives of their self and the perspective of the other by relating and comparing the written data.
- Pairs or groups of three conduct reciprocal or triangular interviews to validate the biographies, clarify, resolve misunderstandings, and make comparisons.
- Everybody creates a meta-cognitive reflection of the learning process through an intercultural diary.
- As an ongoing parallel process the entire class engages in exercises to raise awareness, e.g., with intercultural communication strategies.

## CULTURAL COMPETENCE

Cultural competence is one of the most important goals of the ABC's and is the focus of all our complementary intercultural projects. Cultural competence is a highly complex, multifaceted, dynamic, constantly changing affective and cognitive construct (Bhabha, 1994; Byram, 1997; Finkbeiner & Koplin, 2002; Hofstede, 1997; Larson & Smalley, 1972; Schmidt, 1998; Weaver, 1993). It includes cultural sensitivity, cultural awareness, and empathy, as well as the ability to change perspectives and put oneself into the other person's shoes.

It might be helpful to follow Garner's (1990) model of knowledge representation and apply it to culture. There are three kinds of cultural knowledge: declarative, procedural and situational.

All of them are constructed in a lifelong acculturation process (Finkbeiner & Koplin, 2002) of the self (Finkbeiner, 2005) and they can be referred both to phenomena of Hofstede's (1997) culture one (e.g., art and literature) and culture two (e.g., thinking, feeling and potential acting) as well as to Weaver's (1993) model of culture as an iceberg, where one-seventh of culture is visible (we can see how someone greets, dresses, reacts etc.) and six seventh are invisible (we most often do not know the underlying reasons, values, or the motivation why someone acts the way he or she does).

## Declarative Cultural Knowledge

Declarative cultural knowledge centers on facts about the culture(s) of the self and culture(s) of the other in the sense of Hofstede's culture one; for example, one can name music, literature, and art. Additionally, one knows about the meaning which is attributed to specific words, or to certain colors, shapes, figures, movements, signs etc. within a typical cultural or sub-cultural context.

*Examples.* The color red stands for luck in China, but it signifies danger in the UK and in Germany, and it can be translated as 'that's just right' in Greece.[7] The numbers 888 stand for luck in China, 7 for luck in the United States, 4 for bad luck in Japan, and 13 for bad luck in the UK. Yet, 8 is the figure for prosperity in China and 9 for progress in Thailand.

## Procedural Cultural Knowledge

Procedural cultural knowledge implies that one can talk, act and behave culturally adequately and that one can adjust easily to specific cultural needs.

## Situational Cultural Knowledge

Situational cultural knowledge is, perhaps, the most difficult to grasp for foreign language learners. It sets the fine tone as to when which kind of language (e.g., formal and informal) is used, when and how to behave and how to interpret what is said and done.

Weaver's (1993) model of culture as an iceberg is very helpful in this respect. Students coming from France or Germany attending a USA university might be trapped in their decision making when it comes to the formal or informal code if they simply rely on superficial language markers. One of my students came to the conclusion that due to the fact that there was no "Sie-Form" on the surface level,[8] there would not be any "Sie-Form" under the surface of the cultural iceberg, either. This is a typical cultural trap. Even though students might address their professors with their first name, they would additionally address them with "professor" or "Dr." Things are said more subtle. The students in the U.S. university context would not likely address a female professor with "Mrs.," but with "Ms" or the title.

Situational knowledge not only helps us understand notions of directness and indirectness, but also of physically appropriate behavior, such as body distance, taboo or social acceptance of nudity, touching and kissing, etc. depending on the cultural context. Whereas in the UK a person that shows the soles of his shoes would be identified as someone having the legs up in order to relax, in Saudi Arabia the same person would be identified as rude. Yet, given a specific public context within the UK the person might be considered just as rude. We cannot undervalue the importance of cultural knowledge and the cultural and language decisions derived from them.

## THIRD SPACE

In the introductory scenario at Cologne Station the four-year-old boy seemed to navigate smoothly between different cultural and linguistic worlds. We cannot conclude that the boy actually always navigates so easily in these spaces. We must not deduce that third space is a space that is inherently connected to positive experience or permanently voluntarily entered. The concept of Third Space ought not to be romanticized. It offers a metaphorical leg-room that allows questioning of the self and of the other in a dialogue.

The data that we collected in our ABC's projects, as shown further below, indicate that the ABC's seem to initiate a process which makes participants step out of the dualism of existing worlds and create a new Third Space. It is dynamic, fluid, fuzzy, and non-conforming as well as non-normative. It questions existing beliefs, values and feelings about one's own self and about who we are.

There are valuable resources for third space in Gadamer's (1975) major work "Truth and Method," later refined in writings, such as "Hermeneutics," in which he coins the term "fusion of horizons." Therein he highlights the importance of the self as a social self. Gadamer's horizons can be understood as sensitivity towards differences between the self and the other and between the known and the unknown.

To date, the term third space is most diversely and widely discussed by authors and researchers and it is still far from clear what third space stands for. For instance, "third space" is at the center of attention in Bhabha's *Location of Culture* (1994, p. 53): "The pact of interpretation is never simply an act of communication between the I and the You designated in a statement. The production of meaning requires that these two places be mobilized in the passage through a Third Space." The cultural self is continuously reinvented and co-constructed. This requires ambiguity tolerance and the ability to involve in discourse.

Third space has also been referred to as "third-culture-perspective" by Grosch and Leenen (1998, p. 29), and "third domain" by Kramsch (1995). The concept of third space symbolizes the effort to step away from a binary understanding of who we are as cultural beings. It is not I and you, or the self and the other, but something beyond these binary approaches to self.

It is possible to distinguish between third space on an intrapersonal and on an interpersonal level. For instance, the four-year-old boy created a third space for himself which was neither Persian nor German, but Cologne. The boy might not have had a concept about comparable categories such as national identity and citizenship. Perhaps Cologne signified an emotional space where he could situate himself safely. It allowed him to relate to the teacher without excluding his mother and to talk to his mother without excluding the teacher.

On an interpersonal level third space is co-constructed by two or more participants. Even though it is a space which relates to the single cultures of each participant, it is not simply an overlap. It is a new mental and emotional zone co-constructed by two or more discourse partners.

## THE SELF IN THE ACCULTURATION PROCESS

In order to gain a deeper understanding one's own self during the sojourn to the self and the other at the beginning of the ABC's process, we have developed a model of acculturation. Piaget's (e.g., 1954, 1969) and Vygotsky's (1962, 1978) work were a valuable theoretical basis since acculturation is considered a highly individual and social process. The acculturation model has the "self" in the center. It relates to our former

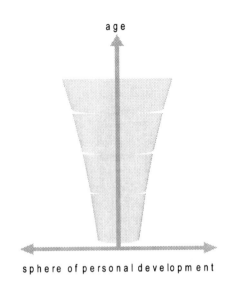

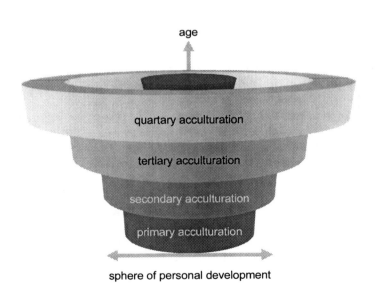

quartary acculturation

tertiary acculturation

secondary acculturation

primary acculturation

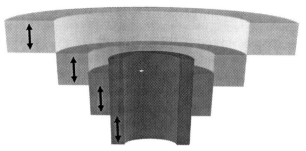

quartary acculturation

tertiary acculturation

secondary acculturation

primary acculturation

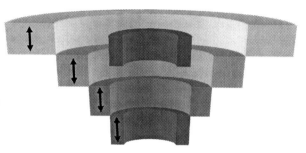

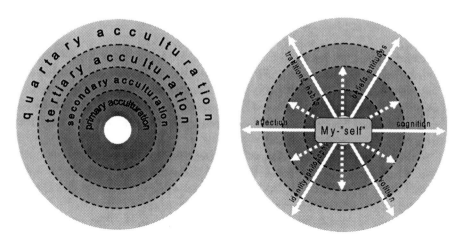

Figure 2.1.   Acculturation model.

design (Finkbeiner & Koplin, 2002), yet further develops and improves it. It now allows the dynamics and fluidity as well as fuzziness of the self to be better portrayed.

First, the model must be understood as an idealized one. Drawing a picture of a continuous and smoothly growing acculturation process is an idealization which does not mirror what actually happens in real life. Depending on critical incidents (such as loss of parents or other close relatives, social deprivation, war situations, divorce, splitting up with a friend) there might be "dents" and "holes" in the picture. When this happens, growth will not be linear. There are different phases in the acculturation process. They can be of different lengths depending on life circumstances. Some phases might be even skipped and then reappear at a later stage in life. Reappearance of things at a later phase, which were important at the first stage, does not imply regression. It only mirrors the dynamics of the acculturation process.

The phases start right from birth or even before birth in the womb. The first phase is called primary acculturation. In this phase the primary cultural facilitator is the mother who carries the child. The unborn in the womb develops into a cultural being who is able to perceive and learn about feelings, such as joy or existential *angst*. It is the child's first encounter with culture. Later it is the family, perhaps the father, grandparents, foster parents, siblings or other care takers who influence the acculturation process of the baby and young child. Children develop cultural identity, and together with it, cultural preferences or ethnic images (Garcia, 1999).

In the second phase, school and institutional acculturation takes place. In some cultures children might not have the chance to enter a school. They enter the work world right away. This means they skip the second phase. In some societies, however, the second phase might run through the entire life. The institutional acculturation might start in the first phase (e.g. kindergartens from 0+).

In the third phase, the workplace culture and the shared language have a major influence on acculturation. They absorb a huge part of the individual's life. Particularly in the fourth stage, which is usually post-labor, former phases might become more important again.

The three-dimensional model was chosen to show that preliminary phases are always there and cannot be deleted. There is always the child in us that we once were. This is crucial, as some participants in the ABC's have problems writing about their lives. The goal is to make students feel safe and comfortable in writing about their lives and to allow them to accept and appreciate who they are.

## THE PRINCIPLES OF RECIPROCITY AND COOPERATION

As the *ABC's Model* only functions in a cooperative setting, it not only triggers cooperation between students, but also the reciprocal endeavor to construct life stories. When writing the autobiography and biography and comparing it, the students start co-constructing their identities together. The following data illustrate this (Finkbeiner & Koplin, 2002).

The first excerpt is taken from the validation process. In this process one of the two ABC's partners was reading the biography to the other one. The biography was about a student who grew up in a Turkish family in Germany.

**Student 1-German:** (starts reading) Growing up in Germany for the last seven or eight years, she can't imagine returning to live in Turkey for her entire life. By experiencing two cultures at the same time, the student may feel like a stranger in the country she is presently living. Christmas is one example.

**Student 2-Turkish-German:** (interrupts) Hmm . . .

**Student 1-German:** Yes?

**Student 2-Turkish-German:** Here I would like to add, also, that it is a positive thing to make experiences in two cultures, because you can pick up the best things you like from both cultures, so you develop a new culture which contains standards from both cultures.

**Student 1-German:** So, would you say that Christmas has now become more familiar to you?

**Student 2-Turkish-German:** I think that Christmas has become a usual celebration for me. I don't celebrate it, but I join Christmas time indirectly for my way. Mainly, Jesus is also a prophet whom we believe and I find it even interesting that his birthday is celebrated every year.

The data show how important the validation and discourse are. Student 2 did not feel comfortable the way she was portrayed in the biography. Instead of accepting the statement that Christmas was one example of how much a stranger she felt, she clarified that; she had incorporated a

Christian celebration in her Muslim religion without violating it. Furthermore, the intercultural diary of student 2 shows how the ABC's process has enabled her to become aware of her own third space, constructed on an intrapersonal level:

*Intercultural Diary—Student 2—Turkish-German*

We had interesting discussions and I sometimes wondered that in some themes I only had a special kind of viewpoint. In this seminar, I learned to consider something in different approaches, too. Every culture has its own approach. Here it is also worth mentioning that mostly—in my opinion—it was easier for me to understand both sides, namely the foreign opinion and the German opinion. I think this was so because I have—in my mind the advantage—to have grown up in two cultures. I am actually foreign but was born and grew up in Germany. So, I developed a new culture for myself—if you can say so—which contains standards from both cultures. Growing up in those circumstances, you can automatically learn to consider a certain aspect from both cultural viewpoints. If you have no knowledge about the approach of the other culture, it can easily lead to misunderstanding and also to prejudices.

Another example is taken from the intercultural diary of a male student who came from Nigeria to Germany to study. The following excerpt talks about the conflict he felt between his mother and himself when he first came to Germany. The data show that even though he is capable of changing perspectives, he is still trying to find his space.

*Intercultural Diary—Student 3—Nigerian*

In the beginning she [the student's mother] was like most German parents: please, don't bring a black man to my house—for her it was: please, don't bring a white woman to my house. So as time went on, she understood that we are men and that as men we are living outside our homeland and we are living in a very different culture. So we were able to make her understand that there is nothing to fear or worry about the German culture or European culture and today she is even more pro Western culture, pro European. Because I would say today, she has a mixed child and she is very much different from the time we left home.

The following example shows the fight and struggle caused by cultural dissonance. It is an excerpt from an autobiography written by a German female student in which she describes meeting a male student from Sudan at a U.S. university during her year abroad:

*Autobiography—Student 4—German*

The Sudanese did not dare look the woman teacher in the eye. For him a woman could not be a teacher and also it was not allowed in his culture to look up to a teacher[sic—i.e, look directly into the teacher's eyes]. The teacher would always tell him to look at her and that he had to learn this if he wanted to live in American society. The poor guy tried his best and looked everywhere—to the blackboard, to the ceiling—but still not to the teacher.

The last example shows that during the ABC's validation process one student became aware of what could be called his religious third space. Even though he did not want to be called a Christian, nor a Muslim, he needed the routine of church which went together with his African belief. In this process he realized that he celebrated his own deep religion:

Validation of Biography—Student 5—African

I know I said I am not religious but after the interview I thought about it again. It's not that I am not religious: I still believe in so much of my African religion. If I say, I'm a Christian or I'm a Muslim, then I have lost my part of identity. The British brought the Christian to our country. Our culture, real culture is how to talk Oracles. I never thought about it before I came to Germany. It affected me here, that I don't go to church.

## THE PERSPECTIVE OF THE
## SELF AND THE PERSPECTIVE OF THE OTHER

The ABC's as well as the complementary intercultural projects we have conducted over the last few years have proven that it is not only important to focus on the perspective of the self, but at the some time on the perspective of the other. The "other" can be a part of oneself in an inner dialogue or it can be another person one is having a dialogue with. The perspectives of both "others" can be accessed through cultural awareness through the ABC's. Cultural relativity of both perspectives is the key to enter third space.

## THE PERSPECTIVE OF THE SELF

The following model shows that it is helpful to illustrate the perspective of the self as well as of the other on three levels: the actual, the hypothetical and the desired level.

Taking Mary's dancing proficiency as an example we will highlight the importance of distinguishing these different levels. We will first refer to the perspective of the self which is self-referential and self-attributed.

Figure 2.2a.

## Perspective of the Self—Actual

The actual perspective is what Mary truly thinks about her "self". This perspective might be based on prior experience. She thinks she is a good dancer.

## Perspective of the Self—Hypothetical

On the hypothetical level the perspective is an assumption. Mary thinks she could be a good dancer, but she does not know this, she probably has never tried.

### The Perspective of the Self and Other I

Figure 2.2a.   Continued.

## Perspective of the Self—Desired

The desired level of the perspective of the self is what Mary desires to be. She thinks she is not a good dancer but she wishes she was.

## THE PERSPECTIVE OF THE OTHER

The perspective of the other is portrayed in the model of the perspective of the self and other I and II. In our example, John stands for the per-

Figure 2.2a.   Continued.

spective of the other. The difference between his perspectives I and II are, that in II he presumes that Mary knows his perspective.

## Perspective of the Other—Actual

In the perspective of the "other" John's actual perspective of Mary as a dancer is rather negative. He thinks she is a poor dancer.

## Perspective of the Other—Hypothetical

So is his perspective of Mary on the hypothetical level: even though he never has seen her dance he assumes that she is a poor dancer.

## Perspective of the Other—Desired

On the level of desire John wishes that Mary was better dancer. This perspective is based on John's judgment derived from his experience with Mary.

The above models help us understand that there might be differences between the perspective of the self and the perspective of the other. This is why conflict and misunderstandings happen between people.

## CONCLUSION

Through intercultural discourse which allows setting free and talking or writing about the perspectives of the self and other, a process is initiated that helps learning and opening one's eyes about who we are, who we think we are, as well as who the "other" is, and who we think the "other" is. Additionally, it creates awareness for the relativity and fuzziness of perspectives.

Intercultural competence acknowledges the relativity of cultural meaning which is no longer situated in first and second, but in a third culture. Our students and teachers need to be prepared for this sojourn to learn about their selves and others in order to enter this third space. The data show that this is not always trouble-free.

The implications offered by the assumption of a third space need to be considered when it comes to teacher education (Finkbeiner, 2004; Hong Xu, 2001; Schmidt, 2001) as well as integration programs targeting linguistic and cultural minorities (Dilg, 1999; Garcia, 1999). This demands curricula that incorporate knowledge about one's own culture(s) and other cultures as well about one's own language(s) and other languages. Knowledge about the self and the other are undoubtedly crucial preconditions for multicultural societies that want to draw upon the hidden wealth that lies in culture and language.

## NOTES

1. McLuhan originally referred to this notion due to technology and media connecting people. In the meanwhile we face the world as a "global vil-

lage" metaphorically everywhere due to the growing globalization and migration.

2. This phenomenon is typical for many young people in Germany. They do not want to identify with the nation, but rather either with Europe or with a particular region.

3. I will focus on the notion of cultural competence further below.

4. We believe that teaching a foreign language successfully requires teaching it in the target language itself. Thus, English is our official classroom language and the required language for papers.

5. This concept is also referred to as "critical language awareness" (Fairclough, 1992, p. 7).

6. English is used as a *lingua franca*, when, e.g., a Turkish, a Spanish and a German learner meet and the only language they share and can lead their discourse in, is English.

7. Coming back from a conference and transiting in London, I became aware of posters at Heathrow Airport that advertised local cultural declarative knowledge and differences. I refer to some of the examples given there.

8. There are two ways to address someone in German: the formal "Sie" with the family name and the personal "Du" with the first name. In professional settings the "Sie" is most likely to be used.

## REFERENCES

Banks, J.A. (1994). *An introduction to multicultural education*. Boston: Allyn & Bacon.

Bhabha, H. (1994). *The location of culture*. London: Routledge.

Bogdan, R.C., & Biklen, S.K. (1994). *Qualitative research for education: An introduction to theory and method* (2nd ed.). Boston: Allyn & Bacon.

Byram, M. (1997). *Teaching and assessing intercultural communicative competence*. Clevedon: Multilingual Matters.

Cummins, J. (1986). Empowering minority students: A framework for intervention. *Harvard Educational Review, 56*(1), 18-36.

Derman-Sparks, L. (1992). *Anti-bias curriculum: Tools for empowering young children*. Sacramento: California State Department of Education.

Dilg, M.A. (1999). *Race and culture in the classroom: Teaching and learning through multicultural education*. New York: Teachers College Press.

Edwards, P.A., Danridge, J., McMillon, G.T., & Pleasants, H.M. (2001). Taking ownership of literacy: Who has the power? In P.R. Schmidt & P. Mosenthal (Eds.), *Reconceptualizing literacy in the new age of multiculturalism and pluralism* (pp. 111-134). Greenwich, CT: Information Age Publishing.

Fairclough, N. (Ed.). (1992). *Critical language awareness*. London: Longman.

Fehling, S. (2005). *Language Awareness und bilingualer Unterricht. Eine komparative Studie*. Frankfurt/Main: Peter Lang.

Finkbeiner, C. (1995). *Englischunterricht in europäischer Dimension. Zwischen Qualifikationserwartungen der Gesellschaft und Schülereinstellungen und Schülerinteressen*. Bochum: Dr. Brockmeyer.

Finkbeiner, C. (2001). One and all in CALL? Learner—moderator—researcher. *Computer Assisted Language Learning, 14*(3-4), 129-151.

Finkbeiner, C. (2004). Cooperation and collaboration in a foreign language teacher training program: The LMR plus model. In E. Cohen, C. Brody, & M. Sapon-Shevin (Eds.), *Learning to teach with cooperative learning: Challenges in teacher education* (pp. 111-127). Albany: State University of New York.

Finkbeiner, C. (2005). *Interessen und Strategien beim fremdsprachlichen Lesen. Wie Schülerinnen und Schüler englische Texte lesen und verstehen.* Tübingen: Narr.

Finkbeiner, C., & Koplin, C. (2000). Handlungsorientiert Fremdverstehen lehren und lernen. *Fremdsprachenunterricht, 4,* 254-261.

Finkbeiner, C., & Koplin, C. (2001). Fremdverstehensprozesse und interkulturelle Prozesse als Forschungsgegenstand. In A. Müller-Hartmann & M. Schocker-v. Ditfurth (Eds.), *Qualitative Forschung im Bereich Fremdsprachen lehren und lernen* (pp. 114-136). Tübingen: Narr.

Finkbeiner, C., & Koplin, C. (2002). A cooperative approach for facilitating intercultural education. *Reading Online, 6*(3). Retrieved July 25, 2005, from http://www.readingonline.org/newliteracies/lit_index.asp?HREF=finkbeiner/index.html

Gadamer, H.-G. (1975). *Truth and method.* London: Sheed and Ward.

Garcia, E. (1999). *Student cultural diversity: Understanding and meeting the challenge* (2nd ed.). Boston: Houghton Mifflin.

Garner, R. (1990). When children and adults do not use learning strategies: Towards a theory of setting. *Review of Educational Research, 60*(4), 517-529.

Grosch, H., & Leenen, W. R. (1998). Bausteine zur Grundlegung interkulturellen Lernens. In Bundeszentrale für politische Bildung (Ed.), *Interkulturelles Lernen. Arbeitshilfen für die politische Bildung* (pp. 29-47). Bonn: Bundeszentrale für politische Bildung.

Hawkins, E. (1987). *Awareness of language: An introduction* (2nd ed.). Cambridge: Cambridge University Press.

Hofstede, G. (1997). *Cultures and organizations: Software of the mind. Intercultural cooperation and its importance for survival.* New York: McGraw-Hill.

Hollins, E.R., & Oliver, E.I. (Eds.). (1999). *Finding pathways to success: Teaching culturally diverse populations.* Mahwah, NJ: Erlbaum.

Hong Xu, S. (2001). Preservice teachers connect multicultural knowledge and perspectives with literacy instruction for minority students. In P.R. Schmidt & P. Mosenthal (Eds.), *Reconceptualizing literacy in the new age of multiculturalism and pluralism* (pp. 323-340). Greenwich, CT: Information Age Publishing.

James, C., & Garrett, P. (1991). The scope of language awareness. In C. James & P. Garrett (Eds.), *Language awareness in the classroom* (pp. 3-20). London: Longman.

Kramsch, C. (1995). Andere Worte—andere Werte. Zum Verhältnis von Sprache und Kultur. In L. Bredella (Ed.), *Verstehen und Verständigung durch Sprachenlernen? Dokumentation des 15. Kongresses für Fremdsprachendidaktik* (pp. 51-66). Bochum: Brockmeyer.

Lantolf, J. (Ed.). (2000). *Sociocultural theory and second language learning.* Oxford: Oxford University Press.

Larson, D.N., & Smalley, W.A. (1972). *Becoming bilingual. A guide to language learning*. New Canaan, CT: Practical Anthropology.

Matthews, M.W., & Kesner, J. (2003). Children learning with peers: The confluence of peer status and literacy competence within small-group literacy events. *Reading Research Quarterly, 38*(2), 208-234.

McCaleb, S.P. (1994). *Building communities of learners*. New York: St. Martin's.

McLuhan, M. (1962). *The Gutenberg galaxy*. London: Routledge & Kegan Paul.

McLuhan, M. (1964). *Understanding media*. New York: Mentor.

Nieto, S. (2000). *Affirming diversity: The sociopolitical context of multicultural education* (3rd ed.). New York: Longman.

Paley, V.G. (1989). *White teacher*. Cambridge, MA: Harvard University Press.

Piaget, J. (1954). *Construction of reality in the child*. London: Routledge & Kegan Paul.

Piaget, J. (1969). *The mechanisms of perception*. London: Routledge & Kegan Paul.

Schmidt, P.R. (1998b). The ABC's of cultural understanding and communication. *Equity and Excellence in Learning, 31*(2), 28-38.

Schmidt, P.R. (1999). Focus on research: Know thyself and understand others. *Language Arts, 76*(4), 332-340.

Schmidt, P.R. (2001). The power to empower: Creating home/school relationships with the ABC's of cultural understanding and communication. In P.R. Schmidt & P. Mosenthal (Eds.), *Reconceptualizing literacy in the new age of multiculturalism and pluralism* (pp. 389-433). Greenwich, CT: Information Age Publishing.

Schmidt, P.R., & Mosenthal, P. (2001). *Reconceptualizing literacy in the new age of multiculturalism and pluralism*. Greenwich, CT: Information Age Publishing.

Spindler, G., & Spindler, L. (1987). *The interpretive ethnography of education: At home and abroad*. Hillsdale, NJ: Erlbaum.

Spradley, J. (1979). *The ethnographic interview*. New York: Holt, Rinehart & Winston.

Trueba, H.T., Jacobs, L., & Kirton, E. (1990). *Cultural conflict and adaptation: The case of the Hmong children in American society*. New York: Falmer.

van Lier, L. (2004). *The ecology and semiotics of language learning. A sociocultural perspective*. Boston: Kluwer.

Vygotsky, L.S. (1962). *Thought and language*. Cambridge, MA: MIT Press.

Vygotsky, L.S. (1978). *Mind in society*. Cambridge, MA: Harvard University Press.

Weaver, G.R. (1993). Understanding and coping with cross-cultural adjustment stress. In M. Paige (Ed.), *Education for the intercultural experience* (2nd ed., pp. 137-167). Yarmouth, ME: Intercultural Press.

CHAPTER 3

# THE ABC's

## A Journey Toward Making
## a Positive Difference

**Judith Marie Osetek**

### ABSTRACT

This chapter is the result of embracing the *ABC's of Cultural Understanding and Communication* (Schmidt, 2001) process and applying it to the role as an elementary classroom educator. The *ABC's* process leads one through a journey of self-discovery that results in a better understanding of career and personal goals in a manner that has a positive impact on both students and families that are a part of the educational process on a daily basis. This chapter explores the importance of engaging students and families on a personal level to be able to better meet student's individual educational interests and cultural needs. What emerges is a strategy of inviting families to become active members of their child's educational experience and to empower culturally diverse families, to adjust to and fit into the school community and to feel comfortable in the ongoing decisions that comprise the school setting. The *ABC's* process brings two people from different backgrounds together and results in a deeper understanding of how the educa-

*ABC's of Cultural Understanding and Communication:*
*National and International Adaptations,* 43–72

tional process is shaped by the relationship of an increasingly culturally diverse society and middle-class educational expectations.

## INTRODUCTION

I am a firm believer that everything in life happens for a reason, that there is a purpose and a means to an end. For a very long time, however, I did not know what my purpose was—how I could contribute to society and make a positive difference. When I set out to fulfill my goal of becoming a teacher, I was very excited. I knew that in this capacity I would certainly be in a position to promote positive social change, or at least touch the lives of my students in a small, yet meaningful way. Most of my coursework related to education focused on various theories, models, strategies and techniques put forth to prepare the teacher to provide the best possible education for students. As pre-service teachers, we were not only required to be experts in our subject areas, we were also expected to demonstrate our ability to deliver this knowledge in the most effective manner to promote student growth and achievement. We were also expected to create a nonthreatening, nurturing and fair atmosphere in an effort to meet the needs of all students, regardless of race, socioeconomic status, gender, etc. At the conclusion of my pre-service teaching experience and coursework related to education, including my Masters, I felt well prepared to begin my professional teaching career.

Unexpectedly, I was offered a position as an English as a Second Language teacher in the school district closest to my home. This was very appealing to me, due to the age of my very young children as well as my own positive memories of attending school in this district. I considered it just one way to give back to the educational community that had such a positive influence in my life. While I preferred to teach in an upper elementary classroom, I saw this as an opportunity to gain experience and begin my teaching career. I also looked forward to working with students of diverse backgrounds, as well as improve my Spanish. That summer, prior to my first year of teaching in this position, I reviewed class notes, books and strategies/techniques that I felt would be particularly useful regarding the population of students that I would be working with, minority students, mostly Hispanic. I spent many hours planning units and lessons, looking forward to implementing them in my classroom setting.

Unfortunately, my enthusiasm and excitement related to teaching in the position of an English as a Second Language teacher turned to disappointment, confusion and frustration. Within the first few weeks of my teaching experience in this capacity, I was met with resistance, indifference, and even negativity related to my students. As time passed, I was disappointed to observe that my students' needs were not being met in their classrooms, or anywhere else in the school community. On the surface they appeared to "fit in" and were signaled out during special occasions when particular holidays such as *Cinco de Mayo* or *Chinese New Year* were "celebrated." However, such celebrations were infrequent and not authentic. The units and lessons that I planned were set aside as I was expected to act more as a tutor for my students to complete unfinished class work, homework assignments, etc. For the first time, I began to reflect more on the teachings in my education classes related to the role of teachers in society to promote a fair and just education for students of all backgrounds. I began to consider seriously what it meant to be denied a fair and equitable education due to one's status in society. I always assumed that the educational system was structured in a manner to afford all students the same opportunities and that simply by going to school would provide all students, regardless of class or race, an equal chance to benefit from a positive and successful educational experience.

I tried to remain positive; I thoroughly enjoyed working in both of my school assignments with dedicated and talented colleagues, not to mention my amazing students. However, I began to doubt my ability to make a positive difference in the lives of my students and began to let the resistance and negativity of the few have a negative impact on my entire teaching perspective. I was unsure of my role and did not follow through with what I felt was right or best for my students. I did not advocate for them to the best of my ability, as I did not feel that I was prepared to stand up for what I believed in. In the back of my mind, I knew that it was my responsibility to advocate for my students and their families to ensure that their needs were being met; I just didn't know how to go about it without overstepping my ground.

Toward the end of my first year as an ESL teacher, again unexpectedly, I was informed by administration that I would need to become certified in Teaching English to Speakers of Other Languages (TESOL) in order to maintain my position with the district. As much as I enjoyed working with my students and their families, I had been hoping to transition into a regular classroom position as soon as possible. Reluctantly, I began the certification process at Le Moyne College. As my story unfolds, you will learn that my educational experience at Le Moyne proved to be invaluable and that my thoughts and judgments regarding my colleagues' attitudes and perceptions concerning my students were premature and unfair. It not only changed my entire perspective on teaching English as a Second Language and teaching in general, it helped me to discover and realize my purpose in life.

The TESOL certification program at Le Moyne College not only prepared me to be a more effective English as a Second Language teacher, but it also prepared me to be a better teacher in any classroom setting. While my entire experience at Le Moyne was positive, it was the Multicultural Literacy class that I had the privilege of taking with Dr. Patricia R. Schmidt, which made all the difference to me, not only as a teacher, but an individual. It provided me with not only the knowledge and tools needed to be an effective teacher of minority students (and students in general), more important, it also gave me the confidence and inspiration to follow through with what I believe in. The growth that I made as an individual during this course, especially related to the *ABC's of Cultural Understanding and Communication* is profound. Going through this process allowed me to make connections related to my own life, how my position in society impacts my interactions with students and families from different backgrounds, as well as other significant people in my life. It helped me pull together and gain a better understanding of semesters of coursework, readings, lectures, etc. related to educational theory, especially as it relates to providing all children with fair, equal and positive learning experiences.

The manner in which Dr. Schmidt conducted her Multicultural Literacy class was centered on the beliefs and practices of the book, *Reconceptualizing Literacy in the New Age of Multiculturalism and Pluralism*, and her *ABC's of Cultural Understanding and Communication* process. Most important, Dr. Schmidt acted as a role model in and out of class, providing us with real life examples from her own experiences and immediate feedback concerning our past and most recent experiences related to this process, thus confirming that her framework is effective, having a positive impact on students and their families. Throughout the course, she created a nonthreatening atmosphere in which we were able to share our experiences and learn from each other. We listened, shared, discussed, questioned, laughed and even cried (men included). We observed firsthand what a powerful process this is. After completing the course with Dr. Schmidt, I now have a structure, or a process to support my educational convictions. My purpose is clear and after having benefitted from going through the *ABC's of Cultural Understanding and Communication* process, I am confident as I prepare and deliver instruction to my students, while at the same time follow through with my convictions as I advocate for them in all situations. After completing Dr. Schmidt's course in Multicultural Education and going through the *ABC's of Cultural Understanding and Communication* process, I am committed to taking action *to fulfill my responsibilities as an educator, striving to ensure the best possible learning experience for all students.*

## AUTOBIOGRAPHY

## Taking Responsibility/Putting Things in Perspective

Writing one's autobiography is certainly a task that requires much thought and reflection. For many of us, reflecting on the past is not always a pleasant experience. I have often thought that without having experienced hard times, the good times would not seem as wonderful. For me, especially more recently, writing has served as a powerful vehicle to vent and understand my thoughts and emotions. I have found that it is a constructive and productive way to organize thoughts, ideas and emotions. Writing my autobiography then, is the beginning of my journey toward making a positive difference in the lives of my students, by understanding how my background and experiences have shaped me. I have learned that my background and past experiences, indirectly as well as directly, have a significant impact on the students and families that I work with. Becoming explicitly aware of how the culmination of my life experiences influence my behavior toward others will help me to adjust my teaching to meet the needs of my students, keeping an open mind and fair approach in my instruction and overall teaching philosophy.

As an adult, I have learned that while my childhood was filled with contradictions, ups and downs, good times and bad times, etc., it was also one in which I was afforded many opportunities and experiences that many people are not as fortunate to have. More important, I have learned that one cannot compare one person's misfortune or bad experience(s) to another's. Everyone's experiences are unique and significant in some way. It's what you do with such experiences once you have the potential to act on them that makes the difference.

## Family

I was born on December 19 in Oswego, New York. My mother says that my due date was actually December 22 and if I were born any closer to Christmas, my name would have been Holly. Shortly after I was born, we moved in with my grandparents, while my father finished college. Upon his graduation, we moved to Rochester, as my father's first job was with *Kodak*.

Through the years, my father has had many educational experiences and is successful at his career as a project engineer at *Alcan Aluminum Corporation* where he has worked for more than thirty years. He makes a hobby out of building computers from spare parts and is a workaholic.

Unfortunately, he is also an alcoholic. If there is such a condition, he may fit the label "functional alcoholic."

My mother is an amazing woman—kind, generous, and hardworking, just to name a few of her admirable characteristics. She is the eldest daughter of seven children and spent most of her young adult life helping care for and raise her siblings. Times were tough and she faced many hardships related to familial matters. She has always been an example of strength and dignity and now enjoys a healthy and more peaceful life. She is also a vegetarian and certified yoga instructor. She makes it a point to go out of her way to educate friends and loved ones on the benefits of healthy eating and exercise. I also have a younger brother, sister, and stepfamily.

## Earliest Memories

My earliest memories begin when I was around four or five year's old. We lived in a pleasant and peaceful neighborhood, on the east side of the river, surrounded by friendly neighbors. Oswego is situated on Lake Ontario and a river runs through it, south to north, dividing the city, east and west. Beautiful trees neatly lined the streets and well-kept parks were easily accessible. In fact, there was one just down the street from our house. I spent a lot of time at this park, eventually obtaining my first job there, as a "park girl." We also lived within walking distance from my elementary school where, as fate would have it, I am now a teacher and where my grandmother retired from teaching. When I picture my neighborhood as a child, I see winters with snow blanketing the streets, the snow banks climbing toward the tree tops and summers smelling of freshly mowed lawns where neighbors proudly and carefully attended to their yards, taking time to pleasantly talk about the day's events.

Writing my autobiography and including the years up until I left home and went to college is somewhat difficult, probably because I have tried to put my past behind me and focus on the present and future. Those early years were the tumultuous ones, when my parents were "on again, off again." My brother and I never knew what to expect. It was very confusing and, of course, we always hoped for the best. At the time, the best was having my parents stay together and work things out.

The most difficult part of living in a dysfunctional family is growing up with friends that had what seemed like "normal" families. My closest friends never knew what went in my house. I rarely invited friends over, as I was afraid of how my parents would act, more specifically, if my father would come home inebriated, causing an embarrassing scene. My mother did not like alcohol and never engaged in excessive drinking. She tried everything to convince my father to get help, vocally and adamantly expressing her unhappiness and disapproval of his actions, or lack thereof. I shared my mother's convictions, however, was not in a position at the time to make a difference, as much as I wanted to and tried. Therefore, I spent a lot of time at friends' houses or just outside. I was a "tomboy," so I enjoyed, even preferred being outside.

As I write, I realize that I don't enjoy the experience of going down memory lane painting a picture of an awful childhood. It certainly wasn't all-bad. But the fact is, as a family unit, much of it was. Things happened that I am not ready to share in great length or detail. I should stress, however, that for the purpose of the assignment related to the *ABC's of Cultural Understanding and Communication*, it is an important and critical step to complete this aspect of the process and one that should be explored and examined carefully. I realize that this is just the beginning for me in learning about myself, how my past experiences influence the manner in which I relate to others from different backgrounds. The more I understand myself, the better I will be able to communicate with others in a positive and productive manner. Already, reflecting on my life and committing my thoughts and emotions to paper, I have discovered what I have been afraid of and what I need to do to not only move forward, but to have the knowledge and courage to share my experiences and help others.

I was very happy to begin kindergarten in the neighborhood school. I never missed a day unless I was forced to stay home due to illness. I loved school and took advantage of all it had to offer. All through K-12, as well as college, I had wonderful, inspiring teachers. In high school, I was on the track for a regent's diploma and took all the advanced courses, my favorite subjects being science, math and Spanish. I was also involved with many extracurricular activities, including yearbook sports editor, ski club, honor society, soccer, and other sports and activities. I know that my mother was always proud of my educational accomplishments and athletic awards. I don't think she ever missed a soccer game and I know she enjoyed them thoroughly.

As I mentioned, I was a "tomboy" as a young child, which naturally led to my interest and ability in athletics. While I enjoyed all sports, especially gymnastics, softball and track, my passion was soccer. I began playing in the local youth soccer program and played through high school and college. It was also through sports that I not only made my best high school and college lifelong friends, it also provided me with a positive outlet related to worries stemming from home.

The most difficult part of school and growing up involved my pursuit for "perfection," coupled with my father's seemingly unending habit of making life very difficult for everyone. I spent many nights comforting my younger brother as my parent's arguing and fighting kept us awake. Without divulging the details, I will simply reveal that it was very difficult to function the next day in school with little to no sleep as well as the images and worries of events that unfolded the previous night and what to expect when we returned home. I remember times during warmer weather when my parents were engaged in an "argument" and I would run around the house frantically attempting to close all of the windows, hoping the neighbors wouldn't hear what was going on. Reflecting on this, I must have looked like a complete idiot, especially since it was done in vain. Even if I did manage to close the windows, they would have already heard anyway!

Many unpleasant happenings transpired over the years during my childhood, things that my brother and I witnessed and endured as a result of our father's alcoholism, that I won't recount now, as such events need to be told with the humor that they now deserve. As I get older, while the difficult experiences associated with alcoholism shouldn't be minimized, I do see the humor and more importantly the "humanness" in all that transpired. Everything that I relate in my writing is an honest reflection of what I experienced and how it impacts me today.

Prior to writing my autobiography, I unknowingly harbored a lot of resentment toward my parents, especially my father and refused to look back. I even blamed some of my failures or failure to go forward in many ways on such past experiences. I realize now that ignoring such issues is not healthy or productive. My story isn't communicated in an attempt to blame anyone, I am simply telling it the way it was and I know that there are others who have had it so much worse. Without going through the experience of writing my autobiography, I may have never reached this conclusion and perhaps would have perpetuated a negative thought pattern regarding my past, which would undoubtedly continue to hold me back and have negative repercussions in my relationships with other people, including my students and their families. I'm not ashamed of this part of my life anymore, rather, I recognize it, accept it and will do my best to use my knowledge and experiences related to alcoholism in a positive way to help others. This writing experience is perhaps the first step toward taking such action.

## Good Times, Bad Times—the Contradiction of Family

I also have many wonderful memories of my childhood. As I mentioned, Oswego is situated on Lake Ontario. As long as I can remember, our family owned a boat that we spent a great amount of time on during summers. My father still enjoys his outings on the boat and sometimes, although not often enough, my own family and I join him. Some of my best memories were spent on this enchanting lake in our boat, the *Lotto*, named after our beloved pet dog (he did not inherit his name after the *NY State Lottery*). I loved the speed of the boat and the freedom I felt in the wide open, with the wind in my hair and the warm sun upon my face. The speed at which the boat crashed into the waves was frightening and thrilling at the same time. I learned how to water-ski at a young age and enjoyed watching my parents ski as well. Our family enjoyed many summer nights on the lake, when the water was "like glass," as my parents often said. I will always remember the sights and smells of those special nights, not to mention the breathtakingly beautiful sunsets.

Unfortunately, many of these experiences were also tainted due to my father's heavy drinking. There were times when we would reach a destination and have to rely on someone else to come and retrieve us, as my mother was much too afraid to ride home in the boat with my brother and me. Foolishly and stubbornly, my father would depart on the boat and we would worry about him until he arrived home safely. Fortunately, today he is a much more responsible boatman. Even though I have had some negative experiences involving the lake, I feel it is a part of me and something I cannot live without. I feel at peace when I am near it. It is one connection and love of something that I share with my father. I know I will always go there and that is where I will find him.

We also spent a lot of time camping during my childhood and this was something I enjoyed, most of the time. I loved the beaches, campfires, new adventures, etc. I did much of what "normal" children did on the surface. I was a Brownie, Girl Scout, participated in summer camps, etc. Again, positive experiences surrounding such events were more often than not, abruptly ended with an unpleasant turn of events stemming from irresponsible alcohol intake on the part of my father.

Aside from boating and camping, my father's favorite pastimes, he was not involved in anything that I did while growing up. This wouldn't have been such a disappointment if there was a good reason for his absence, but passing time in a local bar rather than attending your child's special events sends a negative message. Sadly, he never really took an interest in me until my parents finally divorced. By this time, I was relieved that the marriage ended and regretted that they had not followed through with it earlier.

## College Days

Going away to college was one of the best experiences in my life. I chose SUNY Binghamton for its high academic standards and reputation for a quality education. I also was not sure what I wanted to pursue as a major, although I always knew that I would be a teacher someday. Bing-hamton did not offer a teaching program; therefore, I graduated with a BA in psychology. At the time, I didn't care; I was just happy to be away from home and enjoyed the freedom that came with college. Throughout college, I never talked about my family, unless it was something positive. My friends rarely, if ever, saw my father as my mother was around more often and had remarried. My undergraduate college experience was very positive and is full of many unforgettable memories.

## Early Career

Upon graduation, I had no idea what I wanted to do as far as my career ambitions in the short term. Again, I still knew that I would be a teacher someday. Because I needed money anyway to finance a graduate degree, I went to work. With a BA in psychology, I soon learned that my options were very limited. I began working at the department of social services as a child protective investigator. Going into this position, I was advised that the "burn out" rate was high and no sooner did I find out why. My experiences related to this job were invaluable and taught me many lessons about life; however I knew that I would not make it my lifelong career. After working at this job for about six years, nothing surprises me. As a child protective investigator, I dealt with many issues of child neglect and abuse, ranging from serious physical abuse to sexual abuse. Working intensely with families coping with serious issues over significant lengths of time gave me a new perspective on the human experience-the struggles and obstacles that people are up against and strive to overcome on a daily basis.

Prior to meeting my husband, I applied to the Peace Corps. Just as my husband and I were enjoying the beginning of a wonderful relationship, I learned that I was accepted to the Peace Corps and was given my assignment. Initially, I accepted the invitation and was overjoyed with the prospect of following through with this goal. My departure date was set for February 14, 1992, for Costa Rica. I had always been fascinated by other cultures and languages, especially Spanish and was excited knowing that I would be immersed in a different language and culture. My assignment was to work in the urban area with pregnant and at risk teenagers. Regretfully, I made the decision to decline the invitation, with the notion that I would follow through with this goal someday. After I retire, or after our kids have grown, I will join the Peace Corps, and fulfill this goal with my husband.

Shortly after my husband and I were married, July 22, 1995, we moved to East Greenbush, near Albany. There, I continued to work as a child protective investigator at the Rensselaer county DSS. While I thought that I had seen everything working in this field in Oswego County, I realized that I hadn't seen anything yet when I began working in this region. While living in East Greenbush, on December 29, 1996, the happiest day of our lives arrived when our son Andrew Gregory was born.

## A Teacher

Upon our return to Oswego, I set out to pursue my goal of becoming a teacher. Then, on October 8, 1999, the other happiest day of our lives transpired, when our second son, Alexander Sheldon was born. I completed my Master of Science in Education in the summer of 2001 and began teaching English as a Second Language that fall. I am currently taking Multicultural Literacy as part of a requirement for the TESOL certification program at Le Moyne. Although I enjoy my job more than I thought possible, I hope to teach in a "regular" upper elementary classroom within the next few years. I travel between two elementary schools in Oswego and work with absolutely amazing students. I learn more and more from them every day.

## My Family and Culture

Most important, my husband and I are very proud of our two sons. They surprise us every day with their ability to learn and fill our lives with wonder and awe. Andrew is just finishing Kindergarten and is already smarter than the two of us put together and Alexander is enjoying preschool, following in his brother's foot steps. The positive impact they have had in our lives is tremendous.

While I feel as though I have written at length, I also feel that I have only just begun. I barely discussed my family origins and the celebrations and events associated with these origins. My husband is half Irish and half Polish and even though I am not Polish by decent, I feel more "Polish" than anything. This group's collective history is intriguing and inspiring. Religion has also played a significant role in my life. I also haven't mentioned many significant people and events that have had a positive impact in my life. Due to the time frame in which this assignment was due and my uneasiness associated with writing about myself, I will end now. I know that I will come back to this writing piece and fill in the gaps, adding details and elaborating as experiences continue to unfold and growth is made. This writing has been positive, as it reminds me that I have a lot to be thankful for and there is still so much left to accomplish.

**BIOGRAPHY**

## Introduction

Recently, and initially for the purpose of carrying out the assignment related to the *ABC's of Cultural Understanding and Communication*, I had the privilege of getting to know a unique and wonderful person. This experience was unexpected and, as is the case of many unanticipated events in life, it was also very exciting and rewarding. I met Freddie Cordoba through a family that I have known for the past two years in my role as a teacher. As an English as a Second Language teacher, I have been working with siblings that although are not his biological children, he now refers to as his own, and with great pride. These children have been through many difficult experiences in their short lives, experiences that have left physical and emotional scars that they will carry with them, in some way, for the rest of their lives. Despite their hardships, the children have demonstrated their resilience and courage time and again and their natural desire to embrace all that is wonderful in life. These children are mentioned here, as they play a central and significant role in Freddie's life today. They are his hope for a better future.

Freddie Cordoba was born on September 24, 1966, in the small town of Utuado, Puerto Rico. He is the youngest of twelve children, including nine sisters and three brothers. Utuado is situated inland, in the midwestern part of the island, southwest of San Juan. He lived there until he, his mom and siblings moved to the United States when he was about nine and a half years old. While none of his family still resides in the same homestead, aunts (mother's sisters) and other relatives continue to reside in Puerto Rico.

When I initially approached Freddie to ask him if he would be willing to allow me to interview him and write his life story, he reacted in a very humble manner. He wondered why I would want to write about his life story and not someone elses. I explained to him that I was taking a multicultural literacy class and that I was required to interview someone from a different culture than my own. I went on to explain that I have always been fascinated with Puerto Rico; it's people and culture. I told him that I thought he would be someone that could provide me with many of the questions that I have not been able to find the answers to and provide me with an authentic perspective on his unique background. I explained that gaining a better understanding of his culture would help me as I plan my instruction and interact with my students and their families.

Freddie agreed to participate in my assignment; however, I sensed an uneasiness in his voice. Little did I know at that moment that he agreed to share with me not only his positive memories, but his most painful ones as well ... the intimate details of his life. I had no idea, at the time, that hearing and examining his life story would change my own perspective on life, in essence, the positive impact it would have on me, especially related to my role as a teacher. For that, I am extremely grateful to have had this opportunity, especially to Freddie, for sharing his life story with me.

## Early Memories of Life in Puerto Rico

I began by asking Freddie to think about his earliest memories as a child. Initially, he seemed to struggle with recalling such memories stating, "I remember a few things." A few memories led to many, as he made connections and seemed to enjoy the experience of having the opportunity to share such memories. Not surprisingly, the first memory he related was of his mother. He recalls with intense thought, "My mother was washing clothes next to a river, on a stone. We lived in a stone house with a dirt floor and a wood stove, which consisted of a slab of iron on top of a couple of cinder blocks with wood under it." In order to get a better idea of this setting, I did some research on this area and discovered beautiful photographs of the river that he referred to ... its winding bends and prominently placed stones. With this in mind, I visualized an image of his mother as she carried out her daily routine by the river, young Freddie by her side.

Freddie stopped there, as if he was surprised by his ability to recollect his past in such vivid detail. I then asked him what comes to mind when he looks back on his life at that time. He remembers that at that time some of his siblings were already living out on their own. He recalled that his older brothers were already out working on the farm, in the sugar cane fields, coffee plantations and pineapple fields. He recalls, "Dad actually worked on a farm, picking coffee beans and cutting sugar cane. I remember running through the sugar cane fields. It looks almost like bamboo, like running through fields of bamboo." He elaborates, "I remember my mother walking me by my hand with a sack on her other hand, with two or three loaves of bread. And maybe a quarter pound of cheese and a quarter pound of salami and a canister of water and a thermos of coffee to go bring to my dad. He worked sometimes thirteen hours, fourteen hours a day. He would get up in early morning, five o'clock in the morning, 'till sundown."

## Going to School in Puerto Rico

I asked Freddie to think about his first day of school. He recalled the physical appearance of the schoolhouse stating, "School was nothing but a long ... looked like some kind of a warehouse building, all old wood.

The fencing around it was about seven feet, all concrete." He went on to state, "It was difficult to learn then because there wasn't state of the art stuff like now. You know, the books were all old; all handed down books, donated from other schools." Despite the lack of supplies, books, etc. and difficult learning environment, Freddie feels that he received a good education while he was in school, in both Puerto Rico and the United States. According to Freddie,

> School in Puerto Rico was very strict. They had the rulers and they would put tape at the end and you would get whacked on your knuckles if you didn't do what they said, or if you misbehaved. Sometimes they would stand you up in the corner facing the wall or they would throw raw rice on the floor and roll up your pants and kneel you down on top of that rice. If you forgot your books, or whatever, at home, the next day when you brought them in they would make you get on your knees on top of the rice with the books on your hand and you couldn't put your hand down. It had to be as long as the teacher said. It was very, very strict.

I suggested that was a harsh punishment, one that would not be allowed in schools today. He went on to explain that it was done with permission stating, "Parents would sign a paper saying yes, you can discipline my child. School was taken serious."

## The Significance of a Caring Teacher

Freddie recalled fond memories of a special teacher he had while attending school in Puerto Rico. He remembers,

> There was one teacher. She always used to rub my face when I walked into class. She was a very, very nice woman. She would baby everybody. It was like we were her kids. And anything we did wrong, in her eyes would be right. She would never see any wrong in us.

Hearing him speak about this memory is a significant reminder of the powerful influence that teachers have on students, to make a positive impact in their lives. She made him feel important and special simply by taking an interest in him. After learning of Freddie's difficult and traumatic experiences at home, the importance of this nurturing relationship with his teacher cannot be underestimated.

## A New Life: Leaving Puerto Rico

Like many Puerto Ricans, Freddie and his family left Puerto Rico for the United States in search of a better life.

When we came here it was more money, more opportunities. My father came here at the age of 25 and he worked at the tobacco farms in New Jersey. And he would send money over there (Puerto Rico) to us. It was cheaper living over there. But at the same time, it would be expensive, for us anyway, because there were twelve of us.

I asked Freddie what specifically prompted his family to seek a better life in the United States. Freddie explained,

We couldn't make it over there for the simple fact that my father had a drinking habit and we lost our land and our farm. And he tried to come to the United States so he could make up for that, try to send money over there but it was too late. So instead of him paying off what he owed, he took the money and he sent for us and we all came to the United States.

## A Winter Wonder Land?

In the beginning, life seemed good for Freddie in the United States. He remembers, "The only part I didn't like was when we came from Puerto Rico to here. I had a 'bola de bu', which was like a puss ball under my foot, right in the center of my foot." He goes on to describe how the injury occurred.

In Puerto Rico they have the river, and they had old barges from World War II and stuff like that. And we would jump off of it into the water. And one day, it was raining. It was so bad the day before that it washed down all kinds of metal stuff like shopping carts and I stepped on a bullet with a nail in it. It was rusty, so I almost lost my foot. They operated on me over there in Puerto Rico and the next day, after the operation, we came here.

Landing in New York was quite a surprise, as Freddie had never experienced snow before. He remembers,

I was in the plane with my brother, Edwin, carrying me, one boot on, one boot off and when I looked out the window on the plane, everything was white. Everything was white, everything! And as soon as they opened the door to step off the plane, I turned right around, came right back in. And there was a lady downstairs, who was my father's friend, waiting with coats and hats and gloves and scarves. So that made it a little warm. But having one foot with no boot was tough. They didn't want my brother carrying me because we both might fall. So I got a taste of what a frozen foot felt like. It was snow everywhere!

As evident by the detail and the enthusiasm for which this memory was recounted, Freddie's arrival in the United States had a lasting impression, especially with a little help from Mother Nature.

## Memories of Home, Cooking and Food

I asked Freddie about the significance of food in his life, as I had read that Puerto Ricans revolve around food, a common theme throughout many cultures. He explained,

> We basically survived right off of the farm. We had boiled bananas, green bananas boiled, platanos, green plantains, also boiled. Once they're ripe, all you can do is fry them. And we would have pork, right from the farm. And we would have beef right from the farm and we would have chickens right from the farm. Everything was fresh; we didn't buy stuff from the store—meats and stuff, everything was slaughtered right there. My father would trade … I'll give you this cow for that horse and these two pigs or I'll give you these two rabbits for that chicken and that's how my father did it. That's how we survived over there.

Freddie recalls that his mother was and still is an excellent cook.

> My mother also made white rice with everything. She used to make everything homemade, all the spices and everything. My mother did all the cooking. There wasn't much to clean because, like I said, there was no floor. And the walls were just stone so there was no wiping down of walls and no cleaning of windows because the windows were nothing but wood.

He goes on to describe the living area.

> It was always warm but there was always a scare of snakes and rats getting in the house, coming from the marsh and from the sugar cane field that was right next to it. One of my brothers was bit by a rat on his foot. He got gangrene and they had to cut one of his toes off.

He describes the house as having two rooms, the parlor and the kitchen as one big wide-open room. He remembers a door that would open to a bedroom with a loft at the top.

> That's where all the kids slept. And my mother and father would sleep at the bottom, on the bottom floor. And we had to walk outside to the outhouse, which was, by the way, like a quarter of a mile away. Down the hill, way down by the river.

## Memories of Mother and the Difficult Times

Speaking about Freddie's mother brought back painful memories. He takes time to reflect, as he appears to gather strength to continue,

The memories of my mother in Puerto Rico are sad. She experienced beatings every day. Like I said before, my father was an alcoholic. She would be
locked in the house and my father would go into the sugar cane fields and
my mother was only allowed to come out at lunchtime to bring him food
and then she had to be back in the house. As soon as she got home he would
send one of the people with the horse by there to see if she was home, to
make sure that she was in the house. And he would come home already half
passed out drinking. He would beat her and show her who's the boss.

These memories are etched in his mind, as he was a witness to the
actual beatings. "A couple of times I would crawl into a ball and go in a
room or do something, but I would not be able to protect her because he
was very mean. I was very afraid of him. We all were."
I asked Freddie if his father ever talks about those times.

No, he doesn't talk about it. He doesn't like talking about it. I confronted
him one time about it. And I told him that out of all my brothers, I'm the
only one who's drug free and has been by his side and my mother's side all
the time and how I help him out of every little jam he gets into because he
doesn't speak or write English. He doesn't know how to read or write and
he's blind in one eye, losing sight in the other. And I told him, just remember that the one that you treated the worst is the one that helps you out the
most, and the ones that you treated the best are the ones that want nothing
to do with you now. And he started crying. Inside he is (sorry) but he doesn't
let it be known because he's just stubborn.

## Turning Ten ( ... and Being Robbed of Innocence)

Freddie remembers that when they first came to "the Cape," it was
basically all good in the beginning. But quickly, things went downhill.
Sadly, Freddie remembers an event that unfolded on what he, like all children, hope to be a day filled with fun, happy memories—his birthday.
Freddie recalls,

I remember when I turned ten, in Massachusetts. When I turned ten years
old, how he had started drinking. I remember this, clear as day. How he
started drinking early with his friends and after this we celebrated my birthday. After his friends left, he started on my mother, saying how she was looking at one of his friends and she wanted him. He would start yelling and
screaming at her and I covered my ears and I started yelling and screaming
because I was in shock from hearing what he was saying to her. I covered my
ears and started screaming and yelling for everyone to just shut up and not
ruin my birthday and I remembered him clearly just swinging his arm back-
wards, hitting me with his fist in my mouth, threw me on the floor off the
chair. I was ready to blow the candles out on the cake, then he picked me up

from the floor and then he threw me up against the wall. And my mother ran, while two of my brothers held him, two of my other younger brothers ran into the room with my mother and me and I told my mother, let's get out of here. It doesn't matter where, anywhere, even the street is better than living here. And he walked into the room with a machete and he told my mother 'if you leave me I will find you and I will kill you.' So my mother went into the kitchen that night to light a cigarette and he was sitting at the table with a file, sharpening his machete. So my mother called one of the teachers that spoke Spanish and at that time of the night and the teacher says, "I really don't want to get into it because it sounds like a dangerous situation but I will send the cops over there." The cops never came and we had to jump out our second floor window while my mother was pregnant and we slept in a cranberry bog over night in an old abandoned truck that was there. And one of the bosses from the cranberry bog saw us early in the morning. He got us assistance and he put us up in a hotel and then my mother put an order of protection on him so he wouldn't be able to find out where we were, but he still sent messages with my brother that he was going to kill us.

## Forgiving Father

Due to the abuse his mother endured by his father, Freddie's mother suffered a serious neck injury. Freddie witnessed this beating recalling, "After everybody left (the party), he beat her with the machete with the flat side of the edge. He beat her; he hit her 27 times on her back with it." I asked Freddie what he was thinking and feeling when he saw this happen. He replied, "I was scared to death because he's known to hurt people. Nothing scared him."

I asked Freddie what makes him different from his siblings, that he has stood by his father, despite all the abuse. He states,

I help him because he's my dad. If it weren't for him taking care of me as a child, I wouldn't be here. But I throw the hint out there every once in a while and I remind him of the pain he caused the family and the pain he caused my mother. And he always tells me it's none of my business.

## Down a Long, Rough Road

Freddie's formal education took him through eighth grade. He explained, "I had to be like an adult in the family. I pretty much learned up to eighth grade what I needed to know. What I thought would get me by, but now I think different." I asked him if he felt that he received a good education. He replied,

I was treated pretty fair, because the main thing was I went there to learn. And I would do all my homework. But from the seventh grade on I started experimenting with marijuana and alcohol. I guess it was because of depression. And the family had so many things happening all at once. I just kinda started experimenting with marijuana and drinking and, let me tell you, I regret those days.

After eighth grade, Freddie started working in the cranberry bogs as a picker and from there his drinking and experimenting with drugs became worse. He worked in the cranberry bogs for about three or four years and then started working in construction. Then, he cut down on drugs, but was still drinking heavily. In 1988 he met a girl. He remembers,

She was one of the girls I picked on in school, in sixth grade. We had a child together in 1988 and in 1990 we separated. I continued my life, just out there drinking and doin' drugs and working and I used to go visit my father once in a while. And one day I went over to visit my daughter and I saw blood on her diaper and I confronted her (the girlfriend) about it. She told me she didn't know anything and I started investigating around and it so happens the guy on the third floor was a child molester. We brought him to court on it and we didn't have any proof so he got two years probation and coming out of court, in the heat of the moment I blacked out, I grabbed the gun and I went to the court. I shot him eight times and I ended up doing ten years in prison for involuntary manslaughter. I got out in 1998.

It was difficult for Freddie to share his experiences with me related to this part of his life. And, truthfully, it was also very difficult for me to hear. When he revealed this part of his life, I was caught off guard, completely shocked by what I had learned. As he continued divulging information regarding this part of his life, the thought that I was sitting next to and engaging in a conversation with someone who admittedly committed murder, made me very uneasy. Yet, I continued to listen, as it was obvious that he trusted me and needed to talk to someone. My past experiences as a child protective investigator also came to mind and carried a sense of urgency with it.

Freddie is still in the process of healing and sorting out his negative past experiences and how they affect his life today. I appreciated his honesty and willingness to speak openly and honestly about this period of his life. Freddie earned his GED while in prison and became a mentor. He also met a pastor that had a positive influence on him but not until his seventh year in prison. I asked him how he coped with things for such a long period of time. He replied, "It's very traumatic, it's very traumatic. You are more scared to get released and go back into society than you are to go in there." I asked him if he had any regrets of committing this crime. He replied,

In a way I do. Because everybody has a right to being angry, but you don't have the right to act on that anger. And because it's ten years that I didn't see my daughter. And I just recently saw her, like two years ago, and that's the last I seen of her. I explained to her why I went to prison, cause her mother left that all up to me, to explain that to her. She was only 18 months old. And I explained it to her and then I moved here, to Oswego.

Freddie thought for a while and then spoke,

I also understand where my father's anger came from. He was the only child and his dad also beat him. He was told he would never amount to anything. He never went to school, never, not once. He went straight to the farm. The same thing with my mom. My mom only went up to third grade. I never met my father's parents at all. My mother told us about the way he used to get beating after beaten. He would get fed only if he worked. And his mother and father were also alcoholics. My mother's mother and father were also alcoholics.

We discussed the topic of alcoholism and its devastating effects on people and families. Freddie stated, "Alcoholism is a disease. Just like a person that smokes a cigarette, you won't make it through the day without it."

## Looking Forward

We had a discussion about the positive impact that Freddie has had on the five children, now a part of his life. He hopes they learn from his mistakes and have a better life. I let Freddie know that I admired his dedication to the children and that it takes a lot of courage and strength to tell the truth and speak so candidly about such painful experiences. I suggested that at some point the cycle has to stop and one has to be the stronger person. Without guidance and support from his father and family, Freddie has survived many hardships in life. With this in mind, I believe that Freddie is the stronger person. Because of his perseverance and inner strength, he is in a position in which he has and can continue to make a positive difference in the lives of his children. He looks toward a bright future for them, stating, "I always tell the kids, when you're standing up on that stage and when you're picking up your diploma, the words that are going to come out are, 'thanks for the diploma and if it wasn't for that guy yelling at me all the time, I would never be where I am right now.'"

I complimented Freddie on the positive influence that he has had on his five wonderful kids and their mother. They have so much potential to go places and experience success and happiness in life. I stress that the key is to keep persevering, despite the obstacles, and I now recognize and appreciate that there are many. Like any other student in their school, they too can succeed, graduate from high school and college, moving on to achieve great things. Too often, I hear the words from my students that they cannot do it, putting themselves down, even giving up. Freddie included,

> They're at the age where they need that—discipline, because they never had it from anybody else. And the reason why I yell a lot is because I stress out because they don't want to listen to me. Lately, they have been very, very good kids. Very rebellious sometimes. But it's because what they've been through too. Which is another story.

I suggested that is where he comes in and that it just goes to show that there is a purpose and a meaning in life.

## "Don't Judge a Person Until you Have Walked a Mile in His Moccasins" (Native American Proverb)

I asked Freddie if he felt that being a Puerto Rican has limited his opportunities. He replied,

> Opportunities as far as employment, part of that has to do with me. Committing crimes at an early age makes it hard for people to hire you. I shouldn't blame anybody but myself, but when I look back, the way I was brought up, the way I was raised. Rebellious kid, just didn't care.

We talked further regarding his prison time. He explained why he was convicted of involuntary manslaughter stating, "It means that I did it without; I wasn't in my right state of mind when I did it." I asked him if it was a reaction to what happened to his daughter. He replied, "Yes, because the same thing happened to me. The same thing happened to me as a child and the first thing I thought of was that I don't want my daughter to go through that pain." I asked him if he felt comfortable sharing this experience. He explained that it happened when he was seven or eight years old, while living in Puerto Rico. He recalled, "Someone that claimed to be my uncle, but he wasn't, he was just a friend of my dad."

I understood then and in a deeper, more significant way than I had prior to our in-depth discussions related to my assignment, that Freddie truly has had several difficult/traumatic experiences in life and that I hoped talking about it was helpful for him. He shared that he has talked about some of his abusive experiences a few times with professionals but that he has never confronted anybody. He stated, "It took me a while to be able to trust. I had a trust issue. I thought everyone was just out to get me." I agreed that he had a right to feel that way. There's no reason for anyone to have to go through what he went through as a child. While there's no justification for committing murder, perhaps Freddie didn't know any other way to cope with his experiences, confusion and anger.

I suggested that you can't judge a person or know a person until you've walked in their shoes. Without hesitation, he agreed. I asked him what he thought brings people to the point of abusing drugs and alcohol.

> Some people look towards that for power, some people look towards it to kill the pain of what they been through, how they had it rough. Even though it's not an excuse. It's just like alcohol. Alcohol helps you for the time being and makes you forget, but the next day you feel a headache and you feel worse. And what do you do, you continue to do it to get rid of that head ache—to get rid of that pain again. And so on … it's like a cycle that will keep goin' and goin' and goin'. And the system doesn't see that. Alcoholism is an illness. It's not that they choose to pick up the bottle. They have to pick it up. Some people have to.

Hearing these words gave me a new perspective regarding alcoholism and other illnesses related to drugs and what I can do to understand better and help others in need, including my own father.

## A VERY WISE MAN

I asked Freddie if he felt he has been treated unfairly because he is Puerto Rican. He replied,

> There's a lot of people that think that blacks should stay in Africa and Puerto Ricans should stay in Puerto Rico. But little do they know, we got the same color blood. Yes. In a lot of ways. I get stared down when I sit in restaurants with my partner and I get stared at or followed when we go into a store, especially when she goes her way toward the women or children's clothes and I go my way toward the tools and stuff and people walk by and hang around.

I asked him why he thinks he is treated this way. He stated, "Because they put us all in the same category. Because they think that all Spanish are thieves. Like if a black person walked in, they think that all black people are thieves."

This led to a conversation regarding the role of society and schools. I pointed out that traditionally in textbooks the majority of heroes/heroines and positive role models are white and that minority groups are not deservedly recognized for their positive contributions and achievements in society, or are at best, recognized in a superficial, minimized, even inaccurate manner in comparison to other cultures that have made significant contributions. Children from minority backgrounds don't always have the opportunity to learn about such positive role models to emulate and aspire to be like someday. Freddie replied, "They don't show that, not that I have seen."

In this respect, children from minority groups often don't have as many opportunities to read and learn about relevant and significant role models, indirectly suggesting that they are not as important. They need to read and learn about such events related to their own people and history in order to make significant connections to their own lives, through such relevant literature.

I explained to Freddie that it helps to understand his background, his hardships and why people behave in certain ways. I talked about the importance of learning about people from different cultures, to not make judgments without having accurate information, without getting to know the person and their experiences. I suggested that most people who have gone through what he has experienced would be too angry to have a thoughtful conversation and try to make positive changes regarding their past, but would continue to make poor choices and continue on a path of self-destruction. Freddie made it clear, "Oh, I'm angry. I'm angry, but I don't show it. Being angry is not. " And he stops. He goes on to explain that as much as he tries, it is difficult to find a decent paying job and all of the obstacles that he is still up against.

As much as I would have liked to tell Freddie that everything will be all right, I realize that I am not in a position to make such a statement. All I can do is validate that it's tough and that I don't have the answers but I remind him that he has a future to look forward to. His kids have a bright future, with positive guidance. Freddie expresses his concern regarding the children's biological father, "Their father says, you're not going to be anybody; you're going to be just like me. But I told them their education is very important." He continues, "Juan, he's talking about being an architect. He built an atom and took it to school and got a 100." I reinforce this potential, stating that yes he can be an architect; he can be anything he wants to be. But I remind Freddie that children need guidance and encouragement in order to make such dreams a reality. I tell him that is where he comes in; there is a purpose in life for everything. He is the positive difference in their lives.

I end the formal interview process by congratulating Freddie for doing a great job with the children and encourage him to continue to guide them in a positive direction. Getting to know Freddie and learning about the unique experiences that make him the special person he is today was a privilege and I hope he knows how much I have learned from him and how much he matters.

## CROSS-CULTURAL ANALYSIS OF SIMILARITIES AND DIFFERENCES

Prior to writing Freddie Cordoba's biography, I did not consider that we may share similarities and differences that shape my opinion of him, influencing my behavior toward him, as well as other people from backgrounds different from my own, especially related to minority groups. I knew that we were different and I simply assumed that was just the way it was. In fact, I really didn't give it much thought at all. I accepted our roles in society, which are set in place by factors related to a power structure, which perpetuates an unjust social system. Freddie and his "people" were on the periphery and I was closer to the center, a more privileged "class." I never really thought about how this dominant group ideology impacts one's life, as I have always felt comfortable and safe in my role as an individual that benefits from all that comes with belonging to the group closest to the center. While I have recognized the unfairness of this system, I have not acted in a manner to help make a positive change for those that are not as privileged, based upon ethnic background or other determining factors such as gender, sexual orientation, socioeconomic status, etc., thus aiding in the perpetuation of this system.

Now that I have gone through the *ABC's of Cultural Understanding and Communication* process, I have had the opportunity to learn about and understand what it is like to struggle and face a world of uncertainty and prejudice, based upon the color of one's skin and/or ethnic background. As a result of this process, I have taken the time to genuinely get to know a person from a culture different from my own and through his memories and stories, "feel" his pain and hardships. Prior to this experience, I would not have had the foresight or patience to take the time to genuinely get to know and understand someone "like Freddie" let alone sit next to and remain engaged in a conversation with someone who committed a murder. When I went into this assignment, I had no idea what a powerful impact it would have on me as a teacher and a person. More important, the connection that I made with this individual also had a positive impact on him and his perspective regarding his place in society. Knowing that even one more person values him and his culture makes a positive difference.

## MAINTAINING THE CONNECTION

Since my formal interviews with Freddie related to writing his biography, I have met with him and his family, as follow ups to this experience and as a teacher to the children he acknowledges as his own. During these meetings, he has continued to share aspects of his experiences and culture in a more informal manner. Recently, he was very excited to share family photo albums with me that he borrowed from his mother since our interviews. Although I was in a hurry when he offered me the opportunity to look through these albums, and planned on staying for only a few moments, I stopped and thought about the connection that we had made and how important it is to maintain this relationship. I didn't decide to stay and allow him to share his photo album with me because I felt obligated, but rather, I saw it as a chance to learn even more about him. More important, I felt honored that he would want to continue to share meaningful aspects of his life with me.

We sat down, with Freddie on one side of me and his two daughters on the other, as he pointed out pictures related to memories that he shared with me during the interview process. I was able to see pictures of the home that he described while living in Puerto Rico. He recalls, "Remember when I was telling you about how there were no windows in the house, just openings. This is what I was talking about (as he points to the window). Now you can see what I meant about the danger of animals getting in." As he continues to tell his life story, I see pictures of his siblings, mother, father, aunts, uncles and cousins as they engage in celebrations and pose for other special occasions. I observe a picture of a young boy blowing out birthday candles and wonder if it was a happy occasion or tainted by some unfortunate event related to his father's alcoholism. As Freddie looks at these pictures, I can sense that he is taken back, perhaps reliving this time in his life. I wonder when the last time was that he looked at these pictures, or if he ever had at all. He also looks at them and reports with great pride, "this is my cousin, she's an engineer and this is another cousin, she's a model. This is my father with the instrument I showed you" and so on. He then says in a sad voice, "There were some good times, but it could have been different. It could have been better if it wasn't for my fathers drinking."

## WORLDS APART, YET SO MUCH ALIKE

Alcoholism is a similarity that Freddie and I share, that compels and inspires me to confront my own weaknesses and fears as an individual. Although I enjoyed the experience of writing my autobiography and benefitted greatly from this process, I still held back and did not write at length on the topic that has troubled me the most since my childhood. I have not been able to talk about or share the experiences related to my father's alcoholism with anyone in great depth. Listening to Freddie's experiences triggered memories from my own childhood, in fact, situations that almost parallel his. I wondered if we could have been going through such similar experiences at the same time, only in a different place, as we are near in age. When Freddie shared the painful memories of his father beating his mother with the machete, and fleeing to safety in an abandoned truck in a cranberry bog, I couldn't help but be reminded of the incidents in which my father's alcoholism led to similar altercations and consequences. Until this writing assignment, I was not ready to share some of my most painful memories, even in writing. I think that I am just beginning to confront my struggles related to this part of my childhood.

## THE POWER OF FORGIVENESS

I admired Freddie's ability to talk about his father in such a positive way, especially while referring to his alcoholism. He forgives his father, as he recognizes alcoholism as a disease. Although I am knowledgeable regarding alcoholism as a medical term, I have somehow placed my father in a category of his own, relative to this condition. I have even avoided reading at great length on this topic, as perhaps I do not want to confront the truth related to this terrible disease. For so long, I heard my mother plead with my father to get professional help, that he is an alcoholic and will never "get better" without such intervention and my father holding on to the strong conviction that he was (and is) not an alcoholic.

I believed my father, and therefore, perceived him in light of this. If he was not an alcoholic, then he was just a bad husband and a father that didn't care about his family. I never really thought that my father had a disease, something that he couldn't control. He is an intelligent man and has held a respectful job for many years. If this was so, then why couldn't he control his drinking? I always held this against him. In fact, I was embarrassed by him and thought of him as a weak person. I even hated him at times. After all these years, I have still never confronted him, or even expressed my anger or confusion regarding this. More important, I have never gone out of my way to look at things from his perspective in an effort to help him. After listening to Freddie and relating his experiences to my own, I have to question whether or not I have actually forgiven my father and take the necessary steps to resolve this in a positive way. Perhaps this will not only strengthen my relationship with my father, but also give me the courage to help other children that have gone through or are coping with similar circumstances.

## FALSE ASSUMPTIONS

Admittedly, prior to going through this process, I held negative assumptions about Freddie. I assumed that he was just like the other Puerto Rican men in his fiancé's life that had a negative impact on her and her children, related to abuse and a negative lifestyle. I was always suspicious that my students would be let down again by another "father figure" in their lives. But this time seemed different, especially since I was also getting to know Freddie as an individual, related to my assignment.

Prior to Freddie's involvement with my students, they have had difficult and unpleasant school related experiences. They were constantly being signaled out as troublemakers and spent a lot of time being disciplined in the principal's office. They often became angry and felt that they were being treated unfairly. Since Freddie's involvement with the children, however, they have experienced much more success in school. In fact, teachers involved with my students have recognized and complimented Freddie on his positive impact with the children, regarding the routine he has established with them, his involvement in parent-teacher conferences and his efforts related to supporting their learning at home. Still, teachers assumed that this would not last, and it wouldn't be long before something negative transpired due to his "character" to disappoint the kids. I too, was guilty of these thoughts. Like all parents, Freddie only wants what is best for his children. Understanding Freddie and his circumstances has given me the knowledge and confidence that I need to advocate for and empower my students and their families.

After going through this process, I feel very selfish regarding my negative attitudes related to my own childhood experiences. I have held it against my parents, especially my father, for acting in ways that I deemed unacceptable. While their judgment may have been poor at times, it does not make them bad people, but rather human. Yes, my father is an alcoholic, but he still loved us in his own way and provided us with many things that afforded my brother and I advantages—advantages that Freddie did not have.

Initially, I judged Freddie and wondered why he did not become a stronger person in light of his hardships during his childhood and act in a manner that would set him on a path for a different, more productive life than his father's. Instead, he rebelled and "chose" a life of alcohol and drug abuse, which had an extremely negative impact on his life, and those around him. He regrets choices he made and still struggles with his past behaviors. Now I realize that Freddie didn't really have a choice, or at best his options were very limited. He did not have all of the advantages that I had related to my middle class socioeconomic status and my European-American privileged white background. I had advantages that allowed my family to "hide" the alcoholism and partake in many opportunities that are accessible to someone from my background relative to my ethnicity and socioeconomic status. My parents could afford to buy me equipment to play sports, go on ski outings with the ski club, soccer camps, travel abroad, to list a few. I had access to resources and more options to choose from. Freddie and his family, on the other hand, had to struggle to make ends meet. Freddie did not have access to resources that I had which influenced my ability to focus and channel my anger and confusion in a positive direction.

When I compare my situation relative to Freddie's, I realize how fortunate I was growing up and how the privileges that I took for granted have had a powerful and positive impact on my place in society today. I only had one obstacle to struggle within my life, while Freddie had so many more. Knowing how difficult and painful it was for me growing up as a child of an alcoholic parent, I understand better and appreciate more, after really getting to know Freddie, how much more difficult life has been for him. Not only was alcoholism a negative factor in his life, he also faced hardships related to belonging to an oppressed group. When I put myself in his shoes and think about how I would have "survived" his childhood, I don't know what I would have done and the place I would have in society today.

## TEACHERS CAN MAKE A POSITIVE DIFFERENCE: UNDERSTANDING AND APPRECIATING THE POWER TO EMPOWER

While the assignment for this process did not require interviewing an actual parent or caretaker of my students, my situation allowed me to do so. Prior to beginning this process, I did not think seriously about the idea of fostering a strong home-school connection with this family, other than my understanding that this was the anticipated outcome of the *ABC's of Cultural Understanding and Communication* process. I was simply following through with an assignment, required for this Multicultural Literacy course. Having gone through this experience with a caretaker of my students, I have experienced first hand the positive impact that this process has on, not only the parents/caretakers in relationship to their school involvement but more important, the positive impact it has on their children's educational experiences.

While I began this process toward the end of the school year, I have not yet had the opportunity to continue this process and realize its long-term effects relative to developing and fostering a strong home-school connection and its positive connection to literacy growth. In the short time that I have implemented this approach toward literacy development, I am already seeing the positive impact it has had on my relationship with this family. I better understand their struggles, their fears and their hopes for a better future. They believe that a good education is a key ingredient to a better future. I believe that in an effort to help make Freddie and his family's "dream" a reality, as educators we need to act on what we believe in and build a strong home-school connection with the families in our schools. In this respect, we are validating their experiences and connecting such experiences to the learning process, through literature that is relevant to their lives, that confirms their identity and inspires them to succeed.

## MAKING A POSITIVE DIFFERENCE: AN ONGOING PROCESS

Since the initial writing of this chapter, another school year progresses and I continue in my position as an English as a Second Language teacher. Much has changed, however, especially regarding my approach and attitude toward teaching children from diverse and minority backgrounds. I have learned that becoming a good teacher, in any setting, is a lifelong process. Although I am still learning and making changes as needed regarding my overall planning and instruction, I have made it a priority to go out of my way to get to know my students and their families on a personal level and learn first hand about their cultures, experiences, fears, hopes and dreams. In an effort to accommodate my students' needs, I plan my instruction and selection of materials and literature so that it is relevant and meaningful to their lives.

I have also made a concerted effort to share this information with the classroom teachers with whom my students spend most of their school day. Prior to taking this approach and embracing a more positive attitude regarding the entire school community relative to my ESL teaching position, many of my students seemed hesitant to talk about and share their backgrounds with the larger school community. My enthusiasm and confidence regarding my conviction that this process, the *ABC's of Cultural Understanding and Communication*, is effective and its significant role in my planning and teaching, are reflected in the pride my students exude as they excitedly and happily share their life stories and experiences with me, their classmates, teachers, and the entire school community. And when I observe my students make connections related to their experiences in a manner that fosters positive academic growth, I beam with pride knowing that my students not only did their best, but that I also did my best to help meet their needs.

Another change involves my connection with Freddie and his children, now my former students. They have moved out of state; however, we have maintained contact via email and telephone. Freddie and his family still experience difficult times and worry about the future. As always, I offer encouragement and a genuine concern for their well being. I, as well as the many dedicated and caring teachers that were involved with this family, sincerely miss them and hope they are doing well. The strong home/school connection that was forged with this family as a result of carrying out the *ABC's of Cultural Understanding and Communication* process remains strong. The concern and commitment to making a positive difference in our students lives, even thousands of miles away, is evident through our continued efforts to assist them whether it is through positive thoughts, good wishes, ongoing advice and encouragement, letters or care packages, the genuine concern and commitment that my colleagues have demonstrated toward this family are appreciated and remarkable, a true testament to why we are teachers.

My conviction that everything in life happens for a reason, that there are a purpose and a means to an end, holds even more meaning to me now having completed my TESOL certification and engaging in and embracing the *ABC's of Cultural Understanding and Communication* process.

My purpose *is* clear and I realize now that I, along with many of my colleagues, share the same desire and commitment to make a positive difference in the lives of our students and their families. The ongoing process of becoming a good teacher is challenging and often frustrating, but together we can and do make a positive impact in the lives of our students and their families every day.

## REFERENCE

Schmidt, P. R. (2001). The power to empower. In P. R. Schmidt & P. B. Mosenthal (Eds.), *Reconceptualizing literacy in the new age of multiculturalism and pluralism.* Greenwich, CT: Information Age.

CHAPTER 4

# DOING THE ABC'S

## An Introspective Look at Process

### Stacey Leftwich and Midge Madden

### ABSTRACT

In this study, the researchers were interested in exploring the usefulness of the *ABC's of Cultural Understanding and Communication* in their own practice. Developed by Patricia Ruggiano Schmidt, the model allows participants to explore issues of diversity by taking part in several tasks: writing an in-depth autobiography, interviewing and writing a biography of a person identified as outside one's culture, and completing a cultural self-analysis. This article describes how two university professors embarked upon a study in which they participated in, documented their thinking, and arrived at new understandings of the *ABC's Model*.

> *One must learn by doing the thing;*
> *for though you think you know it you have no certainty, until you try.*
> —Sophocles

*ABC's of Cultural Understanding and Communication:*
*National and International Adaptations*, 73–92
Copyright © 2006 by Information Age Publishing

*The two women perch on stools in the warm kitchen. Hot coffee steams from two mugs and the fire crackles, brightening the dismal day outside. Midge reaches over and turns on the tape recorder. "Tell me about yourself, Stacey," she invites. And so the interview begins. One black woman, a young mother in her thirties, and one white woman, a grandmother in her fifties, turn to one another and start to talk.*

"What about your early school memories, Stacey?" Midge asks.

"Well ... " Stacey pauses. "I remember the Eagles, the Bluebirds, and the Crows. The Eagles were the smart group and I was always placed in that group. That is, until the teacher realized that I was really not that smart. Then never fail, I got moved to the Crows, the struggling readers' group."

"So why do you think this happened?"

Stacey looks puzzled for a moment. "I guess because my Dad was in the military and we moved around a lot. Maybe my records didn't always follow. But I looked good—my mom always dressed me nicely—and I could play the game, you know, talk the talk of the school culture."

"Hmmm. What do you mean, play the game?" Midge looks closely at Stacey.

"You know, the game. I could speak well, listen, follow directions ... do what I was supposed to do." Stacey shrugged.

"Actually, you know, I did the same thing. I was this little girl who so wanted to please the teacher. Shoot, I even looked like Jane in Dick and Jane ... God, I remember those books! Jump up, Spot. Jump up Sally. The "perfect American family!" Midge quipped.

"Yeah, well I used the same kind of books. Only it was a newer version and they put people like me in the stories. I guess to be politically correct, you know, after the Civil Rights movement and all that." Stacey gave a wry smile.

"Hmm. So we both played the game. Both got put in top groups. The only difference is that I was always in the Eagles and you got moved out. But it does sound like we were a lot alike doesn't it?" Midge says.

"Yeah it does, but we're probably not," Stacey muses. "I mean I really don't think our lives were the same. Seriously, Atlantic City versus, where did you grow up, Greenwich, Connecticut? How many black people did you know? How many poor people did you hang out with?" Stacey asks sarcastically.

"Okay, you're right," admitted Midge. "There weren't too many underprivileged kids in Greenwich and I don't think any black kids in my school .... at least I didn't know any. But there were Italians and my mother didn't like me hanging out with them."

Surprised, Stacey asks, "Why not?"

"I'm not sure ... I guess because they lived differently. You know, demonstrative, always hugging, kissing and eating huge meals!" Midge grins. "Boy, that's a stereotype! But my mom's perception of Italians always bothered me. And regardless, I ended up marrying one!"

Stacey laughs. "Stop! Seriously, I find it fascinating that despite our twenty-year age difference, we remember ourselves as good students, always doing the right thing. But you were an Eagle and I was a Crow. How can that be... I wonder if it's background?"

"What do you mean?" Midge asks.

"Well, I don't recall much literacy learning at home. No bedtime stories, scribbling notes, you know all the stuff that makes a good reader. Do you?"

"Are you kidding? My whole life revolved around books—spending hours in my grandfather's bookstore, reading the Bobbsey Twins, Hardy boys, Cherry Ames, Wuthering Heights … you name it, I think I heard it or read it. I loved listening to stories and later reading them. 'Guess I was the original nerd because that was my favorite thing to do!"

"Ha! Nerd I wasn't!," laughed Stacey. "Yeah, maybe I would have read more if books weren't so hard to understand. Or if had had more at home. Or someone reading to me … interesting." Frowning slightly, Stacey pauses for a moment. "And funny. Now I'm a reading professor and so are you. But how did we both get here from such different worlds?"

## OUR QUESTIONS

Over the past two years we have both experimented with implementing the *ABC's of Cultural Understanding and Communication* (Schmidt, 1998) and have been intrigued by its possibilities. But, as we attempted to use this model to learn more about literacy learning and subsequent literacy teaching, we found that something intangible was missing. And we remain puzzled. This chapter discusses our attempts to further unpack the process of the *ABC's of Cultural Understanding and Communication* (Schmidt, 1998). The preceding portrait documents our voices as we questioned our idiosyncratic perspectives about literacy, perspectives we unpack in written literacy autobiographies. A nagging suspicion that we have not yet fully tapped the possibilities of this *ABC's Model* pushed us to rethink our previous attempts at its implementation. We remain two teacher researchers driven by a common question: How can we implement a practice that we don't fully understand?

A second question for both of us became: How might the *ABC's Model* provide further insights into the notion of reflective practitioner and the power of story? In what ways can writing autobiographical and biographical narratives help us to better understand our own practice and consequently help other teachers to do the same? We believe that reflection and writing to articulate such reflective practice offers important insights into the understanding of oneself as teacher and learner (Finkbeiner, 2000). Furthermore, we hold that narrative discourse, in our case simply the telling of our stories, becomes an excellent vehicle through which to probe understandings about literacy learning and teaching. We premise that using the epistemological and methodological frames of reflective practitioner and narrative discourse as lenses through which to examine insights about literacy and literacy teaching offers exciting possibilities for teacher understanding and more effective and equitable literacy practices.

Further, we argue that university faculty and staff developers who would implement the *ABC's Model* in graduate courses and school sites must first engage in the process themselves. Thus, the focus for much of this chapter documents and discusses what happens when we, two university professors, look reflectively and reflexively at our own practice and one another's *and* apply new understandings of self and another to the teaching of literacy. We explain our rationale for the frames of reflective practitioner and narrative discourse, situated within the new and still-evolving paradigm of teacher Research. (Although there exists some debate as to whether teacher research even qualifies, epistemologically and methodologically, as *research* at all [Huberman, 1996; Lytle, 2000; Ray, 1993], we argue that it is a valid and critical paradigm.).

In the second part of the chapter, we discuss adaptations of the *ABC's Model* and specific ways that we have begun to work with teachers in staff development.

## THEORETICAL FRAMEWORK

The notion of reflective practice can be traced back to John Dewey (1933) as one of several paradigmatic orientations to the education of teachers (Zeichner, 1983). In recent years there has emerged a renewed interest in reflective practice, perhaps as a response and a challenge to the prevailing views about the nature of schooling and knowledge (Cochran-Smith, 1994; Smyth, 1989). Holding dissatisfaction with technologically minded policy makers and educational reformers (as exemplified by the call for competency-based curriculum programs and teacher education), the reflective teacher idea offers an alternative to this fixed positivist way of thinking about teaching and learning (DeStiger, 2001; Richardson, 1990).

As university professors in a literacy department, we believe that if we encourage pre service and in-service teachers to reflect upon their knowledge about teaching and their instructional decisions, they will become better at teaching and thinking critically about their teaching. (Finkbeiner, 2001; Gore & Zeichner, 1991; Risko, Vukelich, & Roskos, 2002). But we also believe that as university professors, we must *first* reflect upon our own unique knowledge and understandings about teaching and learning before we ask other teachers to do the same. We question as well the process of such reflection and how this reflective process might impact our future teaching and learning (Risko et al., 2002). We propose that analyzing narrative discourse, specifically our life stories/autobiographies, might be a way to study the process of reflecting on our own practice as researchers and instructors of practicing teachers.

Schon (1983) examines numerous descriptive papers and empirical research addressing teacher reflection. But few studies look specifically at the reflective thinking of the teacher educators and researchers; nor do they provide insights into ways to *teach* or support reflective thinking. While much research argues for the importance of reflective thinking, many studies also conclude that developing deep levels of reflection is difficult and provide few clues for why this is so (Risko et al., 2002). We propose that the *ABC's Model* might serve as a vehicle through which to examine further ways to develop deep levels of reflective thinking.

Examining the second epistemological and methodological frame of narrative discourse, we find much research to support it, particularly the writing and study of autobiography. Witherell (1991) writes that two central reasons explain the rich use of narrative in teaching: coherence of the self as expressed in autobiography and the power of story in suggesting possibilities for human action. She writes: "Whether inventing, reading, or listening to stories, reading or writing journals and autobiographies, or conducting oral history interviews, the teller or receiver of stories can discover connections between self and other, penetrate barriers to understanding, and come to know more deeply the meanings of his or her own historical and cultural narrative" (p. 94). Those participating in such activities are enabled to "leap into the other" (Ozick, 1986, p. 65), visualizing the experience and emotions of the other.

Although narrative ways of knowing have often been devalued in empirical research, the power of narrative is its ability to allow the self to locate and relocate its voice in its social and cultural context (Brody & Witherell, 1991). We hold that the narrative form, in our case autobiography, allows us to reorganize, reassess, and realign our life experiences so that they are continuously integrated into our present personal schema (which embraces our social and historical culture) and ultimately into the schema for the community (Brody & Witherell, 1991; Finkbeiner & Koplin, 2002). As this chapter will show, immersing ourselves in the writing of personal narratives and in the reflective analysis of our own and each other's life stories enabled us to move to deeper levels of knowing ... about ourselves and about one another. And consequently, we believe that we will be able to more effectively read and analyze the autobiographies of the elementary teachers in our ongoing work in professional development with the *ABC's Model*.

Finally, believing that learning occurs best in the doing of the thing and we suggest that our teaching will be more credible and effective if we ourselves first participate in the *ABC's Model*. Yes, we concur that the *ABC's Model* seems ideal when teaching teachers about diversity issues and helping them to study how this knowledge of diversity impacts their literacy practice. "But," we ask, "What about the teachers who teach the teachers? University faculty and staff developers? How might an in-depth look at our own life stories and each other's impact our understanding of teaching literacy more effectively and equitably to diverse populations? And how might "doing" the *ABC's Model* further our understanding of its purpose and possibilities?"

## OUR STORY

And so we begin. Revisiting the opening portrait, we show two very different women grappling first with self-understanding, then reaching beyond self into another's perspective. In this section of the chapter, we offer additional information about ourselves gleaned from our autobiographies and interviews.

Stacey is a mid-thirties African American educator, wife, and mother of a two-year-old daughter. She has been a teacher for eleven years, moving from elementary classroom to a fellowship in doctoral studies. Receiving her Ph.D. degree in literacy in 1999, Stacey now teaches as an assistant professor at a mid-Atlantic state university.

Midge has taught for twenty-five years, beginning like Stacey, as an elementary teacher. She is of European American origin, in her mid-fifties, married for thirty-five years, mother of five children, and recent grandmother. As an elementary teacher and reading specialist, she spent ten years in public schools before moving to college teaching where she worked primarily with "at risk" minority students in reading and writing basic skills courses. Completing a Ph.D. degree in literacy in 2000, Midge now teaches literacy courses and works in schools with in-service teachers. She currently teaches at the same mid-Atlantic state university as Stacey.

We have known each other for two years, working together asynchronously before actually meeting the first year. (Midge had taken over Stacey's classes mid-semester when Stacey took an emergency maternity leave.) Since then, our professional relationship has grown. As we discussed in the beginning of the chapter, we share many common interests as well as some differences.

In charting similarities and differences, we find differences in our early school learning. Stacey talked of fears in school—of being judged as a reader with difficulties, floundering in humiliating moments unable to answer teacher questions. She believes that this has impacted her confidence as a learner, making learning difficult even in college and graduate school. Midge recalled excelling as a student in elementary and high school academics, but admitted that even though she received "A's" she rarely spoke out or reflected on her learning.

But we also found similarities. School taught us little about using our knowledge to critique and/or to change our worlds. We had mastered literacy in its narrow sense we *could* read and write proficiently. But we had not experienced the critical literacy which Friere (1993) so passionately taught—"read the word in order to read the world." Schooling had *not* taught us to question and to think against the grain or status quo. More important, schooling in elementary school, high school and college had not pushed us to seek answers or to suggest and implement solutions.

Graduate school presented us with similar challenges. Both of us came to doctoral programs, hampered by what it means to learn. To us learning meant listening, taking notes, fulfilling course requirements, memorizing content ... certainly, not questioning or challenging the instructor or curriculum. Stacey's decision to pursue a doctoral degree came with fear of being labeled as a struggling student yet again. Midge struggled to think critically and to voice dissenting ideas. We both began to critique schooling that had demanded little of its learners in terms of independent thinking and critical literacy and we recounted similar experiences of initial frustration in our doctoral programs.

A conversation between Stacey and a professor illustrates her bewilderment as a new doctoral student:

> **S:**   Honestly, Dr. J, I don't understand why this project is incomplete. I followed your written directions ...
> **Dr. J:**   But Stacey, that's not enough.
> I provided possibilities for your research and you must decide how and what you will study.
> **S:**   Just tell me what you want, Dr. J!
> **Dr. J:**   No, Stacey. Part of learning is finding your questions and deciding how to go about answering them. Go back and think again; give me a revised proposal next class.

In recounting this memory, Stacey talks of her struggle to take ownership of her learning. The notions of self-directed study and inquiry-based curriculum presented many challenges as Stacey sought to learn the culture of the university in her doctoral program.

Midge shared a parallel story about her dissertation writing at a similar inquiry-based university program. Conducting the research had challenged Midge, but the writing had stretched her limits. From 1996 to 2000 she worked and reworked chapters and research results, seeking a way to best relate her research findings. And ultimately, it was the telling of a story—writing a narrative—that worked. But much uncertainty prefaced this realization. She told about the sense of dread that monthly meetings with her chair had brought. "What does all this mean?" Susan would ask. "I-I-I'm not sure," Midge would respond. Susan would offer some insights, pose some questions, then end the meetings with, "You need to look over this again. What are you trying to tell others about basic writing and a critical pedagogy?" Susan pushed Midge to reach deep within to find her writer's voice. She never stopped her intuitive questioning, her words of encouragement, or her unwavering belief that Midge would somehow figure it all out. And in doing so, Midge learned much about the kind of teacher she strived to be. Her chair not only directed the dissertation but modeled inquiry at its finest.

As we shared graduate school experiences, we began to articulate evolving understandings about teaching and learning. We discovered that we both harbor like visions and that our doctoral studies have served as the catalyst for these new understandings. Constructivism—validating the knowledge of others and co-constructing course content with our students—intrigued us. Finding ways to enact feminist and critical pedagogies in literacy teaching also drove us to hypothesize possibilities. We believed that asking students to speak freely is not easily accomplished. We pushed to define the conditions that make a *safe* classroom where all might speak. And we agreed that this classroom can never be *a* or *one* discourse community, but rather must be worked as a "heterogeneous site-in-struggle" (Himley, 1997, p. 46) wherein we take into account the power differentials represented in the larger cultural dynamics implicit in all classrooms.

One of our conversations focused solely on how we seek to realize these ideas in our classrooms. We laughed about how our doctoral program professors had referred to "Aha" moments arising from reflections about beliefs and practice. Doubters, we quipped, "Sure, that might *really* happen!"

Midge talked about her past six years, experimenting with co-constructed course syllabi and critical literacy practices and chasing the elusive critical classroom. As she told of her experiences and shared her vision, Stacey listened intently. But when Midge paused, a noticeable silence followed and then Stacey spoke,

> You know, I'm not a constructivist at all! I talk all the time of constructivism and inquiry approaches but I don't *do* these things in my classrooms! I teach like I was taught in grade school!

That "Aha" moment surprised both of us.

In another conversation, we sought to unpack our understandings of critical, constructivism, and inquiry learning. We bounced ideas around, agreeing that our passions move us to further work in these areas. And we acknowledged the difficulty of such work. Stacey believes that the demands of teaching the content of a course often prevail, leaving little time for students to ask questions, create inquiry projects or to reflect upon their learning. Midge works hard to provide opportunities for students to voice their questions, but feels that time constraints work against her, as well, and she often compromises course content. Both of us expressed dissatisfaction with our present practice, wanting to move closer to our vision of teaching critically.

## OUR DATA COLLECTION AND FORMS OF ANALYSIS

These are the thoughts and actions that led us to this study. We began by collecting evidence of our new insights and learning over a six-month period from a variety of sources: (a) our written autobiographies, (b) a series of audio-taped discussion meetings, (c) audio-taped, focused discussions to gain different cultural perspectives, (d) a written chart of similarities/differences between the researchers' life stories, and (e) a critical literacy framework created to guide our teaching in future classes and professional development.

We analyzed data following the constant comparative method of Glazer and Strauss (1967). We read and reread our own and each other's autobiographies, taking notes on similarities and differences in social and historical culture. We listened to audiotapes of conversations about our life story writings, taking more notes and asking questions for clarification. Themes emerged which produced categories that supported the research questions. We charted these themes and studied the chart carefully for evidence that would answer our questions about the usefulness and effectiveness of the *ABC's Model*. We also compared the *ABC's Model* as described in the literature to the *ABC's Model* that we had implemented. We looked at the *real* and *imagined* process, finding some interesting differences with implications for future studies.

## SO WHAT DID WE LEARN?

In looking at ways that our participation as research subjects in the *ABC's Model* has impacted our understanding of teaching and learning, we asked two questions: "What have we learned by going through the process of writing and sharing our narrative life stories?" and "What have we learned about the *how* of reflective thinking and the difficulty of developing deep levels of introspective thinking with ourselves (and ultimately, with our students)?" Careful analysis of our data suggests four conclu-sions: (1) talk is critical to understanding self and others; (2) think-alouds to make visible "our thinking about our thinking" prove a useful heuristic; and (3) reading life texts through a critical lens fosters a deeper probing and fuller understanding of literacy acquisition and addresses differences across race, class, gender, and culture.

## The Impact of Talk

Talk is important, but, further still, critical talk is more important. An overarching: finding that emerged from this study suggests that talk is essential to building a deeper understanding of others. A simple, but powerful notion. Yet, so often in classrooms we eschew talk because it takes *time*. We push our students to reflect and write, but *we, the teachers,* frame the talk and structure the time. Stacey and I found that the more we talked, the more we shared and the more comfortable, (safe?) we became with our sharing. Tentative admissions of doubts and insecurities changed to freely shared confidences about continuing frustrations in our practice. Our talk moved from personal reflections about our lives and our teaching to question how this *ABC's Model* and a critical perspective on our teaching might inform one another. Our new understandings, arrived at together through talk, suggest several implications for our teaching and teachers who aspire to a critical classroom.

First, understanding the context of the classroom is key. We learned that it is imperative to carefully consider questions such as "Who are the students?" and "What works with whom and under what circumstances" in order to successfully enact a critical practice. Our first conversations were indeed awkward as Stacey and I danced between our black and white identities. But as we continued to come back to issues of race in our con-versations, these issues became easier to voice and we began to grapple with the realities of equity and literacy.

Second, we find that teachers must pay close attention to creating opportunities for forming relationships between teacher and students and among students before they address volatile topics such as racism and inequity. Both of us envision a classroom where students might speak their minds freely and we worry about how to create this kind of space. For us, researchers who researched our own thinking, creating space in our lives for lots of conversation provided a familiarity with one another, creating a kind of comfort zone. Only then did we venture into places of discomfort wherein we confronted cultural dissonance. Midge, particu-larly, struggled to understand schooling and learning from Stacey's per-spective and questioned how white teachers might truly understand their students of color. We conclude, too, that there exists a very different notion of community for the critical classroom, involving first, the acknowledgment of different positions of power held by students and teacher, and secondly, the recognition that a sharing of ideas can never be complete, mutual understanding and reciprocity, but must remain fragile and asymmetrical (Young, 1990).

## The Importance of Thinking Aloud

A second conclusion addresses the "how" of reflective thinking. As we engaged in the process of reflection, we questioned how we might transfer our increased self-awareness as learners to our practice as university teachers and facilitators of professional development courses. In discussing what we learned about ourselves from our autobiographies and about each other from our series of interviews and conversations, we consciously stopped at different intervals to reflect aloud on what we were doing and how we were thinking. And we charted "thinking aloud" as we talked. We found that making *explicit* the *implicit* led us to a deeper understanding of our nascent theories about creating safe classrooms that invite honest talk about politically-charged issues. We theorized that this making *explicit* the *implicit* might help teachers (*our* students) examine and articulate their thinking—in a word, become self-reflective—in order to better understand the power of reflection upon their practice.

## Reading Lift Texts Through a Critical Lens

As we talked and moved to deeper levels of understanding ourselves and each other, we realized that we were using a multilayered process to read and interpret our life texts. And a critical literacy framework began to evolve. In this section, we discuss this framework in terms of interpreting our own autobiographies or life stories; however, we also have begun to explore the framework's possibilities with teachers in professional development and we discuss these findings in the implications of our chapter.

According to the fifth step of the *ABC's Model*, participants create a *Home-School Connection Plan for Literacy Development*. For us, **because** our research involved studying the processes of the *ABC's Model* as **participants,** our home-school plan became the development and teaching of a framework to help teachers read life stories (autobiographies and biographies) through a critical lens. We believe that teachers who know how to critically analyze narratives will be better able to design and implement literacy plans for their diverse student populations. Teachers must understand how to read their own life texts *against the grain* as well as. others' life texts. And they must be able to use multiple lenses when unpacking these stories.

We have identified three interrelated dimensions in our critical literacy framework. In the first dimension, we teach our students to *read against the grain*. Readers question the text and ask, "What is the untold story? Who is the speaker and what wondrous things might he or she be telling us?" Barry Lopez (1987) reiterates the power of story in *Arctic Dreams* when he tells readers that the most treasured places in a culture are often not visible to the eye but are rather brought into focus through the drama of narrative or song. So, too, do we now understand the marvels of a life story. And we know that we must teach others to look beyond commonly accepted understandings and stories of other cultures.

An example of reading a text *against the grain* occurred when Stacey tried to clarify an excerpt from Midge's autobiography. The excerpt read:

> "Let me down! Let me down!" squealed the laughing blonde child. Running across the lush green lawn, she clapped her hands delightedly.
>
> "Come catch me, Alley. Come catch me!" she chanted. Then she disappeared into a grove of trees fragranced with the powerful, sweet scent of magnolia blossoms. Two blue eyes peered through swaying branches.
>
> "Boo!"
>
> "Help!" screamed the startled child. She tore across the grass toward the big house, with Alley close on her heels. Two huge black hands hoisted her up onto massive shoulders.
>
> "I caught you!" grinned Alley. And he carefully handed her into her grandmother's outstretched arms.

"What's the point you're trying to make here, Midge?" Stacey asked. "I mean, you say in the next line that you remember a carefree childhood in a sleepy Georgia town, oblivious to racism and prejudice. And perhaps you do. But when I read your story further and then go back to this excerpt, I read it differently. You say you always wondered why you could call Alley by his first name but he called you "Miss Midge" and your parents and grandparents "Mr." and "Mrs." But did you ever ask an adult why this practice was accepted? I see a white child growing up in a world where racism still existed."

In Midge's eyes, this excerpt simply evoked memories of a happy, carefree childhood. But, to Stacey, the words spoke a very different meaning.

In the second dimension of our critical literacy framework, we ask readers to concurrently *try* to understand texts from their own individual perspective and from the viewpoints of others. Embracing Rosenblatt's reader response theory, we believe that readers must juxtapose their idiosyncratic interpretations with each other's to come to a fuller understanding of texts. Thus, we challenged ourselves to unpack the cultural bias that we bring to the text and to listen to the perspective of one who lives a culture.

When we read and shared our autobiographies, we first looked for the story. But in so doing, Stacey observed, "You know, you need to know who's telling the story, don't you? I mean how else can you get at the meaning behind the mere recitation of events? And maybe, just maybe, there's more than one story." It was then that we began to try to read and understand from each other's perspective ... in a sense, to walk in another's shoes. And this was hard! We listened to each other's interpretations and we did learn. Yet, we felt that this was not enough. Midge questioned how she might gain deeper understanding of what it means to grow up black in New Jersey, observing, "We talk, yes, but I want always to know more about your life, Stacey. How can I do so without being intrusive?" And Stacey countered, "Yeah, you and I kid about white privilege—you know I joke a lot—but we could push deeper. I mean, honestly, growing up in the south, did whites—you too—feel *better* than others, like black or Mexican people?"

As we grappled with naming multiple understandings of our life texts, we began to move into the third dimension of our critical framework. In this dimension, we read in order to move beyond the text. We believe, like Freire, that the goal of all literacy is to *read the word in order to read the world* (Freire, 1993). This dimension pushed us to take what we had learned about each other's culture, question the status quo, and attempt to situate ourselves with others in the larger world.

An example of this occurred when we began to talk about our students of color in our undergraduate classes and how we might rethink ways that the university supports these students. Midge argued that in some sense we perpetuate the sorting and tracking that many kids of color experience in high school. "You know, we require all incoming freshmen to pass basic skills tests *before* enrolling in many credit-bearing courses; many who fail are students of color. Do we do these kids an injustice by placing them in non-credit basic skills courses? These are the kids who have little money and we ask them to take out *more* loans for non-credit courses. What if we instead provided scaffolded support in intro college courses?" Stacey agreed, observing, "Yeah, maybe as instructors we could even add focus groups or extra sessions where we provide added help for our struggling students. I know this sounds unrealistic, but ..." We struggled with this third dimension of challenging the status quo and continued to search for ways to structure conversations about politically-charged issues.

## WIDENING THE LENS:
## MOVING FROM PROCESS TO APPLICATION

Although this chapter documents the evolving understandings of the *process involved in learning* the *ABC's Model,* we have begun to explore ways to implement what we have learned. In this final section, we share some of these experiences. We hope that other faculty and teacher educators involved in professional development might benefit from our ideas. And we invite them to join us in seeking ways to open up honest dialogue across diverse groups that might engender deeper mutual understanding and more effective and equitable literacy practices.

We find that providing opportunities for talk *before* we write autobiographies and biographies is essential to creating safe spaces where all can tell their stories. But we also conclude that many teachers—us included—have never been taught how to *talk* such talk. As we have discussed in this chapter, we have developed a three-dimensional framework that scaffolds teachers in learning to think, talk, and write critically. Our work has begun to show the possibilities of such a framework.

Much of our work to date has focused on teaching readers to take different stances as they read—to understand initial interpretations but to color those interpretations by looking for other meanings. After first responses to a piece of text, we ask, "Who is writing this text? What do we know about him or her?" Then we push teachers to step outside and read from another's perspective.

In one professional development session, we introduce a short, provocative text entitled *The Colonel* written in 1978 by poet Carolyn Fourche. In the excerpt, written as an interview, the colonel rants about his country's people. Although not directly stated, readers can infer that the colonel is some sort of dictator in a Spanish country. He boasts of silencing his enemies and spills human ears on the table to make his point! Most readers react strongly to this graphic piece, interpreting the colonel as a kind of Fidel Castro. But we push teachers to consider the cultural bias that they bring to the text ( i.e., in this particular instance, the belief that democracy and freedom are worth fighting for), and we challenge them to step into the shoes of the colonel. Jim jumps in, suggesting, "Well, perhaps this ruler, the colonel, is simply trying to bring order to a country fraught with chaos and violence. Maybe he **has** to counter violence with more violence in order to bring eventual calm." Interestingly, other readers begin to rethink original interpretations, and all agree that there may indeed be more than one way to read this text.

In another session, we focus on the second dimension of our critical literacy framework. Again we select a provocative text (texts must be radical or provocative in the sense that they stir up emotions and invite strong response); this time, we use the wordless picture book *Why* by Nikolai Popov (1996). The text opens with a fight between a frog and a mouse over an umbrella, but the illustrations tell a different story of war and its consequences. Teachers first read the book silently, then react to the text in 14 words or less. A text rendering follows where each reader simply reads what he or she has written. We silently listen to each response with no commentary. Groups of four then share responses and discuss again, and then, come to a group interpretation of *Why*. At this point, teachers begin to understand how multiple interpretations of the same text enrich and broaden individual interpretations. And they understand reader response theory as a way to look critically at a text.

Finally, we have done some work with the third dimension—moving beyond an individual interpretation to consider ways the texts bump against social and political issues in the broader society. We use life stories written by Latino high school seniors from Wakima, Washington and we invite teachers in pairs to read two or three in silence. These life stories differ from the commonplace notion of autobiography. We explain that it takes two persons to write a *testimonio*, the interviewer and the person whose story he or she tells **and** more important, the interviewer must find a story that reflects the lives of others and a universal experience (Bodeen, 2002). Teacher pairs then select one *testimonio* and reread to unpack the social and/or political issues that they find in the text. In so doing, we begin to uncover the difficulties of living as a Latino in Wakima, Washington; but, we also see shared difficulties that all Latinos living in the United States face and we begin to consider the oft hidden inequities in their lives. Disrupting commonly held meanings, validating others' interpretations to gain deeper meanings, and reading texts to understand more about our world become essential to reading through a critical lens. When we ask teachers to write autobiographies, interview and compose biographies of persons from different cultures, and use their findings to better teach literacy, we find that we must first show teachers *how* to examine the texts they create. For us, our critical literacy framework has proved an excellent tool.

## CONCLUSION

Vinz (1996) writes that "continuously as we make one choice after another, the mosaic of our teaching life deepens and takes other shapes" (p. 140). So too have the teaching lives of both of us deepened and changed as a result of participating in the *ABC's Model*. Juxtaposing our autobiographies and listening to each other's life stories has enabled us to reach across differences of race, age, childhood experiences, and family histories to acknowledge and more importantly to *name* similarities.

As we look hard at our different approaches to current teaching, this introspection gives rise to new questions. We ask: "How might we build on difference to find similarities and common goals. What is it that draws one person to another ... pushes one to work to understand the other? And how can such an intangible phenomena be nurtured and fostered?" We search for an answer. And conclude that reading life texts through a critical lens becomes critical. We argue that in choosing to participate in this ABC's study and in choosing to learn about difference, the mosaic of our teaching lives has indeed taken new shapes and our passion for learning has intensified. Although acquaintances before the study began, the *ABC's Model* has enabled us to begin a conversation—conversation that has brought both of us to new awareness of different perspectives about the culture of schooling. And, in recognizing and acknowledging differences, we have found a common vision that calls for continued inquiry into the art of teaching. Virginia Woolf envisioned teaching not as the practice of domination but rather, the "art of human intercourse; the art of understanding other people's lives and minds" (Woolf, 1938, p. 50). We embrace her definition of teaching as we continue to work toward its realization.

Our study has attempted an introspective and shared look at the process and possibilities of the *ABC's Model* that targets multicultural awareness and reflective practice. Through writing life stories and engaging in conversations across time, we have gained critical insights into one another's lives and perceptions of teaching and learning Acknowledging like goals, together we work to realize the possibilities of literacy communities at their best—fostering critical awareness, encouraging intellectual talk among students and teacher, examining and challenging the status quo. As teacher educators, we strive to create conditions so that other teachers can *and will* speak their differences and consequently learn to question and defend their thinking. We know now that each time we meet a new group of teachers, each group will decide its own agenda and its own possibilities ... it remains for us as teacher educators to show the way.

# APPENDIX A

## Critical Literacy Framework

| Disrupting the Ordinary | Validating Multiple Viewpoints | Focusing on Sociopolitical Issues |
|---|---|---|
| ⇩ | ⇩ | ⇩ |
| Reading Against the Grain | Reader Response Theory | Reading the Word to Read the World |
| **The Role of the Reader** | **The Role of the Reader** | **The Role of the Reader** |
| • Problematizing text<br>• Asking questions<br>• Taking an oppositional stance/devil's advocate | • Considering text from individual perspective and viewpoints of others concurrently<br>• What's the untold story? | • Going beyond the personal<br>• Challenging and/or questioning the status quo |

*Source:*   Madden and Leftwich (2003).

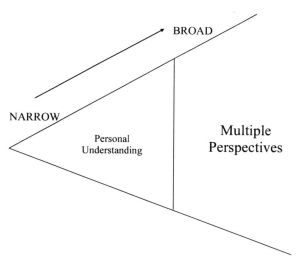

*Source:*   Madden and Leftwich (2003).

Understanding Reader Response

## APPENDIX B

1:45-2:00

- Think back to the stories from this morning
- Show of hands, how many told stories of empowerment/disempowerment?
- What does this mean for us as learners? (chart)
- What does this mean for us as teachers? (chart)
- Do you think it safer to talk about times of empowerment?  Why?
- In this strand we're looking at ways to move beyond the safety of our stories and push our thinking so that we can help our students do the same
- As university professors (share concerns of teachers about their students' ability to question text and think critically)

2:00-2:15

- You were asked to read an article on critical literacy
- We're going return to this article to outline dimensions of critical literacy and provide you with a teaching framework
- Introduce Critical Literacy Framework (a framework that you can use to move beyond literal and interpretive comprehension)
- Today we will focus on the second dimension with a short text

2:15-2:30

- Give 15 minutes to read text and write PERSONAL interpretation (What does this text mean to you?)

2:30-2:50

- Give 20 minutes to share their interpretation and write a GROUP interpretation

2:50-3:00

- Make explicit that personal interpretation comes from schema/life text
- Listening to others will give multiple perspectives and broaden our schema, creating deeper meaning of text

# REFERENCES

Bodeen, J. (2002). Seeking light/Buscando Luz. In J. Bodeen (Ed.), *Seeking light in each dark room* (pp. 11-14 ). Yakima, WA: Blue Begonia Press.

Brody, C., & Witherell, C. (1991). Story and voice in the education of professionals. In C. Witherell & N. Noddings (Eds.), *Stories lives tell* (pp. 257-279). New York: Teachers College Press.

Cochran-Smith, M. (1994). The power ofteacher research in education. In S. Hollingsworth & H. Sockett (Eds.), *Teacher research and educational reform* (pp.142-165). Chicago: The University of Chicago Press.

Dewey, J. (1933). *How we think*. Lexington, MA: D.C. Heath.

DeStiger, T. (2001). *Reflections of a citizen teacher: Literacy, democracy, and the forgotten students of Addison High*. Urbana, IL: NCTE.

Finkbeiner, C. (2000). Handlungsorientierter Usericht (Holistic and action-oriented learning and teaching). In M. Byram (Ed.), *Routledge encyclopedia oflanguage teaching and learning* (pp.255-258). London: Routledge.

Finkbeiner, C. (2001). One and all in CALL? Learner-moderator-researcher. *Computer Assisted Language Learning, 14*(3-4), 129-151.

Finkbeiner, C. (2002). A cooperative approach for facilitating intercultural education. *Reading Online, 6*(3). Online: http://www.readingonline.org/newliteracies/litindex.asp ?HREF +/newliteraciesltinkbeiner

Finkbeiner, C., & Koplin, C. (2002). A cooperative approach for facilitating intercultural education. *Reading Online, 6*(3). Retrieved July 11, 2005, from fttp://www.readingonline.org/newliteracies

Freire, P. (1993). *Pedagogy of the oppressed*. New York: New Continuum.

Freire, P., & Macedo, D. (1996). A dialogue: Culture, language, and race. In P. Leistyna, A. Woodrum, & S. Herblom (Eds.), *Breaking free: The transformative power of critical pedagogy* (pp. 199-228). Cambridge, MA: Harvard Educational Review.

Glazer, B.G., & Strauss, A.L. (1967). *The discovery of grounded theory: Strategies for qualitative research*. New York: Aldine De Gruyter.

Gore, J.M., & Zeichner, K.M. (1991). Action research and reflective teaching in pre-service teacher education: A case study from the United States. *Teaching and Teacher Education, 79*(2), 119-136.

Himley, M. (1997). *Political moments in the classroom*. Portsmouth, NH: Heinemann.

Huberman, M. (1996). Focus on research moving mainstream: Taking a closer look at teacher research. *Language Arts, 73*(2), 124-140.

Lopez, B. (1987). *Arctic dreams*. New York: Charles Scribner's Sons.

Lytle, S. (2000). Teacher research in the contact zone. In M. Kamil, R. Barr, P. Mosenthal, & S. Herblom, (Eds.), *Handbook of reading research III*. New York: Longman.

Ozick, C. (1986). The moral necessity of metaphor. *Harper's Magazine*, pp. 64-65.

Popov, N. (1996) *Why*. New York: North-South Books.

Ray, R. (1993). *The practice of theory*. Urbana, IL: National Council of Teachers of English.

Richardson, V. (1990). The evolution of reflective teaching and teacher education. In R. Clift, W. Houston, & M. Pugach (Eds.), *Encouraging reflective practice in education*. NewY ork: Teachers College Press.

Risko,V., Vukelich, C., & Roskos, K. (2002). Preparing teachers for reflective practice: Intentions, contradictions, and possibilities. *Language Arts, 80*(2), 134-144.

Schmidt, P.R. (1998). The *ABC's Model:* Teachers connect home and school. *Nation Reading Conference Yearbook, 47*,194-208.

Schon, D. (1983). *The reflective practioner: How professionals think in action*. New York: Basic Books.

Smyth, W. (1989, March-April). Developing and sustaining critical reflection in teacher education. *Journal of Teacher Education*, pp. 2-9.

Van Manen, M. (1995). On the epistemology of reflective practice. *Teachers and Teaching: Theory and Practice, 1*(1), 33-50.

Vinz, R. (1996). *Composing a teaching life*. Portsmouth, NH: Heinemann.

Witherell, C. (1991). The self in narrative: a journey into paradox. In C. Witherell & N. Noddings (Eds.), *Stories lives tell* (pp. 83-96). New York: Teachers College Press.

Woolf, V. (1938). *Three guineas*. New York: Harcourt Brace.

Young, I.M. (1990). *Throwing like a girl and other essays in feminist philosophy and social theory*. Bloomington: Indiana University Press.

Zeichner, K. (1983). Alternative paradigms in teacher education. *Journal of Teacher Education, 34*, 3-9.

CHAPTER 5

# INVESTIGATING THE ROLE OF AWARENESS AND MULTIPLE PERSPECTIVES IN INTERCULTURAL EDUCATION

**Claudia Finkbeiner and Sylvia Fehling**

## ABSTRACT

The chapter focuses on the European project MOBIDIC in which the roles of multiperspectives and language awareness are investigated. This project has strong connections to *the ABC's of Cultural Understanding and Communication* (Schmidt, 1998). The MOBIDIC project is situated in Content and Language Integrated Learning (CLIL) classes in Europe. It was conducted with partners in Poland, France, Germany and England. The project, the goals and the data collection procedures will be described and some exemplary results will be presented and discussed.

*ABC's of Cultural Understanding and Communication:*
*National and International Adaptations,* 93–110

## INTRODUCTION

In this chapter we report on MOBIDIC, a European research study on Modules of Bilingual Didactics and Methodology for Teacher Training. MOBIDIC is a Comenius-2-Project, which started in October 2001 and was finished in December 2004. Between September and October 2002 the data were collected. The research grant was awarded by the European Union.

Four countries participated: Poland, France, Germany and England. Our team of teachers, teacher trainers, and researchers consisted of 16 people. The group met several times in order to design, discuss and evaluate research and educational issues. The meetings alternated among all project members' countries.

## "BILINGUAL" CLASSES IN EUROPE—CLIL CLASSES

The term "bilingual" used in our acronym does not refer to immersion programs in North America (Swain & Johnson, 1997) but to "bilingual classes" in Europe. These classes are coined by the term Content and Language Integrated Learning (CLIL) (Finkbeiner & Fehling, 2002, p. 10; Fehling & Finkbeiner, 2002, p. 23). In Content and Language Integrated Learning (CLIL), subjects such as history, geography, politics, and biology are taught in a foreign language (Fehling, 2002b, p. 213).

A foreign language (FL) is used as the instructional language. The focus is on subject knowledge rather than facility in the FL. This means that teaching the subject matter is more important than on the language skills.

The students who participate in CLIL classes usually have a high proficiency in the foreign language. When they graduate from grammar and high school, they are fluent in the foreign language. Another goal of CLIL is the development of intercultural competence. In our project we define intercultural competence as the ability to change perspectives and develop a meta-cognitive awareness with respect to both language and culture.

## THE GOALS OF THE MOBIDIC PROJECT

The MOBIDIC project is closely related to the ABC's Model, since it focuses on intercultural education and follows Schmidt's paradigm of "Know thyself and understand others" (Schmidt, 2001, p. 390). Both the ABC's (Schmidt, 1998) and MOBIDIC have in common, that their overall goals are cultural understanding and communication.

The specific goal of MOBIDIC was the development of instructional modules to foster Content and Language Integrated Learning (CLIL). The study's purposes were (a) to collect and evaluate data on what actually happens in selected CLIL classes in Poland, France, Germany and England to define the status quo, (b) to develop methods to raise language and cultural awareness, (c) to design approaches that integrate multiperspectives, and (d) to find ways of triggering intercultural learning and contribute to a long-lasting effect of intercultural education beyond the classroom.

Another goal was to deepen European partnership and to foster mobility among teachers in Europe. In this way, the MOBIDIC project fully complied with article 126 of the European Maastricht Treaty, which can be seen as the constitutional basis of a unified Europe (Finkbeiner, 1995, pp. 1389). Above all, we aimed at the common goal to improve the education of students and teachers who were involved in bilingual teaching.

## CONNECTING MOBIDIC TO THE ABC'S

We are responsible for the design and evaluation of the data collected in the MOBIDIC study. Intercultural learning together with language and cultural awareness are at the core of our interest. Our research is strongly connected to the ABC's of Cultural Understanding and Communication (Finkbeiner & Koplin, 2001, 2002; Schmidt, 1998, 2001). Both the European research study MOBIDIC and the ABC's Model have much in common.

Examples are:

- they focus on intercultural education;
- they teach intercultural education in a declarative and in a systematic, and process-oriented approach of first-hand cultural experience;
- they are situated in the field of teacher training;
- they follow a continuing lifelong learning approach in teacher training;
- they use an action-oriented and holistic approach (Finkbeiner, 1995);
- they relate to the same theoretical sociocultural foundations and bases (Finkbeiner, 2001, 2002b) as highlighted in the introductory chapter (Finkbeiner & Schmidt, in this volume);
- they are not normative nor prescriptive but draw conclusions from the data collected in each case;

- they are both individualistic, subject-oriented, and social at the same time;
- they follow Schmidt's paradigm of "Know thyself and understand others" (Schmidt, 2001, p. 390);
- they celebrate differences and thus follow a multi perspective approach;
- they systematically incorporate literacy activities;
- they allow people to think about their own culture(s) and other cultures.

The ABC's and MOBIDIC act as mutual catalysts that have the potential to recipocally support each other.

Additionally, the MOBIDIC project has a strong focus on the second language issue. This is due to the multilingual situation in Europe (Finkbeiner, in this volume).

## LANGUAGE AWARENESS AND CULTURAL AWARENESS

Language and cultural awareness are key to the MOBIDIC project. Language awareness is defined as "a person's sensitivity to and conscious perception of the nature of language and its role in human life" (Donmall, 1985, p. 7). Cultural awareness is:

> the concept of reflexivity, i.e., the idea that insight into experience of the practices of systems of meaning of other cultures is of significance for the individual's cultural understanding of self and their own identity. [...] The development of CA [i.e., cultural awareness] is a development from ethnocentrism to relativity, including among other things an engagement with national stereotypes, or a development of the realisation that the world can be seen from many different perspectives, e.g., national perspectives. (Risager, 2000, pp. 159-162)

Thus, language and culture can be seen as the two sides of the same coin. According to Humboldt (1922, cited in Baron, 2002, p. 42) language and culture belong together: "Each language expresses the subjectivity of the culture with which it is historically interwoven and which it determines, at the same time, as means of expression."[1]

When talking about culture, we must consider different goals and values. This is influenced by different acculturation factors (Finkbeiner & Koplin, 2002; Finkbeiner, this volume). Relevant factors in the MOBIDIC project are the educational setting, the language situation, and, intercultural teaching scripts.

## MULTIPLE PERSPECTIVES:
## BEING AWARE OF DIFFERENT SCRIPTS AND SCHEMATA

The script and schema theories were of major importance in the MOBIDIC project. Scripts refer to knowledge which is organized around hundreds of stereotypic situations with routine activities. Examples are riding a bus, visiting a dentist, placing an operator-assisted telephone call, asking for directions, and so on (Bower, Black, & Turner, 1994, p. 538).

Schemata are knowledge structures which contain generic information about aspects of the world, such as different types of objects, people, situations and texts. They arise from repeated exposure to similar experiences, and are used to make sense of new instances of such experiences. (Semino, 2000, p. 525)

Scripts and schemata are important in the context of language and cultural awareness: Different schemata become clear if you contrast the concepts of, English and German words, such as "dragon fly" versus "Libelle" or "mother country" versus "Vaterland" (Finkbeiner & Fehling, 2002, p. 20). Whereas the term "dragon fly" in English refers to the dragon-like look, "Libelle" refers to the wings which make the fly look like scales. Another example is, that in English the term "mother country" relates to the country in which the mother was born, in German the equivalent term "Vaterland" refers to the father's home.

## EDUCATIONAL SETTINGS IN THE
## MOBIDIC PARTNER COUNTRIES

The MOBIDIC partners were Poland, France, Germany and England. Different universities, teacher training institutes and schools participated in the study. When one is committed to a research project across national borders, one has to consider additional "other" borders (i.e., differences in the educational systems, curricula, and in teacher training).

Poland and France have a centralized school system. The system in Germany is non-central and lies within each of the 16 states. In England, the Local Education Authorities (LEA) are responsible for the financing and maintenance of most state schools, but the curriculum follows the National Curriculum (Sturm, 1999).

Consequences from international literacy studies,[2] are a lot more difficult to implement in a non-central than a central system. Additionally, a federal system makes national comparisons more difficult due to the differences in curricula, textbooks, and teacher education in each federal state.

Furthermore, there are differences in teacher profiles. Teachers in Germany, for example, have to major in two or three subjects. University students studying to become a teacher can choose combinations, such as a foreign language plus a content matter subject (geography, history, biology etc.). In contrast to this, students in Poland, France, and England usually study only one main subject.

The role of Content and Language Integrated Learning (CLIL) differs among the European partners: While Poland has just recently started implementing CLIL in schools, early German CLIL programs had been implemented in 1969 (Finkbeiner & Fehling, 2002, p. 11).

The interest in CLIL in the UK has developed from the nineties onwards, especially in schools with special status such as Language Colleges. In France, CLIL was introduced in 1992.[3]

## LANGUAGE SITUATIONS IN THE PARTICIPATING MOBIDIC COUNTRIES

Within the participating MOBIDIC countries, there are the following language situations: The mother tongues of the biggest majority of the pupils participating in the project were Polish in Poland, German in Germany, and French in France. Yet, there are a growing number of students whose mother tongue is different from the first instructional language: Those children and/or their parents have a migration background. For instance, the following mother tongues were represented in German classes participating in MOBIDIC: Turkish, Persian, Russian, French, Bosnian, Croatian, and Italian.

In the CLIL classes that we examined, the foreign languages which were used as main instructional languages were English in Germany, Poland, and France; German in Poland and France; French in Germany and Poland.

## THE THREE PROJECTS WITHIN THE MOBIDIC PROJECT: PHASES AND TOPICS

The MOBIDIC project integrated three simultaneously ongoing projects: (a) the MOBIDIC CLIL school project, (b) the MOBIDIC CLIL teacher training project, and (c) the MOBIDIC research study. All three projects were closely coordinated and pursued the goals as expressed above.

The study included different phases. These phases were:

1. planning and design
2. implementation
3. evaluation
4. design of new modules
5. European teacher training courses.

Within the school project there were four main topics that were taught in all participating CLIL classes. The topics agreed upon unanimously were:

Topic 1:   Migration
Topic 2:   Treaty of Versailles
Topic 3:   Urban development in the 19th century
Topic 4:   European Union

All topics were part of the curricula in all MOBIDIC countries. Most of the topics were either taught in geography, in politics or history CLIL classes.

No requirements nor specifications were given to the partners about how to teach or what material to use. This was done to avoid a bias with respect to the teaching and learning approach. Instead of standardizing the teaching and learning methods, our interest lay in the difference. For example, we were interested in culturally different teaching scripts in the participating countries.

We expected to gain insight into (a) what was appreciated as valuable in CLIL teaching in the different European partner countries, and further-more, (b) what could be considered as a "must" and (c) what was obviously a complete taboo with respect to teaching methods and content. With respect to all the differences in the teaching scripts in the participating MOBIDIC countries, we were designing a framework of what all partners considered a "good" CLIL class, taking language and cultural awareness, multiple perspectives and intercultural learning as quality measurement.

## ACTION RESEARCH

The MOBIDIC research study, just as the ABC's (Schmidt, 1998), was designed as an action research project. This allowed for direct implementation of the results into teacher training courses during the research process. This teacher training project was conducted in January 2004. It took place at St. Martin's College Carlisle and Ambleside, England. Teachers from Germany, Poland, France, and England participated. Additionally, we held local implementation training sessions in Warsaw, Paris, Frankfurt, and Kassel.

## DESIGN, RESEARCH QUESTIONS, HYPOTHESES

The study consisted of quantitative and qualitative components, including a complex video study and a set of different student and teacher questionnaires. With reference to the "migration" unit the research questions were:

- What prior knowledge and preestablished concepts do students have before the lesson plans on migration start in the CLIL lessons?
- Can we identify multiple perspectives with respect to the topic from the students' point of view before the lessons have an impact?
- Can we identify multiple perspectives with respect to the topic when teachers teach the topic in CLIL classes?
- How do teachers approach the topic?
- How do teachers deal with non-anticipated, student-initiated perspectives on "migration?"
- What differences can we perceive when we compare the teachers' approaches to the topic and the students' concepts?
- What differences are there on a cross-cultural scale when comparing the data from Poland, France, and Germany with each other?
- What effect do the lessons on migration have on students' concept formation? Are there differences between the concepts elicited prior and posterior to the unit?

Based on the research questions we formulated the following assumptions:

We expected differences in the perspectives chosen by the teachers in the different classes examined when teaching the topic "migration." Furthermore, we were prepared to identify differences in the prior knowledge and preestablished concepts concerning the topic "migration" between German, French, and Polish students. We wondered whether we would identify multiperspectives among the students even before the lessons on migration would have had an impact. We also expected differences in the core words used by the different groups to describe the phenomena of migration. We believed that there were different underlying schemata between the Polish, German, and French students connected tated with the language use. Last, we were hoping that the lessons on migration would affect students' concepts and perceptions of migration.

We administered a set of questionnaires to pupils at the age of 16 to 18 ($n = 193$) at three secondary schools in Poland, three secondary schools in Germany, and one secondary school in France. All schools had a strong CLIL profile. The teachers used a foreign language as the instructional language for teaching the subject matter in history, geography etc.

The participating teachers had to design lesson plans for each topic. The topic "migration" is particularly interesting in the MOBIDIC context, because it is quoted as a mandatory topic in all participating European school curricula and it is of highest relevance in the 21st century in a European as well as in a worldwide context (Finkbeiner, 1995; this volume).

According to our literature and data base review, "migration" can be applied to human beings and animals as the following definitions show:

> Migration, movement of people, especially of whole groups, from one place, region, or country to another, particularly with the intention of making permanent settlement in a new location. Humans have migrated since their emergence as a species. Their original differentiation into ethnic groups appears to have been a result of the isolated development of separate groups of people who migrated from a central point of origin, perhaps in Africa or Central Asia. Even in the Stone Age, however, this isolation was not complete, for migrations resulted in a complicated pattern of blood relationships through widely separated groups. (Retrieved March 21, 2005, from http://encarta.msn.com/encyclopedia_761569913/Migration.html)

> Animal Migration, seasonal or periodic movement of animals in response to changes in climate or food availability, or to ensure reproduction. Migration most commonly involves movement from one area to another and then back again. This round-trip, or return migration, may be of a seasonal nature, as in the spring and autumn migrations of many birds. Or it may require a lifetime to complete, as in various species of Pacific salmon that are born in freshwater streams, travel to ocean waters, and then return to the stream where they were born to breed before dying.(Retrieved March 21, 2005, from http://encarta.msn.com/encyclopedia _761557464/ Animal-Migration.html)

In particular, with the topic migration we were hoping to find hints in the data as to the influences of different aspects of cultural and language awareness as well as the existence of multiperspectives when teaching the topic migration to CLIL classes.

**Table 5.1.  Instruments Used in the MOBIDIC Study**

|  | *Videography* | *Questionnaire* |
|---|---|---|
| **Student** | | |
| Language awareness/ cultural awareness | CLIL-COLT[a] | MIGRA-ANTE/ MIGRA-POST |
| Multiperspectives | CLIL-COLT | MIGRA-ANTE/ MIGRA-POST |
| Code switching | CLIL-COLT | EFBS/ ATTITUDE-CLIL |
| Student evaluation lesson | | EVA I/ EVA II |
| Attitudes CLIL | | ATTITUDE-CLIL |
| **Teacher** | | |
| Teaching methods/ languages | CLIL-COLT | |
| Language awareness/ cultural awareness | CLIL-COLT | TEACH-CLIL |
| Multiperspectives | CLIL-COLT | |
| Code-switching | CLIL-COLT | |
| School system | | TEACH-CLIL |

[a]The CLIL-COLT (Finkbeiner & Fehling, 2003) is a version of COLT (Spada & Fröehlich, 1995) adapted for CLIL purposes.

## OVERVIEW OF THE DATA COLLECTION PROCEDURES

We used the following data collection procedures in the MOBIDIC study as listed in Table 5.1. We collected data on the concepts, schemata, and scripts pertaining to the term "migration" before and after the unit (MIGRA-ANTE and MIGRA-POST). We used questionnaires immediately after the lessons (EVA: Evaluation sheet). We administered questionnaires to the students on attitudes concerning CLIL (SA-CLIL). We collected data on the CLIL lessons through evaluation of videotaped lessons, transcription, categorization of critical CLIL key sequences.

The teachers who participated in the project filled out the two teacher questionnaires (TEACH-CLIL and SCHOOL-CLIL). This was done in order to obtain information on different teaching methods concerning CLIL and on the specifics of the school systems and CLIL in the different European countries.

Furthermore, a video study was conducted in French, German, and Polish CLIL classes. It was the aim of this qualitative video study to record CLIL lessons, to analyze them systematically, and to compare the findings with the results gained from the quantitative part of the study. In each participating school, an introductory lesson and a follow-up lesson on the topic "migration" were taped.

## THE MIGRA-ANTE QUESTIONNAIRE

The following questions were given in the MIGRA-ANTE questionnaire to evaluate the concepts on migration students might have already had before the lesson started:

- What do you associate with the term migration?—Please write down 10 to 15 terms in your mother tongue and in the foreign language.
- Please, complete the following sentence: "Migration is ..."
- Please, write spontaneously a sentence about "migration" in the foreign language.
- Does migration mean the same for you in your mother tongue than in the foreign language? Please give reasons for your answer.
- Please, draw a mind map concerning the topic "migration."

A comparative analysis and a systematic content analysis were carried out. The following steps were implemented: (a) data entry, (b) formation of alphabetical lists, (c) formation of quantitative lists, (d) first reading, (e) content analysis and interpretation, (f) categorization, (g) second reading, (h) third inter-rater reading: verification of categories, (i) qualitative lists, (j) cross-cultural analysis, and (k) similarities and differences.

For the topic "migration" we obtained the following categories and subcategories across all participating countries:

- *Direction of movement:*   immigration, emigration, resettlement.
- *Inland migration:*   inland migration, village, village-city, emigration to the village, emigration to the cities, emigration to the cities/village.
- *Reasons for migration:*   (political, religious) persecution, unemployment, famine, poverty, violation of human rights, war/civil war, revolution, oppression.
- *Migration of animals:*   whales, birds, storks, salmons etc.

The set of differentiated answers to the sentence completion task "Migration is ..." complemented the results above.

The following examples illustrate how students responded to the sentence beginning "migration is ..." in the sentence completion exercise within the categories found in our analyses.

*Direction of movement: "Migration is ..."*

- "There are different types of migration: Emigration, immigration, and inland migration."
- "The movement of people (immigration, emigration)."
- "The movement of people from one country to another to settle down."

*Reasons for migration: "Migration is ..."*

- "The resettlement of people to another country because of political, social reasons."
- "The movement of people, who immigrate to a foreign country to live freely and to practise their religion."
- "The movement of people within a territory (e.g., to find a job, to improve their personal situation)."

The results of the MIGRA-ANTE questionnaire helped us to gain an insight into how the topic "migration" was dealt with in the participating countries. We obtained interesting data that can serve as the basis for further research studies in this field. For instance, we made the following observations: While the participating German students mainly associated migration with "immigration" (migration *into* the country), many Polish students associated the same term mainly with "emigration" (migration *out of* the country into another country) and "inland migration." The students in Germany predominantly mentioned countries, from which major groups of immigrants in Germany originate (e.g., Turkey, Russia), whereas the students in Poland associated migration with popular target countries (e.g., Germany, the United States).

Our data have historical value, because they were gathered about two years before Poland became a European Union member. Today there is a new reality for a new kind of migration which seems to change the direction of movement. There is a new labor migration from Germany to Poland due to unemployment in Germany. Therefore, if the research data were collected today, the results might be different.

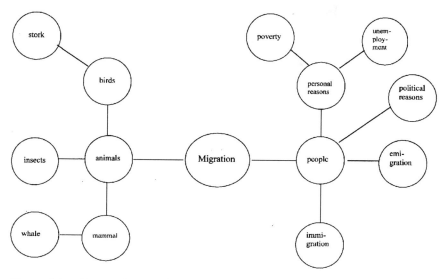

Figure 5.1.    Perspectives on the concept of migration.

We discovered that the majority of students had different perspectives regarding the concept of the term "migration." This is illustrated in Figure 5.1.

## THE VIDEO STUDY

As mentioned above, in each participating country several lessons were videotaped: an introductory lesson on the topic "migration" and a follow-up lesson with exercises and/or group work. The teachers had the chance to reflect verbally on their lessons. This was also videotaped and evaluated by us. The pupils evaluated their lessons with the help of a questionnaire.

The video evaluation was done with the help of the COLT (Communicative Orientation of Language Teaching) observation scheme (Spada & Fröhlich, 1995). This scheme provides an analytic framework for documenting communication and interaction in second language (L2) classrooms. The COLT scheme was developed to identify features of communication and interaction which make second language acquisition more effective, as Spada and Fröhlich (1995, p. 1) emphasize:

> Depending on the user's goals, the scheme may be used to describe particular aspects of instructional practices and procedures in L2 classrooms, to

investigate relationships between teaching and learning, to sensitise novice teachers to different aspects of the instructional process or to encourage more experienced teachers to reflect on teaching practices.

The COLT observation scheme was originally designed for traditional second language classrooms. In order to investigate CLIL classes we added the following subcategories: (a) perspective (b) code-switching (c) language and cultural awareness.

*Perspective:*   Perspective means having different view points on the same topic during the lesson. In the context of "migration," different perspectives could be "migration of human beings" and "migration of animals." These are either introduced by the teacher or the pupils.

*Code-switching:*   The CLIL subcategory code-switching focuses on the change between the official instructional language (German in Germany; Polish in Poland; French in France, etc.) and the target language (e.g., English).

We learned that some of our participating teachers were prepared for changes of perspective. In one of the lessons, however, the teacher started explaining the phenomenon of migration with reference to human beings. He did so in a very authentic way by relating to the students' personal lives. One student suddenly raised his hand and mentioned that not only human beings migrated but also animals. The student introduced a new perspective with his statement in class. We gave this a rating in our observation scheme. Yet, when we reviewed this scene in the video, we saw that the teacher did not respond to this new perspective. He ended the discussion by stating: "Stay focused and do not get sidetracked by stuff like that."

With respect to code-switching, we observed that the lessons were held almost exclusively in the foreign language and code-switching was a very rare phenomenon. Consequently, no *language* awareness episodes could generally be observed. We did not discover episodes in which the foreign language was contrasted with the official classroom language.

On the other hand, *cultural* awareness episodes could be detected. This was achieved by contrasting aspects of migration in different countries including the political, economic, and social conditions under which people in different countries live.

It was difficult to gather evidence as to multiple perspectives, code-switching and language awareness in most classrooms. The reason for this might lie in the fact that these goals cannot easily be achieved and therefore, impose challenges on the teachers as well as on the researchers in the field of teaching CLIL. Additionally, there might still be a missing awareness for the role of awareness of language, culture, multiperspectives, and code-switching in CLIL classes.

## LESSONS WE LEARNED

The results of the MIGRA-ANTE questionnaire and the video study together helped us to gain a deeper insight into how the topic "migration" was taught in CLIL classrooms in all participating countries.

A few of the lessons we learned were:

*First lesson—the issue of formats in international project collaboration.* The European grant regulations forced us into tight scheduling and there was not sufficient time for detailed discussion and exhaustive feedback, particularly at the beginning. Due to the time constraints, we were forced to develop the instruments as fast as possible, so that the project could get started.

This caused an intercultural conflict within the group. The reason for this lay in the decision we made with respect to the kind of format to use for our instruments. For instance, in order to evoke students' schemata and concepts, we had decided to use a *mind map* as a research tool. One of our partners, who worked as a teacher trainer, was upset about this and told us that *mind maps* would not necessarily be used in schools in her country. Of course, if the students are not familiar with certain research formats, there is the danger of bias. This is why we opened a discussion on that subject matter. The result was that the other teachers from the same country actually supported our suggestion and mentioned that they quite frankly thought that *mind maps* were frequently used in their schools. Here we were confronted with the phenomenon of two opposing opinions as to what can be considered part of an established teaching and learning script in one country. This mirrors the dilemma and difficulties in cross-cultural research. For future studies it would be very helpful to inquire in a large-scale quantitative study what formats are used in the different countries and how often. This would make research across different countries easier.

*Second lesson—The role of mother tongue and foreign language in word association.* In the MIGRA-ANTE questionnaire, the students were asked to answer the following question. "What do you associate with the term 'migration'?—Please write down 10 to 15 terms in your mother tongue and in the foreign language."

The focus of this question was to investigate whether the students' script of "migration" differed between the mother tongue and the foreign language. Unfortunately, this could not be analyzed, since most students just translated the mother tongue associations concerning "migration" into the foreign language. Therefore, we learned that in future projects we would strictly divide our instruments into separate mother tongue and second language research instruments. These would have to be given to the students separately, so that the two languages could be investigated independently.

*Third lesson—the personal factor—biography.*   In regard to the video study a CLIL lesson was taped in France. The CLIL instructional language was German. The class consisted of nine girls and two boys between 15 and 16 years. Nearly all of them had a migration background. The first task in the lesson involved an exercise in which each student had to show on a world map where he or she came from. This was highly motivating for the students. They were active and interested in answering questions regarding where they and/or their families came from. Most of the children were born in France but their parents came from Morocco, Tunisia, Turkey, Italy, Algeria and Egypt. Only one girl was native French. The fact that the teacher personally involved the students and took their biographical background seriously bears strong connections to the ABC's Model (Finkbeiner & Koplin, 2002; Schmidt, 1998).

In the beginning of the above example, we can see the teacher relied on the autobiographical and personal involvement. He then switched his *focus* to the historical and political context without relating back to the students' personal lives and migrations. If the ABC's Model had been implemented by the teacher it would have enabled the students to fully grasp the concept of "migration."

This is the point where we see huge power in the ABC's Model implemented in such lessons. In future European projects, the *ABC's of Cultural Understanding and Communication* (Schmidt, 1998) can serve as a vehicle for facilitating understanding and creating awareness for different perspectives on the topic. The ABC's used in this way would not only enrich each single classroom discussion, but also contribute to better and deeper understanding of the different partner countries once shared in the European language community.

## NOTES

1. Originally the Humboldt (1922) citation was in German and quoted in German (Baron, 2002, p. 42).
2. For example, such studies are the second wave of the PISA Study (Programme for International Student Assessment) (Retrieved March 21, 2005, from: http://www.pisa.oecd.org)
3. Retrieved March 21, 2005, from http://www.mobidic.org/m-o-b-i-d-i-c/.

## REFERENCES

Baron, R. (2002). *Interculturally speaking—"Landeskunde," intercultural learning and teacher training in Germany from an American perspective*. München: Langenscheidt-Longman.

Bortz, J. (1999). *Statistik für Sozialwissenschaftler* (5th ed.). Berlin: Springer.

Bower, G.H., Black, J.B., & Turner, T.J. (1994). Scripts in memory for text. In R.B. Rudell, M. Rapp Rudell, & H. Singer (Eds.), *Theoretical models and processes of reading* (pp. 469-581). Newark, DE: International Reading Association.

Donmall, G. (1985). *Language awareness*. NCLE papers and reports 6. London: Centre for Information on Language Teaching and Research.

Fehling, S. (2002a). Methodische Überlegungen zur Erforschung von Language Awareness. In S. Breidbach, G. Bach, & D. Wolff (Eds.), *Bilingualer Sachfachunterricht: Didaktik Lehrer- Lernerforschung und Bildungspolitik zwischen Theorie und Empirie. Schriften zum Bilingualismus und bilingualen Sachfachunterricht* (Vol. 1, pp. 161-172). Frankfurt/M.: Lang.

Fehling, S. (2002b). Language awareness in content and language integrated learning. In C. Finkbeiner (Ed.), *Wholeheartedly English: A life of learning. Festschrift für Johannes-Peter Timm* (pp. 213-221). Berlin: Cornelsen.

Fehling, S. (2005). *Language Awareness und Bilingualer Unterricht: Eine komparative Studie*. Frankfurt: Peter Lang.

Fehling, S., & Finkbeiner, C. (2002). Evaluation von Schulleistungen im bilingualen Sachfachunterricht. In C. Finkbeiner (Ed.), *Bilingualität und Mehrsprachigkeit. Modellet Projekte, Ergebnisse* (pp. 20-30). Hannover: Schroedel.

Finkbeiner, C. (1995). *Englischunterricht in europaischer Dimension. Zwischen Qualifikationserwartungen der Gesellschaft und Schülereinstellungen und Schülerinteressen. Berichte und Kontexte zweier empirischer Untersuchungen*. Bochum: Brockmeyer.

Finkbeiner, C. (2001). One and all in CALL? Learner-moderator-researcher. *Computer Assisted Language Learning, 14*( 3-4), 129-151.

Finkbeiner, C. (Ed.). (2002a). *Wholeheartedly English: A life of learning. Festschrift für Johannes-Peter Timm*. Berlin: Cornelsen.

Finkbeiner, C. (2002b). Foreign language practice and cooperative learning. In C. Finkbeiner (Ed.), *Wholeheartedly English: A life of learning. Festschrift für Johannes-Peter Timm* (pp. 109-122). Berlin: Cornelsen.

Finkbeiner, C. (2003). What teachers think about how students read. In B. Di Biase (Ed.), *Developing a second language. Acquisition, processing and pedagogy of Arabic, Chinese, English, Italian, Japanese, Swedish* (pp. 73-94). Melbourne: Australia.

Finkbeiner, C., & Fehling, S. (2002). Bilingualer Unterricht: Aktueller Stand und Implementierungsmöglichkeiten im Studium. In C. Finkbeiner (Ed.), *Bilingualer Unterricht. Lehren und Lemen in zwei Sprachen* (pp. 9-22). Hannover: Schroedel.

Finkbeiner, C., & Fehling, S. (2003). *Adapted version of the Spada & Fröehlich (1995) COLT (Communicative Orientation of Language Teaching Observation Scheme)*. Unpublished manuscript.

Finkbeiner, C. & Koplin, C. (2001). Fremdverstehensprozesse und interkulturelle Prozesse als Forschungsgegenstand. In A. Müller-Hartmann & M. Schocker-v.-Ditfurth (Eds.), *Qualitative Forschungsansätze im Bereich Fremdsprachen lehren und lernen* (pp. 114-136). Tübingen: Narr.

Finkbeiner, C., & Koplin, C. (2002). A cooperative approach for facilitating intercultural education. *Reading Online, 6*(3). Retrieved March 21,2005, from:

http://www.readingonline.org/newliteracies/lit_index.asp?HREF=/
newliteracies/finkbeiner/index.html

Finkbeiner, C., & Schnaitmann, G. W. (2001). Darstellung und Diskussion der Lehr- und Lernforschung in der Jahrtausendwende. In C. Finkbeiner & G.W. Schnaitmann (Eds.), *Lehren und Lernen im Kontext empirischer Forschung und Fachdidaktik* (pp. 9-31). Donauworth: Auer.

Hawkins, E. (1987). *Awareness of language: An introduction* (2nd ed.). Cambridge: Cambridge University Press.

James, C., & Garrett, P. (1991). The scope of language awareness. In C. James & P. Garrett (Eds.), *Language awareness in the classroom* (pp. 3-20). London: Longman.

Risager, K. (2000). Cultural awareness. In M. Byram (Eds.), *Routledge encyclopedia of language teaching and learning* (pp. 159-162). London and New York: Routledge.

Schmidt, P.R. (1998). The ABC's of cultural understanding and communication. *Equity and Excellence in Education, 31*(2),28-38.

Schmidt, P.R. (2001). The power to empower: Creating home/school relationships with the ABC's of cultural understanding and communication. In P.R. Schmidt & P.B. Mosenthal (Eds.), *Reconceptualizing literacy in the new age of multiculturalism and pluralism* (pp. 389-433). Greenwich, CT: Information Age Publishing.

Semino, E. (2000). Schema and script theory. In M. Byram (Ed.), *Routledge encyclopedia of language teaching and learning* (pp. 525-527). London and New York: Routledge.

Spada, N., & Fröhlich, M. (1995). *COLT: Communicative orientation of language teaching observation scheme. Coding conventions and applications*. Sydney: National Centre for English Language Teaching and Research (NCELTR).

Sturm, R. (1999). Bildung und Kultur. In Bundeszentrale für politische Bildung (Ed.), *Informationen zur politischen Bildung: Großbritannien*. Retrieved March 21,2005, from: http://www.bpb.de/publikationenl021222878100
14360029029023937315,0,0,IZPB_262_Bildung_und_Kultur_050402.html

Swain, M., & Johnson, R.K. (1997). Immersion education. A category within bilingual education. In R.K. Johnson & M. Swain (Eds.), *Immersion education: International perspectives* (pp. 1-16). Cambridge: Cambridge University Press.

Wolff, D. (2002). Bilingualer Sachfachunterricht in Europa: Ein Überblick. In C. Finkbeiner (Ed.), *Bilingualität und Mehrsprachigkeit. Modelle, Projekte, Ergebnisse* (pp. 5-11). Hannover: Schroedel.

CHAPTER 6

# REVEALING AND REVISITING "SELF" IN RELATION TO THE CULTURALLY DIFFERENT "OTHER"

## Multicultural Teacher Education and the *ABC's Model*

Jyotsna Pattnaik

## ABSTRACT

The chapter shares findings from course projects that used Schmidt's ABC's model in two universities. The purposes of the projects were to allow present and future teachers to perceive commonalities and differences in human experiences, understand and analyze the unique challenges faced by new immigrants, and reflect on their own privileged experiences as members of the majority group, as well as their responsibility as teachers of immigrant children. The study highlighted the importance of instructional strategies that use personal narratives for self-revelation and self-reflection

*ABC's of Cultural Understanding and Communication:*
*National and International Adaptations,* 111–141

to help white pre-service/in-service teachers identify and deconstruct privilege and hierarchy and connect to immigrant children and their families. The authors suggest the implementation of the ABC's model in a variety if courses including diversity courses, methods courses, and discipline-specific courses. In addition, the impact of the ABC's model will be even greater and sustained in courses founded on the "critical race theory" which engages students in systematic analysis and evaluation of white racism and white privileges. The author emphasizes the need for follow-up/longitudinal research to explore the long-term impact of the *ABC's Model* on research participants.

## INTRODUCTION

My interview with Sophindh spanned approximately three hours.... At times, during the interview, I felt that I was getting too close to personal information and revelations, but he seemed eager to share his memories and feelings. I was taken by his honesty and his willingness to express his lowest moments with such candor. As we talked at his desk ... several staff members had to interrupt to ask Sophindh to do a task or make a phone call in Khmer. The offhanded, even brusque manner in which some of our staff members spoke to him embarrassed and pained me, I wanted to cry out to them, "Don't you appreciate whom you're talking to? Can't you remember, or haven't you ever realized, that this man represents the living history of the war in Cambodia? Why don't you treat him with the respect he deserves? " I began to imagine what it might feel like to be disregarded.... The years of regret and frustrations that this man has experienced are almost too much for his slender frame to bear, and yet despite all that he has endured in his life, he continues to work diligently every day. (Elaine)

When we got to the topic of discrimination, I found the most difference in our lives. I was very surprised to hear some of his experiences and the experiences of his family members.... They (his family) have received bad looks from people. They have not been helped in stores, even one right here. This really came as a shock to me. I have shopped at the store that he was talking about. Whenever I went there, I have been bombarded by salesmen. I never thought that this was a discriminatory town.... When he lived in Oklahoma, his daughters were teased on the school bus by some older boys. They told the girls that they were "dirty Mexicans and they should go back to where they came from." When he and his wife went to talk to the principal of the school, she would not punish the boys, and in fact recommended that the girls attend a class on getting along with others. This was appalling to me. I could not imagine the rage and anger that I would feel as a parent if the principal would not take action. (Karla)

The above excerpts are taken from the papers submitted by two female Caucasian students for course projects in two teacher education programs (one in the midwest and the other in the west-coast). For their projects, students in these courses were required to interview first generation immigrants. Through comparing their own life experiences with that of their interviewees, Elaine and Karla explored commonalities and differences between their own mainstream lives, with the lives of their interviewees, lives on the margins, lives separated by boundaries of race/ethnicity, social class, language, and religion. Elaine and Karla, pre-service teachers, also learned about the personal, financial, social, and institutional challenges new immigrants face in the United States. Furthermore, Elaine and Karla learned of their own taken-for granted privileges being English-speaking, white, middle class, protestants in a highly race, class, language, and faith conscious society. Hopefully, Karla and Elaine's experience will aid in their development as teachers of children from diverse cultural backgrounds.

The need for the development of "critical cultural consciousness" (Gay & Kirkland, 2003) between pre-service and in-service teachers is justified on the basis of the changing demographics in the nation's schools, college campuses, and the society (Camarota, 2001); the global work environment and the diverse workforce (Krishnamurthy, 2003); as well as the multicultural and inclusive ideological telos on which a pluralistic democracy is founded (Pattnaik, 2001). The U.S. Department of Commerce (1996) projects that by the year 2050, minority students from African American, Asian American, and Latino communities will constitute close to 57% of all students in the United States. However, 90% of teachers and teacher education students currently are white middle class females (Ladson-Billings, 1999). Therefore, Howard (2003) reminds teacher educators to reconceptualize the way new teachers are prepared and how to provide them with attitude, knowledge, and skills that will be appropriate and effective for teaching children from diverse backgrounds. Highlighting the importance of multicultural education for teachers, Gay and Kirkland (2003) maintain, "teachers knowing who they are as people, understanding the contexts in which they teach, and questioning their knowledge and assumptions are as important as the mastery of techniques for instructional effectiveness" (p. 181). Although scholars in multicultural education recognize the larger structural reforms that are required to bring educational equity to all children, they have also emphasized the role of individual teachers to reach out to all children in their classrooms, however small the impact may be (Anyon, 2001). Townsend (2002) justifiably argues that "deliberate actions are needed to move pre and in-service teachers toward the effective use of culturally responsive pedagogy to ensure that we "Leave no teacher behind' (p. 737).

This chapter is based on course projects designed by a teacher educator to foster multicultural understanding among students enrolled in teacher education courses at two universities. The course projects were based on Patricia Ruggiano Schmidt's (1998a) *ABC's of Cultural Understanding and Communication*. They required that a pre-service or in-service teacher write an *autobiography*, write a *biography* of a first generation immigrant after conducting in-depth interviews with the person, and finally construct a *cross-cultural analysis* comparing and contrasting the two life stories. The purpose of the project was to allow present and future teachers to perceive commonalities and differences in human experiences, understand and analyze the unique challenges faced by new immigrants, empathize with new immigrants, and reflect on their own privileged experiences as members of the majority group, as well as their responsibility as teachers of immigrant children.

## REVIEW OF LITERATURE

The following postmodern movements in social science research have influenced the inception as well as the direction of this particular study: the post-structural and feminist movements (Alpert, 2000; Beyer & Liston, 1992; Lather, 1992), interpretive inquiry (Erikson, 1986; Lincoln, 1989) and contemporary scholarly interest in narrative studies (Bell, 2002; Connelly & Clandinin, 1988; Elbaz, 1991; Rossiter, 2002; Spigelman, 2001). These above approaches also come under the platform of qualitative research as opposed to quantitative research/positivist inquiry. Despite their individual uniqueness, all the above perspectives join their voices against the scientific authority of positivism, as "one and the only best way" approach to generate and validate knowledge about the world. Their legacies of multiple epistemologies and recognition of multiple perspectives as the bases for inquiry were integrated into the methodological model adopted for this study.

### Feminist Perspectives

Feminist perspectives have contributed significantly to the understanding, purpose, methods, and directions of inquiry in educational research. By discarding master narratives as normative truth, postmodern feminist researchers highlight self-reflexive nature of inquiry and the feminist epistemology offer forms of knowledge that are alternative to the existing masculine assumptions about legitimacy and significance (Alpert, 2000; Thompson & Gitlin, 1995). Moreover, other aspects of feminist inquiry, such as the relational spirit and the search for meaning in connection, the situated nature of knowledge, as well as its focus on voice, authority and positionality (Maher & Tetreault, 1994) are of particular relevance to this study. Through sustained interaction and interviews with a first generation immigrant, participants revisited as well as reconstructed their own experiences, beliefs, and perspectives. In addition, the self-reflexive process of inquiry enabled students to realize the positionality characteristics (such as race, social class, gender, language, religion) that impact the life experiences, cultural values, and beliefs of their own and that of their interviewees.

Nonwhite feminist scholars such as bell hooks, Gloria Anzaldua, Chandra Talpade Mohanty, and Gayatri Spivak have contributed to current research on examining "Whiteness" with their call for "white people to locate themselves within structures of privileges and to shift perspectives from naïve notions of pluralism to understanding the ways in which unacknowledged white supremacy inhibits any authentic project for diversity" (Hytten & Adkins, 2001, p. 437). Participants in the study under discussion, were allowed opportunities to compare their privileged experiences (being white) with that of their nonwhite interviewees.

Because of the fact that the study relied heavily on writing of autobiographies and biographies, it will be appropriate to discuss the problems of narrative as a research methodology and the ways these concerns were addressed in this study.

## Narrative: A Research Methodology

Writing of autobiographies/biographies fall into the category of narrative studies. The possibilities of narrative as a research methodology are many. The adoption of narrative as a research methodology has drawn many intellectual and professional concerns. Thomas (1992) writes, "Narrative as a genre presents post-modernist problems, not least the relation of language to reality and what may count as evidence or data" (p. introduction). Phillips (1993) perceives narrative research as a political stand rather than an epistemological one and continues, "There are many cases in the social sciences (including educational research) where the beliefs, and resulting narratives—of the individuals concerned are not particularly insightful or causally enlightening" (p. 9). In narrative studies, the potential threats to "rigor" (expected from any research methodology) come from two major fronts: the trustworthiness of the experiences told/written and the possible misinterpretation of these experiences by the interpreter-researcher.

In this particular study, I made a conscious effort to ensure methodological rigor. Because of the fact that participants' autobiographies revealed their own life experiences especially in an atmosphere of mutual trust and privacy (between participants and myself, the instructor/ researcher), I perceive no threat to trustworthiness/validity in student-produced autobiographies in this study. Students wrote the biographies of their interviewees based on the audio-taped recording of their interviews. Interviewees read their own biographies written by students for possible misinterpretations.

## Multicultural Education: A Critical Analysis

While the ongoing challenge to multicultural education comes from the conservative right, the field has faced severe criticisms from its proponents in recent years. For example, multicultural units and lesson plans are rejected as isolated segments without any relevance to the central curriculum. Therefore, multicultural units and lesson plans are perceived as additive rather than transformative approaches to multicultural curriculum (Banks, 1997). The focus on heroes, food, and festivals is criticized for fostering a tourism approach in students. In addition, scholars also argue that multiculturalism has taken a reductionist agenda encouraging cultural essentialism (May, 2000), where "ethnicist discourses seek to impose stereotypic notions of common cultural need upon heterogeneous groups with diverse social aspirations and interests" (Brah, 1992, p. 129).

## Cultural Autobiographies: A Different Approach to Study Culture

The failure of those mentioned above approaches in enhancing preservice teachers' understanding of ethnically diverse students and their families has led to an alternative approach that advocates defining and studying cultures from an individual/personal perspective (Florio-Ruane, 1994). The proponents of this approach focus on "the development of one's own cultural identity as a necessary precursor to cross-cultural understanding" (Zeichner, 1993, p.15). Writing of autobiography is the primary focus of this particular approach. Using students' autobiography as a vehicle for personal and academic growth is not new in teaching. The implications of autobiographies for students have been recognized from many vantage points, such as: students defining themselves and their philosophies of life (Shull, 1991); students validating and clarifying their personal experiences (Nicolini, 1994); students gaining insights into their personal development (Karpaik, 2000), students connecting with community and place in constructing landscapes and personal meaning (Newman, 1995); students constructing their personal identity (Kehily, 1995);

students fostering individual and social self-consciousness through their autobiographies (Kass, 1995). Researchers have also identified the value of autobiographies for classroom and pre-service teachers, such as teachers constructing and reconstructing their personal practical knowledge (Beattie, 1995; Elbaz, 1991); continuing professional education for teachers (MacLeod & Cowleson, 2001); and fostering individual and social self-consciousness among students (Kass, 1995). The value of autobiographies in the context of cultural learning has recently been advocated by theorists and researchers (Florio-Ruane & de Tar, 1995), such as allowing minority students to connect with their cultural backgrounds through their autobiographies (Allison, 1995). The writing of cultural autobiography is based on the underlying assumption that "ethnicity" and "culture" will no longer be perceived as the study of "others." Here, the study of self creates a context to explore and connect to the experiences of the "other."

## ABC (Autobiography/Biography/Cross-Cultural Analysis): Constructing Self from the Other

The ABC's of cultural understanding model connects closely to the "cultural-historical activity theory" (Gutierrez, Asato, Santos, & Gotanda, 2002, p. 336) that accepts the role of culture in language and human development (Moll, 2000). The primary purpose of the model is to enable students to realize the influence of culture in their own and that of their interviewee's beliefs, values, and experiences and to accept diversity and difference as resources of learning (Engestrom, 1999; Moll, 2000).

When applied with white pre-service/in-service teachers, the *ABC's Model* addresses some of the important aspects of the "anti-racist" pedagogy suggested by Derman-Sparks and Brunson-Phillips (1997). First, it helps participants in developing deeper self-knowledge about one's racial and cultural identity and the ways racism has shaped this identity through writing autobiographies. Second, interviewing and writing biographies of a culturally different person helps strengthening one's understanding and knowledge base about racially and culturally diverse groups though empathy and de-centering. The *ABC's Model* does not encourage essentialist interpretations of groups or reductionist notion of culture. It allows pre-service and in-service teachers to perceive the overlapping space between the individual and the social/cultural. The *ABC's Model* also intends to move students beyond what Rotherberg (2000) refers as "food court" to critically reflect over white privileges and racism in the American society and the influence of "whiteness" on self and minority communities.

Researchers have adapted the *ABC's Model* in various ways and have reported positive findings. From her ongoing research, Schmidt (1998a,b, 1999, 2001) reported that *ABC's Model* enabled teachers to reflect on their own attitudes toward differences, to modify their literacy instruction for diverse students, and the model enhanced teachers' academic and cultural knowledge of students. From adaptation of the model with pre-service teachers in her literacy methods course, Xu (2000a) recommends that, "Teacher educators must create opportunities such as the adaptation of the *ABC's Model* to guide pre-service teachers to explore diversity while teaching diverse students in all subject areas" (p. 141).

The author of this article has infused the *ABC's Model* over the years in varieties of ways into undergraduate and graduate level courses. Besides adapting the model into undergraduate-level diversity courses, I have also adapted the model into early childhood education masters' level core courses. For example, students have been engaged in course projects that allowed them opportunities to use the *ABC's Model* with individuals in Japan. Students in another course project interviewed newly immigrant parents in the United States to understand differences in child-rearing beliefs and practices between their own and that of their interviewees; differences in perceptions regarding the role of parents, teachers, and family members; the challenges faced by immigrant parents in early childhood centers; and their own role in designing culturally appropriate policies, curriculum, and pedagogical strategies to meet the needs of immigrant children and their families. Students have invariably shared their positive learning from these projects. Here is a student's response:

> The biggest challenge in interviewing Anna was my fear of offending or getting too personal with my questions. Many times I am curious about something regarding one of my students and do not have the courage to ask these personal questions.... This project has helped me better understand the importance of an open dialogue with my students and their parents. Only when we truly understand where a child is coming from can we effectively teach and guide them to their fullest potential. (Clara)

It is important to mention here that discussion of diversity were infused into all courses that I teach and therefore the course projects that adapted the *ABC's Model* were not additive rather integrated very well into the courses.

## FIRST-GENERATION IMMIGRANTS: A CULTURE IN TRANSITION

The researcher deliberately chose first generation immigrants for the interview phase of the projects for the following reasons. First, there have been a steady influx of new immigrants to the United States in the last ten years, an increase of almost 1 million immigrants in U.S. public schools (Garcia, 2002). Most of the immigrant populations have settled in the major urban cities. However, rural Midwestern towns have also experienced a change in their demographic pattern because of the employment of immigrant workers in poultry industry and agricultural sectors. Second, the new immigrants' lack of knowledge of the mainstream culture accompanied with the mainstream culture's apathy to deal with the problems faced by the new immigrants affect the adaptation and accommodation of the new arrivals into the new social order. In addition, there have been educational trends what Gutierrez et al. (2002) label as "backlash pedagogies ... that prohibit the use of students' complete linguistic, sociocultural, and academic repertoire in the service of learning" (p. 337). The result is manifested in poor academic achievement and high dropout rates of the limited English proficiency children. Third, Laosa (1989) suggested that variables such as characteristics of the communities of origin, the background of the child and the family, the challenges and constraints faced in the country of entrance, consideration of the person's life cycle at which immigration takes place should be considered while dealing with first generation immigrant children and families. This can be possible if one explores the life experiences of immigrants within a very nonthreatening environment. Moreover, Owocki and Lohff (1995) suggest that the acculturation struggle of these children and families should not be viewed from the macrocultural ideals but from the immigrant' perspectives. Therefore, the process of interviewing and writing biographies of recent immigrants by white pre-service teachers is very important in this context. The cultural analysis that resulted from students writing and comparing their autobiographies with life experiences of their interviewees, hopefully, will enable them to understand and empathize with new immigrants and develop strategies to connect with immigrant children and families.

## METHOD

The method of data collection and analysis followed the procedure of qualitative research (Lincoln & Guba, 2000). This section describes the setting, participants, procedures, and the data analysis.

### Setting

The study took place in two public universities, one in the Midwest and the other on the west coast. The university in the Midwest had a student population of about 13,000 of which only 13% were nonwhite. The university receives its student population from the neighboring farming communities and from the city/suburbs. The population of new immigrants has been increasing in cities in Missouri, in suburbs, and in rural areas. The majority of the university's international students manage to find jobs in these two neighboring cities or in other places of the United States after graduation and join the pool of new immigrant work force.

The university in the west coast is located in an urban city in California. The student population is around 32, 000. The majority of the students in the Master's in Early Childhood Education program are white female classroom teachers teaching in very diverse settings in public schools or preschool/child care programs around the area.

## Participants

I, the researcher, was born in India, and earned university degrees in my native land. My doctoral degree research in teacher education took place at a Northeastern university in the United States. My research revolves around the preparation of teachers for early childhood education.

The 34 volunteers, white, mainstream participants in this study were students in two teacher education programs. The participating students in the Midwestern university were enrolled in an undergraduate course related to diversity. The participating students in the university on the west coast were enrolled in an early childhood graduate level course that infused multicultural education into all aspects of the course. Five students of color were enrolled in both classes. However, I only selected papers of the white female students; they consented to the use of their papers for analysis. Because of the personal aspects involved in writing one' s autobiography, I have used pseudonyms. It is appropriate to mention here that some students in the Midwestern university interviewed international students in the university.

## Data Source

The following data sources were used for the study.

1. Personal journal writings.
2. Writing of autobiographies.
3. Writing of biographies of a new immigrant.
4. Cross-cultural analysis paper.

## Procedure and Data Collection

Before the inception of the study, I shared the purpose and procedure of the research and sought participants. The assignments were required for all students in the two courses and fulfilled the requirement of partial grading for the course. Therefore, from the very beginning of the semesters, I clarified the difference between the completion of the assignment and the participation in the study. I also defined the meaning of participation in the study which meant giving permission to the instructor/researcher to use the data for presentation and publication.

The study proceeded through the following three phases:

*Phase 1.* In the first phase, students wrote some personal journal entries on topics such as "have I ever been discriminated against and how it felt," "reflecting on my own biases," "my experiences with somebody who was different from me," which culminated in an in-depth writing of autobiography. I also provided some guidelines for possible themes (such as key events in one's life including influence of family, culture and religion on personal perspectives, hopes/aspirations, failures/successes, painful and enjoyable moments, union and separation) to be included in the paper and student were allowed to add their own dimensions into it. Students had the choice of inclusion, omission, or deletion of any of their personal experiences at any point in the research. The degree of candidness was left open to individual choice and decisions. Students submitted their autobiographies for review. I reviewed the autobiographies for detail, comprehensiveness, and reflections/clarifications (if any).

*Phase 2.* In the second phase, each participant identified and interviewed a "first-generation immigrant." The interview focused on themes included in participant's autobiographies as well as the interviewee's experiences in the United States and in his/ her own country. Participants audiotaped and transcribed the interview(s). Interviewees also read their biographies to ensure accuracy in information and interpretations. Written permission was sought from the interviewees to use this information for the class as well as research purposes and the assurance to maintain anonymity was provided. Participants submitted the biographies for my review. I provided feedback on following criteria: comprehensiveness, detail, and clarity. After the review by the researcher/instructor, if required, students contacted their interviewee to prepare the final draft of the biography paper.

*Phase 3.* Participants compared and analyzed their own autobiographies with the biographies of their interviewees to write the commonalities and differences in their life experiences, their understanding of other perspectives, societal injustices toward new immigrants, and incorporation of this learning in their future career and life. While analyzing the data, I contacted individual students for further clarifications if required.

## DATA ANALYSIS

The data analysis could be described as a process of inductive reasoning (Goertz & LeCompte, 1981). The data was collected which focused on the inquiry under consideration. Yet, there were no predetermined categories to which the data needed to be matched. Initial "units of meaning" (Lincoln & Guba, 1985) were developed from the textual analysis of each individual participant's written autobiography, biography, and cross-cultural analysis papers. Major categories emerged consequently through a "constant comparison" method of comparing students' writings (Bogdan & Biklen, 1994).

The findings of the two studies are reported here under two themes: Typical (the themes that appeared more than 70% of participants' papers) and "atypical" (the themes that were very important for the purpose of the study, although appeared in less than 50% of participants' papers).

### Typical Themes

The typical themes that emerged from the data analysis were: (a) Understanding culture and cultural lenses; (b) Acknowledging cultural differences; (c) Discovering similarities in human experiences; (d) Empathizing with the other; (e) Overcoming fear of non-communication; (f) Acknowledging the value of the project for personal life and professional teaching career.

*Understanding of culture and cultural lenses:*   One of the objectives of this project was to enable Caucasian participants in this study to realize that they belong to a culture and that their positionality within the culture of their family and race shapes many of their perceptions and practices in life. This point is very important because educational researchers have pointed out that many white people including classroom and pre-service teachers are not accustomed to perceiving their affiliations in an ethnic group (Baumann, 1996; Pearce, 2003). Pearce aptly argues, "This inability to recognize one's own culture leaves intact the idea that whiteness is a neutral place from which to look at others" (p. 275).

Although many students have not explicitly articulated their understanding of the meaning of "culture," their papers expressed an understanding of the influence of culture on their outlook and ways of life. For example, the value of religion as an important cultural lens appeared in more than 90% of participants' autobiography. "Family" was another important cultural aspect that appeared frequently in participants' papers such as family values, traditions, and customs.

One of the participants, Lavonne, provides her deeper understanding of culture (her own and that of others) through a metaphor.

> We generally judge others based on our fund of knowledge. While we might possess a general understanding of a culture, that is not enough. Culture can be seen as the background of a picture of a person. The details are all of the aspects of a person's life that add colors and richness. The more you come in contact with the picture, the more details you come to see and appreciate. When communicating with people from a different culture, it is important to understand their point of view. This is the picture's perspective. From their vantage point, you will have a better understanding of who they are.

The excerpts below demonstrate participants' identification and acknowledgment of cultural influences on their lives.

> Another big influence on my life is religion. Being a Southern Baptist, my preachers know how to get their points across to you and they make sure the point will stick with you for a very long time. Most of the decisions I have made are based on my religion—is my religion for or against it? What would God think of that? (Kim)

> My family influenced my life in many ways.... My family did not attend church because my parents did not want to fight over which church their children were going to attend. They decided to let us choose when we were old enough. We were always taught to believe in God and there was a heaven etc. (Cathy)

The two above excerpts highlight the fact that religion (Christianity here) has played an important role in both these participants' experiences.

*Acknowledging cultural differences.* Many participants moved beyond the meaning of culture to examine cultural differences between their own and that of their interviewee. Sometimes they struggled between whose view is better and at other times they accepted these differences as a part of their cultural and individual beliefs and experiences. For example, Aimee compares the interviewee's openness with her conservative attitude toward interracial dating.

> This person had worked with many different races for jobs, church-related activities and other places. He said that he gets along with people from other ethnic groups well. He has never dated anyone outside of his races,

but it would not bother him to do so. I, on the other hand, have not really had much contact with other races.... I don't have a problem with interracial marriages, but, truly, I do not feel I could ever date anyone from another race. (Aimee)

The writings of Ann and Joy portray their learning of differences in cultural traditions and philosophies between their own and that of their interviewee.

Another difference between us is the concept of "freedom." Risa expressed an unbelievable awe of how American women make all their decisions and create their own experiences. Risa feels that she has gained more day to day personal freedom after coming to this country, yet overall her actions and decisions are closely guided by her family. Family interest and happiness comes before her own interest. It sounded strange to me, yet I realized that both of us grew up knowing only our ways. I do not know whose way is better. Yet, this interview provided us an opportunity to understand and interpret each other's practices and point of views. (Ann)

We talked about the arranged marriage system in Sri Lanka. Sunita's parents' marriage was arranged. Sunita said that her parents are very happy and the family is very close. Sunita seems to be very comfortable with that concept. According to her, arranged marriage system has been very successful in her country. I still have a hard time accepting the concept of arranged marriage. Yet, I wish that the majority of children in the United States could enjoy a stable home and family. As a child, I have gone through the trauma of parental divorce. (Joy)

*Discovering similarities in human experiences.*   Participants in the study discovered similarities in human experiences irrespective of their memberships in different cultural groups. In fact, in the reflection section of their papers, almost all the participants shared that they discovered many similarities between them and their interviewees, something that they did not expect before the interviews. Describing a common reference point, Allison writes,

She describes her relationship with the family as that of companionship. They can talk about anything.... This is especially true, when facing new situations that you have to think and adapt to. Having your family as a sounding board is very important and I am fortunate to enjoy it myself.

Comparing her adolescent and teenage years with her interviewee, a Taiwanese immigrant, Beth states:

One thing that was similar with our parents is the importance that they put on education. While growing up, Audrey's mother as well as my mother constantly reminded us to focus on studies, not on boys or anything else.

Students also realized how commonalities of experiences connect people of different cultures in spite of the barriers of language and other cultural traditions. Rebecca established that human bond while interviewing Pamella, a first generation immigrant from Germany. They both broke down in tears while sharing the death of beloved persons who changed the paths of their lives.

> I never thought that people were similar around the world. I also thought it would be hard to ask questions to someone that didn't speak my language fluently. This was not hard for us though. Pamela also thought it would be hard because I spoke too fast. We both had a devastating death in the family that changed us. We have grieved, mourned, and tried to get on with life. However, we both have realized that it is hard to get over something like that.... I found that we can relate if we look further than just the outside of someone. (Rebecca)

*Empathizing with the "other":*   Listening to the story of their interviewees, most of the students realized the discrimination that their interviewees have experienced in this country. They discovered and interpreted the reasons for the immigrants' problems. Sometimes ignorance and the "cultural supremacy" attitude of Americans pose a problem for immigrants and, at other times, the language barrier poses a problem "of not being able to understand them" (Kristin). Frequently, the anti-immigrant movement in the country adds to people's perception of these new immigrants as "threats to the economic interest of the country" (Jeremy). After interviewing Kirabel, a first generation immigrant from Ethiopia, Amy writes:

> Because he did not know the language very well, he was very quiet, and children many times made fun of him because they did not know why he did not communicate with them ... many kids asked him why he looked so healthy because people in Ethiopia were supposed to be sick ... many students even told him to go back to where he came from. His story made me remember my days as a student, and the cruel remarks made to me about my features. When I compared my suffering to what Kirabel went through I am astonished at the level of maturity he had. Kirabel realized that the students who were making fun, and being hurtful did not know what they were saying ... they already had preconceived notions and prejudices about Ethiopia from their families. (Amy)

After interviewing Olatumi, an immigrant from Ghana, Summer's empathy led her to understand Olatumi's life experiences:

> The main difference between us is that she had experienced many instances of discrimination. These experiences obviously had an impact on how she

felt about certain things. I was surprised to hear that she thought education was different for her as a "black" student than it was for a white student. While the quality of education was not the question, it was more the social experience in education. She felt that teachers catered more to the students they had known for extended periods of time and simply overlooked her as a student.

It is also interesting to note in Summer's excerpt and in many other participants' papers the expressions, "surprised," or "shocked," when describing their interviewee's life experiences. It highlights two very important aspects. First, many participants were caught off guard with their interviewee's life experiences which were beyond their own imagination. Second, while the participants may have been exposed to minority experiences through news media, movies, and other such channels, they were able to more critically analyze information related to the person interviewed.

The above excerpts also highlight how the stories of their interviewee's life served as powerful medium to move participants cognitively and emotionally. Not only that they were able to empathize with their interviewees, they also critically analyzed the economic, social, and cultural factors that contribute to people's treatment of others. Participants also articulated an understanding that misinformation is the root of stereotypes and discriminatory behavior among people. These excerpts validate the recommendations made by narrative researchers to incorporate stories and case studies into teaching and learning (Bruner, 2002; Dominice, 2000; Rossiter, 2002).

*Overcoming fear of non-communication.* By providing participants opportunities to interact with a person from a different cultural background, the project allowed them to realize that when knowledge is co-constructed through exploring "self-in-relation to others," (Gensch, 2000) rather than as disinterested observers, it becomes more compelling and meaningful to the learner. For example, a person's construction of someone unfamiliar and the consequent fear resulting from that construction may have come from media, stories, and other such sources, rather than authentic, personal, and meaningful experiences. Invariably, participants in the study admitted that interviews with a culturally different person enabled them to overcome the barriers of communication that they feared before the interview. Here are excerpts from Ann and Elizabeth's reflections.

I must admit that when this assignment was given, I was extremely nervous about talking with someone from such a culturally different background....
In the end I found this assignment to be very rewarding. I interviewed Risa, a nineteen-year-old from Jakarta. I think in the beginning, my fear was basi-

cally of the unknown. I knew nothing of Risa's culture, what her experiences were, how she felt about things.... What I forgot in my misplaced fear, was that Risa does not know anything about me either. The chasm was quickly overcome when we began our interview sessions.... I was even surprised to find that language was not a barrier. If either one of us did not understand, we would ask again or reword the statement until we understood each other. What I was anticipating as a bad experience was actually an honor and a privilege and enjoyable. (Ann)

The time I spent talking with her really gave me an opportunity to let my guard down that I sometimes put up and around others that are different from me. (Elizabeth)

*Acknowledging the value of the project for professional teaching career.*   Participants' written papers clearly revealed how this experience was valuable to them as a person and as a teacher/future teacher. Tiffany wrote:

I think that this experience has helped me to learn about myself and my way of thinking. I plan to become an elementary teacher one day. I think I will have more compassion with students from different cultures now. I want to learn about their values and beliefs. Each child is unique and people need to understand where the child is coming from.

After interviewing Tammy, a Russian immigrant, Vicki wrote:

Interviewing Tammy was an experience that I feel will be of great value to me as a future teacher. It gave me the opportunity to reach out to someone from another ethnic origin and to learn about them as a person. I think as a teacher it will be important for me to be able to recognize the differences in people as individuals not just as a perceived image portrayed by the society of their culture. Also one really nice result of this project is that I have made a new and interesting friend.

Involvement in this project enabled participants in the study to develop instructional strategies. Gay and Kirkland (2003) rightfully maintain that the process of critical reflection can be internalized by "turning critical thoughts into transformative instructional actions" (p. 186). Students visualized strategies to use in their classrooms and with immigrant parents. Connecting with children and parents from other cultures, exposing white, mainstream children to cultures of new immigrants through unit/lessons on friendships, common festivals, writing of autobiographies/biographies, and strategies to involve parents were mentioned by students.

For immigrant children form different countries, who do not speak English, it is important to speak slowly.... As a teacher, I should use many pictures, cues, facial expressions, and simple terms to explain what I am talking about. (Alisha)

As a teacher, I will have to communicate with children and their parents that are of different races than my own I think it will be a good idea for all teachers to set aside time just to meet the families of their students in order to get to know them and to get better understanding of each other's differences and commonalities. (Linda)

This interview has helped me at a personal level. For the first time in my life, I got a friend from another culture. I would include a unit on friendship … the children should learn ways to make friends with people from other cultures and adopt problem solving techniques for when they are in a disagreement. (Jodi)

As highlighted in the above excerpts, participants in this study realized the importance of integrating the "cultural capital" (Bourdieu, 1973) that immigrant children bring to their classrooms that includes the cultural norms, social practices, ideologies, language, and behavior (Tyrone, 2003). This realization is very important for teachers and future teachers because minority children's "cultural capital" is frequently not accepted or recognized by teachers and other members of the mainstream society.

## Atypical Themes

Two important themes that appeared in less than 50% of participants' papers were: Acknowledging one's own privileged experiences and reflecting on one's own biases toward other groups.

*Acknowledging one's own privileged experiences:*  Students' written papers demonstrated their ability to compare life experiences of their own and that of their interviewee. However, the privileged aspects of their own experiences were explicitly articulated by some students.

I interviewed Betty, a twenty-six-year-old woman from Panama. She came to the Unites States six years ago with her American husband, an Air Force officer. The biggest difference I discovered between us is our experiences with "discrimination." She is discriminated against a lot more than I am. As a female in a male dominated society, I did experience some discrimination. Betty's biggest complaints are about her work place, a Wal-Mart super center: when people make fun of her accent, and when people label her as a certain culture.... Customers at work treat her rudely sometimes because of the way she talks. (Debby)

Elaine compares the privileges she has enjoyed compared to her interviewee, Sophindh. She reflects:

If one's life can be summarized in a theme, the theme of Sophindh's life seems to be that of a man who has never been allowed to make choices for himself. His life has been the mercy of his uncle the Buddhist monks, the communist, and then his American sponsors.... A comparison between my life and that of Sophindh's life leaves me feeling privileged and fortunate. Although my family struggled financially, we were wealthy compared to the rural inhabitants of Cambodia.... We lived with generalized fears of nuclear destruction during the Cold War, but never actually experienced the horrors of war I also had the overwhelmingly encouraging feeling throughout my life that I had choices! Even during dark depressing time of my life, I not only had the perception of choice, I had the freedom to actually make choices.

The above excerpts from participants' papers highlighted one very important aspect of feminist theory, the development of a sense of "caring" for a person who was a complete stranger before the onset of this project. The ABC's process involved participants in a caring relationship with their interviewees and enabled them to "seeing others thickly as constituted by their particular human face, their particular psychological and social self.... taking seriously or at least being moved by one's particular connection to the other" (Flanagan & Jackson, cited in Herr, 2003). These excerpts also highlighted an important point for teacher educators; that we may need to shift our multicultural teaching focus "from looking at others to the ways in which the dominant culture, in effect, creates the category of "other" (Hytten & Adkins, 2001, p. 439).

*Reflecting on one's own biases toward other groups.*   This particular theme appeared only five (out of 34) students' papers. They showed anger or resentment toward people who have demonstrated biased attitude or actions toward their interviewee.

Here are two excerpts from Cynthia's paper, one from autobiography and the other from the cultural analysis section:

I do have biases toward other races. I think it is lack of experiences. There were not very many other races besides whites where I grew up. My parents did not like to socialize with the few blacks in the town due to the fact that my father was almost killed by a gang of black people when he was younger. This has influenced my biases.

After the interview with a recent immigrant from Nigeria, she writes:

Personally I envy this young woman's ability to love people of all races. By getting to know her, I feel ashamed of the biases I might hide deep inside of me.... She is a wonderful person. I am glad I got to know a little about her.

As mentioned before, a majority of the participants' written narratives did not reveal their personal biases. In fact, some students' papers indirectly referred to their lack of biases toward people who are different from them. Researchers have reported the inability of white pre-service teachers in their studies to identify personal biases that color their perceptions toward minority students in their classrooms (Lawrence, 1998; McIntyre, 1997). However, from their research with white teachers, Marx and Pennington (2003) report that participants in their study became highly critical of the ways in which they constructed their beliefs about children. It is appropriate to mention here that the findings of Marx and Pennignton's study may have been influenced by their use of "critical race theory" as the central focus of their courses which engaged students in systematic analysis and evaluation of white racism and white privileges.

## DISCUSSIONS AND IMPLICATIONS

To enhance multicultural understanding of pre-service and in-service teachers, teacher educators have adopted various strategies and models over the years and Schmidt's (1998a) *ABC's of Cultural Understanding and Communication* is an important effort in this direction. In this section, my discussion will connect the *ABC's Model* with existing theoretical and research perspectives on cross-cultural learning while highlighting specific examples from this particular study. I will also provide directions for future research.

### Autobiographies: Stepping Stone for Cross/Cultural Learning

Consistent with findings of other researchers (Duff, Brown, & Van Scoy, 1995; Parsons & Matson, 1995; Solas, 1992), the findings of this study reiterate the influence of "writing autobiography" for participants' cultural understanding. The findings of the study are consistent with research studies (Finkbeiner & Koplin, 2002; Pattnaik, 2001; Schmidt, 1998a,b, 1999; Xu, 2000a,b, 2001) that have used the *ABC's Model* to further cross-cultural learning of teacher education students. Participants in this study deconstructed their life experiences by exploring their cultural lenses that determine their individual autobiographies. They also realized the taken-for granted privileges that they enjoy being members of the majority group. The context of writing autobiography/biography allowed students to step out of their social and cultural roles/contexts to critically analyze those roles/contexts (Marinara, 1992).

All the participants received first hand information of new immigrants' perspectives and problems. To gain a cross-cultural perspective, one's own life history (autobiography) became more meaningful when connected to a culturally different person's history (biography). When autobiography became a context as well as the medium to write and interpret biography of a culturally different person, its importance became multifold as was evident in this particular study. Sometimes one's own historical landscape converged with that of the other as a result of perception of commonalities and other times it diverged with the understandings that different life styles and ways of life are natural and normal for human beings. Interestingly, there were times participants stood between these two landscapes unable to decide which one is better or even preferred one over the other. Consequently, engagement in this process of writing autobiography and biography of their interviewee enabled participants to explore themselves as thinkers and to articulate their own voices (Florio-Ruane, Detar, & de Tar, 2001).

## Self-Reflection

Engaging teacher education students in self reflection of their own beliefs and practices has been recognized as an important step in achieving "critical multiculturalism" (Houser & Chevallier, 1996; Moore, 1996). The process of self-reflection needs to begin with an understanding that one's perception of self is socially constructed. Many social, cultural, and economic factors influence this construction. This understanding accompanied with cross-cultural exposure and interaction will facilitate the process and outcome of self reflection (Aaronshon, Howell, & Carter, 1993; Sutton, 1993). In this study, cross-cultural exposure was alleviated to a level which was personal, interactive, and experiential through the use of the *ABC's Model*. In addition, experts in multicultural education argue for fostering a "general reflective ethos" among teachers and suggest that teacher education programs need to adopt training techniques that foster criticalness as a habit of mind (Gay & Kirkland, 2003) and as a reflexive attitude and action. Therefore, adoption of the *ABC's Model* or other such strategies that allow pre-service and classroom teachers opportunities for sustained critical reflection throughout their learning experiences will help learners adopt critical reflection as a reflexive attitude and action. In the *ABC's Model*, self-reflection is embedded within specific social/cultural contexts, rather than as an abstract intellectual practice. Explaining reflexivity, Danielewitz (2001) maintains:

> Reflexivity is an act of self-conscious considerations that can lead people to a deepened understanding of themselves and others, not in abstract, but in relation to specific social environments ... [and] foster a more profound awareness ... of how social contexts influence who people are and how they behave. (pp. 155-156)

In addition, participants' written narratives included more candid and honest self-revelations and evaluation which might have been difficult and uncomfortable for some, if they were asked to share their personal beliefs and experiences related to racial and cultural differences and stereotypes in a more open and public forum (Millner, 2003). For the majority of the participants in this study, the writing of autobiography, biography of a first immigrant, and cross-cultural analysis clearly revealed a process of "transformational learning ... to foster positive life changes in learners ... gaining a more critical and empowered perspective" (Rossiter, 2002, p. 4). Dana, a participant in this study writes,

> I was forced to write down who really I am and what I really think and believe about myself and my life. It was a nice opportunity to reflect on what makes me who I am.

It also moved participants beyond the past and present to visualize and construct the future experiences for their personal and professional lives. Hopefully, the experience gained during the projects will be more enduring and enlightening than that of occasional field trip(s) to an ethnically diverse school or neighborhood where the "other" still remains distant from the self. I also hope that engagement in the process of cross-cultural understanding has helped participants to acquire skill in conducting research and will be transferred to their own classrooms so that they will be able to engage their students in similar research activities.

## Critical Pedagogy/Critical Literacy

In this study, the *ABC's Model* took participants in a journey that began with self reflection and headed toward a critique of many forms of societal dominations under which new immigrants are continually oppressed. In a way, the *ABC's Model* can very well be embedded within critical pedagogy and critical literacy traditions that perceive pedagogy and literacy as vehicles to understand and challenge the unequal distributions of privilege, power, and domination (Brady & Kanpol, 2000; Shor, 1992). Through dialoguing with a first generation immigrant, participants in this study realized the challenges that new immigrant face in a new society because of their language, color, physical appearance, country of origin, religion, cultural differences, and their sense of powerlessness. The value of dialogue and interaction as a part of critical pedagogy is rightly acknowledged by educational theorists and researchers. Boyce (1996) writes:

> Dialogue, a long-valued element of Freire's critical pedagogical practice, facilitates the voicing of difference and enables difference to reside openly within relations rather than be suppressed. (n.p.)

Participants also reflected on their own role as critical pedagogue to empower immigrant children and families. The use of the ABC model has enabled me, the instructor/researcher in this study, to overcome learners' resistance to a pedagogical approach that is transformatory in purpose, process, and outcome. Critical educators have reported many forms of learner resistance to critical pedagogy (Boyce, 1996; Moss, 2001; Shor, 1992). The *ABC's Model* allowed students to identify societal practices of oppression, discrimination, and subordination through connection and reflection. Participants in this study were critically impacted by their engagement with the *ABC's Model* resulting in a broader perspective and critical self-reflection on their current and/or future teaching practices.

## Classroom Implications of the ABC's Model

Experts complain that most of the research studies focus on pre-service teachers' attitude and knowledge aspects rather than examining intervention strategies that prepare strong multiculturally effective teachers (Sleeter, 2001). As an intervention strategy, the ABC model has many advantages. From their research with university and high school students in Germany, Finkbeiner and Koplin (2002) state "Our students' cross-case analyses indicate that use of the *ABC's Model* led to increased and differentiated understanding of cultures and a desire to extend knowledge about cultural customs, concepts, and values" (n. p.). After learning the *ABC's Model*, pre-service and in-service teachers may also use this strategy with children in their classrooms in order to prepare multiculturally effective future citizens. Classroom teachers who have used this strategy with children in their classrooms have reported positive results (Schmidt, 1999, 2001). After using the *ABC's Model*, invariably, all the participants in the study shared ideas to facilitate children's multicultural understanding. For example, Tanya, a pre-service teacher, writes,

> As a future teacher this interview taught me that if you have any questions or concerns, do not be afraid to confront the person with these questions. I now look upon these experiences as good learning experiences for my students not something to be ignored.

Ruth, a classroom teacher, writes,

This will help me in my classroom because I will not assume that I understand a student or his/her family situation. Instead, I will take the time to get to know them.

## CONTINUING THE DIALOGUE: A POSTSCRIPT

Banks and Banks (2004) has identified some major tasks for educators who shoulder the responsibility of educating minority and immigrant children. These tasks include:

- Highlighting the connection between ethnicity and social disadvantage and consequent lack of proper provision in schooling for immigrant children.
- Recognizing the pressure for assimilation and consequent loss of culture among immigrant children.
- Understanding the importance of fostering personal and social identity.
- Development of self-esteem among immigrant children.

It is appropriate to mention here that open discussion with students on these above-mentioned tasks need to be embedded as a postscript of the *ABC's Model* in order to extend the implications of the *ABC's Model* beyond college/university classrooms. Based on insights gathered from their engagement in the *ABC's Model*, students need to be provided opportunities to engage in meaningful discussions on their multicultural responsibility as future and practicing educators. Bringing the *ABC's Model* from an individual realm to the social sphere of the classroom is an important yet challenging task to be dealt with by researchers/instructors intelligently and carefully.

## FUTURE DIRECTIONS

Based on my own research with the *ABC's Model*, I present here some future directions for researchers interested to employ the *ABC's Model* for multicultural inquiry. While reflecting on the societal practice of discriminations and unfair treatments of new immigrants, participants in this study (who were predominantly white) were unable to identify their own biases toward people who are different from them. VanGunten and Martin (2001) shared a similar concern from their own study and cautioned that teacher education and student's inability to reflect on their own attitudes toward race, class, and gender could affect their abilities to become effective educators. From a study with white pre-service teachers, Marx (2001) reported participants' racism in the form of low expectations, resentment, and antipathy toward English language learners of color although all participants described themselves as nonracist and non-prejudiced. Therefore, future researchers may deliberately design their course as a site of self-transformation of pre-service/in-service teachers and use the *ABC's Model* for such transformation.

A second line of research using the *ABC's Model* could focus on life stages (such as pre-service, beginning, and seasoned teachers) and life experiences (especially with diversity) that may contribute to participants' willingness to change and commitment toward multicultural education.

Third, there is a need for follow-up/longitudinal research to explore the long-term impact of the *ABC's Model* on research participants. Longitudinal research may also provide researchers ways to understand whether participants' change in attitude and classroom practices are temporary or sustained. Researchers may also be able to explore what factors contribute to (or deter) participants' long-term commitment to multicultural education.

## CONCLUSION

The study highlighted the importance of instructional strategies that use self-revelation and self-reflection as key components in helping white pre-service/in-service teachers to identify and deconstruct privilege and hierarchy and connect to immigrant children and their families. In the context of this particular study, the *ABC's Model* validated the current argument of using personal narratives as a valid method of educational research and personal growth (Spigelman, 2001). The *ABC's Model* also embraces both the dimensions of multiculturalism identified by Castle (2004), "recognition of cultural diversity and the social equality for members of minorities" (p. 25). Not only participants in the study realized many differences in cultural practices between their own and that of their interviewees, they also learned the struggles, challenges, and unfair treatments received by new immigrants. If used properly, the *ABC's Model* can be used as an emancipatory paradigm that prepares teachers and children to challenge and rectify oppression in schools and in the larger society. The need for an emancipatory approach to multicultural education has been reiterated by Garcia and Willis (2001) in their essay on multicultural literacies.

The *ABC's Model* has far reaching potential for teacher educators teaching a variety of courses including diversity courses, methods courses, or discipline-specific courses. However, when using the *ABC's Model* in courses that do not focus exclusively on multicultural education, one important point needs to be considered. The discussion of diversity must be embedded in all aspects of the course: course objectives, content, and assessment. Otherwise, making a single project based on the *ABC's Model* may turn to what Banks' (1997) refers as "additive" and may not accrue the desired results.

## REFERENCES

Aaronshon, E., Howell, M., & Carter, C. J. (1993). *Preparing monocultural teachers for a multicultural world: Attitudes toward inner city schools in education classes.* (ERIC Document Reproduction Service No. ED 378 135).

Allison, L. (1995). Autobiography in multicultural classrooms: Bridging expressivism and social constructionism. *English in Texas, 26*(3), 37-41.

Alpert, B. (2000, April). *On the contribution of qualitative inquiry to the development of reflective, constructivist and feminists perspectives in student teachers.* Paper presented at the annual meeting of the American Educational Research Association. New Orleans, LA.

Anyon, J. (2001). Inner cities, affluent suburbs, and unequal educational opportunity. In J. A. Banks & C. M. Banks (Eds.), *Multicultural education: Issues & perspectives* (pp. 85-103). New York: John Wiley & Sons.

Banks, J. (1997). *Teaching strategies for ethnic studies* (6th ed.). Boston: Allyn & Bacon.

Banks, J. A., & Banks, C. A. (2004). *Multicultural eduacation: Issues and perspectives.* New York: Wiley.

Baumann, G. (1996). *Contesting culture: Discourse of identity in multiethnic London.* Cambridge: Cambridge University Press.

Beattie, M. (1995). New prospects for teacher education: Narrative ways of knowing teaching and teacher learning. *Educational Research, 37* (1), 53-70.

Bell, J. S. (2002). Narrative inquiry: More than just telling stories. *TESOL Quarterly, 36*(2), 207-218.

Beyer, L. E., & Liston, D. P. (1992). Discourse or moral action? A critique of postmodernism. *Educational Theory, 42*(4), 371-403.

Bogdan, R. C., & Biklen, S. K. (1994). *Qualitative research for education: An introduction to theory and method.* Boston, MA: Allyn & Bacon.

Bourdieu, P. (1973). *Cultural reproduction and social reproduction. In R. Brown (Ed.), Knowledge, education, and cultural changes (pp. 56-69).* London: Tavistock.

Boyce, M. E. (1996). Teaching critically as an act of praxis and resistance. Retrieved April 2004 from http://newton.uor.edu/FacultyFolder/MBoyce/1CRITPED.HTM

Brady, J. F., & Kanpol, B. (2000). The role of critical multicultural education and feminist critical thought in teacher education: Putting theory into practice. *Educational Foundations, 14*(3), 39-50.

Brah, A. (1992). Difference, diversity, and differentiation. In J. Donald & A. Rattansi (Eds.), *Race, culture, and difference* (pp. 126-145). London: Sage.

Bruner, J. S. (2002). *Making stories: Law, literature, life.* New York: Farrar, Straus, & Giroux.

Camarota, S. A. (2001, August 2). *U. S. population and immigration. FDCH congressional testimony.* Washington, DC: Research Center for Immigration Studies.

Castles, S. (2004). Migration, citizenship, and education. In J. A. Banks (Ed.), *Diversity and citizenship education: Global perspectives (pp. 17-48).* San Francisco: Jossey-Bass.

Clandinin, D. J., & Connelly, F. M. (2000). *Narrative inquiry: Experience and story in qualitative research.* San Francisco: Jossey-Bass.

Connelly, F. M., & Clandinin, D. J. (1988). *Teachers as curriculum planners: Narratives of experience.* Toronto, Ontario, Canada: OISE Press.

Danielewicz, J. (2001). *Teaching shelves: Identity, pedagogy and teacher education.* Albany, NY: State University of New York Press.

Derman-Sparks, L., & Brunson-Phillips, C. (1997). *Teaching/learning anti-racism.* New York: Teachers College Press.

Dominice, P. (2000). *Learning from our lives: Using educational biographies with adults.* San Francisco: Jossey Bass.

Duff, R. E., Brown, M. H., & Van Scoy, I. (1995). Reflection and self-evaluation: Keys to professional development. *Young Children, 50*(4), 81-88.

Elbaz, F. (1991). Research on teachers' knowledge: The evolution of a discourse. *Journal of Curriculum Studies, 23*(1), 1-18.

Engestorm, Y. (1999). Activity theory and individual and social transformation. In Y. Engestorm, R. Miettinen, & R, Punamak (Eds.), *Perspectives on activity theory* (pp.19-38). Cambridge, UK: Cambridge University Press.

Erickson, F. (1986). Qualitative methods in research on teaching. In M. C. Wittrock (Ed.), *Handbook of Research on Teaching* (3rd. ed., pp. 119-161). New York: Macmillan.

Finkbeiner, C., & Koplin, C. (2002). A cooperative approach for facilitating intercultural education. Reading Online, 6(3). Retrieved February 20, 2004 from http://www.readingonline.org/newliteracies/lit_index.asp?HREF=/newliteracies/finkbeiner

Florio-Ruane, S. (1994). The future teachers' autobiography club: Preparing educators to support learning in culturally diverse classrooms. *English Education, 26*(1), 52-56.

Florio-Ruane, S., & deTar, J. (1995). Conflict and consensus in teacher candidates' discussion of ethnic autobiography. *English Education, 27*(1), 11-39.

Florio-Ruane, S., Detar, J., & de Tar, J. (2001). Teacher education and the cultural imagination: Autobiography, conversation, and narrative. Manwah, NJ: Lawrence Erlbaum.

Garcia, G. E., & Willis, A. I. (2001). Frameworks for understanding multicultural literacies. In P. R. Schmidt & P. B. Mosenthal (Eds.), *Reconceptualizing literacy in the new age of multiculturalism and pluralism* (pp. 3-31). Greenwich, CT: Information Age.

Garcia, E. (2002). *Student cultural diversity: Understanding and meting the challenge* (3rd ed.). Boston: Houghton Mifflin.

Gay, G., & Kirkland, K. (2003). Developing cultural critical consciousness and self-reflection in preservice teacher education. *Theory into Practice, 42* (3), 181-187.

Gensch, N. (2000). *Coaching the voice of the feminine.* (ERIC Document Reproduction Service No. ED 451 103).

Goertz, J. P., & LeCompte, M. D. (1981). Ethnographic research and the problem of data reduction. *Anthropology and Education Quarterly, 12,* 51-70.

Greene, M. (1993). The passion of pluralism, multiculturalism and the expanding community. *Educational Researcher, 22*(1), 13-18.

Gutierrez, K. D., Asato, J, Santos, M., Gotanda, N. *(2002).* Backlash pedagogy: Language, and culture and the politics of reform. *The Review of Education, Pedagogy and the Cultural Studies, 24,* 335-351.

Herr, R. S. (2003). Is Confucianism compatible with care ethics? A critique. *Philosophy East and West, 53*(4), 471-489.

Hillis, M. (1993). Multicultural education and curriculum transformation. *Educational Forum, 58*(1), 50-56.

Hinchey, P. H. (1994). Introducing diversity: We don't have to wait for a program. *Action in Teacher Education, 16*(3), 28-36.

Houser, N. O., & Chevalier, M. (1996). *Multicultural self development in the preservice classroom: Equity education for the dominant culture.* (ERIC Document Reproduction Service No. ED 397 045).

Howard, T.C. (2003). Culturally relevant pedagogy: Ingredients for critical teacher reflection. *Theory Into Practice, 42* (3),

Hytten, K., & Adkins, A. (2001). Thinking through a pedagogy of whiteness. *Educational Theory, 51*(4), 433-450.

Kanpol, B. (1992). Postmodernism in education revisited: Similarities within differences and the democratic imaginary. *Educational Theory, 42*(3), 217-230.

Karpiak, I. (2000). Writing out life: Adult learning and teaching through autobiography. *Canadian Journal of University Continuing Education, 26* (1), 33-44.

Kass, A. A. (1995). Who am I? Autobiography and American identity. *College Teaching, 43*(3), 93-99.

Kehily, M. J. (1995). Self narration: Autobiography, and identity construction. *Gender & Education, 7*(1), 23-31.

Krishnamurthi, M. (2003). Assessing multicultural initiatives in higher education institutions. *Assessment & Evaluation in Higher Education, 28*(3), 263-277.

Ladson-Billings, G. (1999). Preparing teachers for diverse student populations: A critical race-theory perspective. *Review of Research in Education, 24,* 211-247.

Laosa, L. M. (1989). *Psychological stress, coping and development of Hispanic immigrant children.* (ERIC Document Reproduction Service No. ED 395 018).

Lather, P. (1992). Critical frames in educational research: Feminist and post-structural perspectives. *Theory into Practice, 31*(2), 87-99.

Lawrence, S. (1998). Research, writing, and racial identity. Cross disciplinary connection for multicultural education. *Teacher Educator, 34* (1), 41-53.

Lincoln, Y. S., & Guba, E. G. (1985). *Naturalist inquiry.* Beverly Hills, CA: Sage.

Lincoln, Y., & Guba, E. (2000). Paradigmatic controversies, contradictions, and emerging confluences. In N. K. Denzin & Y. S. Lincoln (Eds.), *The handbook of qualitative research* (2nd ed.) (pp. 163-188). Thousand Oaks, CA: Sage.

Lincoln, Y. (1989, April). *The making of a constructivist: A remembrance of things past.* Paper presented at the International Conference on Alternative Paradigms for Inquiry, San Francisco.

MacLeod, D. M., & Cowieson, A. R. (2001). Discovering credit where credit is due: Using autobiographical writing as a tool for voicing growth. *Teacher and Teaching, 7* (3), 239-256.

Maher, F. A., & Tetreault, M. K. (1944). *The feminist classroom: An inside look at how professors and students are transforming higher education for a diverse society.* New York: Basic Books.

Maher, F. A., & Thompson Tetrealut, M. K. (2001). *The feminist classroom: Dynamics of gender, race, and privilege.* Lanham: Rowman & Littlefield.

Marinara, M. (1992). *Stirring the ashes of public discourse.* (ERIC Document Reproduction Service No. ED 357 338).

Marx, S. (2001). *How whiteness frames the beliefs of white female pre-service teachers working with English language learners of color.* (ERIC Document Reproduction Service No. ED457 119).

Marx, S., Pennington, J. (2003). Pedagogies of critical race theory: Experimentation with white preservice teachers. *Qualitative Studies in Education, 16*(1), 91-110.

May, S. (2000, April). *Multiculturalism in the 21st century: Challenges and possibilities.* Paper presented at the annual meeting of the American Educational Research Association, New Orleans, LA.

Mc Intyre, A. (1997). *Making meaning of Whiteness: Exploring racial identity with White teachers. Albany:* State University of New York.

Milner, H. R. (2003). Reflection, racial competence, and critical pedagogy: How do we prepare preservice teachers to pose tough questions? *Race, Ethnicity, and Education, 6*(2), 193-208.

Moll, I. (2000). Inspired by Vygotsky: Ethnographic experiments in education. In C. Lee & P. Smsgorinsky (Eds.), *Vygotskian perspectives on literacy research: Constructing meaning through collaborative inquiry* (pp.256-268). New York: Cambridge University Press.

Moore, J. A. (1996). *Empowering student teachers to teach from a multicultural perspective.* (ERIC Document Reproduction Service No. ED 394 979).

Moss, G. (2001). Critical pedagogy: Translation for education that is multicultural. *Multicultural Education, 9*(2), 2-11.

Newman, V. (1995). Compelling ties: Landscapes, community and sense of place. *Peabody Journal of Education, 70*(4), 105-118.

Nicolini, M. B (1994). Stories can save us: A defense of narrative writing. *English Journal, 83*(2), 56-61.

Owocki, G., & Lohff, E. A. (1995). Book review: *Crossing cultural borders: Education for immigrant families in America,* by Concha Delgado-Gaitan and Henry Trueba. *Bilingual Research Journal, 19*(2), 337-341.

Pattnaik, J. (1997). Cultural stereotypes and preservice education. *Equity and Excellence in Education, 30*(3), 40-50.

Pattnaik, J. (2001). "Multicultural belief": A global or domain-specific construct? An analysis of four case studies. In P. R. Schmidt, & P. B. Mosenthal (Eds.), *Reconceptualizing literacy in the new age of multiculturalism and pluralism* (pp. 33-62). Greenwich, CT: Information Age Publishing.

Parsons, S., & Matson, J, (1995). *Through the looking glass: An autobiographical study by two science educators.* Paper presented at the Annual Meeting of the National Association of Research in Science Teaching, San Francisco, CA.

Pearce, S. (2003). Compiling the white inventory: The practice of whiteness in a British primary school. *Cambridge Journal of Education, 33*(2), 273-289.

Phillips, D. C. (1993). Gone with the wind? Evidence, rigor, and warrants in educational research. In J. Tooley (Ed.), *Papers of the annual conference of the Philosophy of Education Society of Great Britain* (pp. 4-11). Oxford: Philosophy of Education Society of Great Britain.

Rositer, M. (2002). *Narrative and stories in adult teaching and learning: ERIC Digest.* (ERIC Document Reproduction Service No. ED 473147).

Rothenberg, P. (2000). Beyond the food court: Goals and strategies for teaching multiculturalism. *Feminist Teacher, 13*(1), 61-73.

Schmidt, P. (1996, December). *Autobiographies, interviews, and cultural analyses.* Paper presented at the Annual Meeting of the National Reading Conference, Charleston, South Carolina.

Schmidt, P. R. (1998a). The ABC's of cultural understanding and communication. *Equity and Excellence in Education, 31*(2), 28-38.

Schmidt, P. R. (1998b). The *ABC's Model*: Teachers connect home and school. In T. Shanahan & F. Rodriguez-Brown (Eds.), *Forty-seventh yearbook of the National Reading Conference* (pp. 194-208). Chicago: National Reading Conference.

Schmidt, P. R. (1999). Know thyself and understand others. *Language Arts, 76(4),* 332-340.

Schmidt, P. R. (2001). The power to empower: Creating home/school relationships with the ABC's of cultural understanding and communication. In P. R. Schmidt & P. B. Mosenthal (Eds.), *Reconceptualizing literacy in the new age of multiculturalism and pluralism* (pp. 323-340). Greenwich, CT: Information Age Publishing.

Shor, I. (1992). *Empowering education: Critical teaching for social change.* Chicago: The University of Chicago Press.

Shull, E. M. (1991). *Memoir writing: Evoking the authentic voice.* (ERIC Document Reproduction Service No. ED 341 059).

Sleeter, C. E. (2001). Preparing teachers for culturally diverse schools: Research and the overwhelming presence of whiteness. *Journal of Teacher Education, 52*(2), 94-106.

Solas, J. (1992). Investigating teacher and student thinking about the process of teaching and learning of using autobiography and repertory grid. *Review of Educational Research, 62*(2), 205-225.

Spigelman, C. (2001). Argument and evidence in the case of personal. *College English, 64*(1), 63-87.

Spindler, G., & Spindler, L. (1987). *The interpretive ethnography of education: At home and abroad*. Hillsdale, NJ: Lawrence Erlbaum.

Stotsky, S. (1993). The *uses and limitations of the writer's personal experiences in writing theory, research and instruction*. (ERIC Document Reproduction Service No. ED 359 511).

Thomas, D. (1992). *Putting nature to the rack: Narrative studies as research*. (ERIC Document Reproduction Service No. ED 346 461).

Thompson, A., & Gitlin, A. (1995). Creating spaces for reconstructing knowledge in feminist pedagogy. *Educational Theory, 45*(2), 125-150.

Townsend, B. L. (2002). Leave no teacher behind: A bold proposal for teacher education. *Qualitative Studies in Education, 15* (6), 727-738.

Tyrone, H. C. (2003). Culturally relevant pedagogy: Ingredients for critical teacher reflection. *Theory Into Practice, 42* (3), 195-202.

U.S. Department of Commerce. (1996). Current population reports: Populations projects of the United States by age, sex, race and Hispanic origin: 1995 to 2050. Washington D.C: Author.

VanGunten, D. M., & Martin, R. J. (2001). Complexities and contradictions: A study of teacher education courses that address multicultural issues. *Journal of Intergroup Relations, 28*(1), 31-42.

Verhesschen, P. (2003). The poem's invitation: Ricoeur's concept of mimesis and its consequences for n*arrative* educational *research*. *Journal of Philosophy of Education, 37* (3), 449-465.

Xu, H. (2001). Preservice teachers connect multicultural knowledge and perspectives with literacy instruction for minority students. In P. R. Schmidt, & P. B. Mosenthal (Eds.), *Reconceptualizing literacy in the new age of multiculturalism and pluralism* (pp. 389-433). Greenwich, CT: Information Age.

Xu, S. H. (2000a). Preservice teachers integrate understandings of diversity into literacy instruction: An adaptation of the *ABC's Model*. *Journal of Teacher Education, 51*(2), 135-142.

Xu. S. H. (2000b). Preservice teachers in a literacy methods course consider issues of diversity. *Journal of Literacy Research, 32*(4), 505-531.

Zeichner, K. (1993). *Educating teachers for cultural diversity*. East Lansing, MI: Michigan State University National Center for Research on Teacher Learning.

CHAPTER 7

# THE COMPLEXITY AND MULTIPLICITY OF PRE-SERVICE TEACHERS' EXPLORING DIVERSITY ISSUES

**Shelley Hong Xu**

## ABSTRACT

In this chapter, I will draw findings from two studies to compare pre-service teachers' experiences with exploring diversity issues while they were enrolled in a literacy methods course. Both studies were conducted from Au's theoretical framework of "diverse constructivist orientation" (Au, 1998) and employed Schmidt's ABC's model (Schmidt, 1999) as a means to collect data. The comparison will focus on two pre-service teachers, who were in a different school setting for the field experience. The chapter will conclude with discussions and implications for literacy teacher education and future research.

*ABC's of Cultural Understanding and Communication:*
*National and International Adaptations,* 143–160

# INTRODUCTION

As a future teacher, I fear that my cultural background has sheltered me from other cultures. I know I can learn a lot from students about other cultural backgrounds. With an open mind and experiences, I can adapt to students from other cultural backgrounds and help them succeed. (Joan)

Joan's response to the question "How does your cultural background influence you as a future teacher?" is representative of those from pre-service teachers who have just finished a diversity (or multicultural education) course. They are often predominantly young pre-service teachers from European American middle class backgrounds, who make up a majority of the teaching force (Ladson-Billings, 2000; Nieto, 2000, 2002). Most pre-service and in-service teachers have had inadequate or limited contact with people from other linguistic and cultural backgrounds. Teachers' knowledge about their students could be affected by stereotypes and misperceptions of people from other backgrounds different from their own that are presented in the media and in school curriculum (Lewis, 2001; Nieto, 2002). While the teaching force is predominantly from mainstream cultures, information from the National Center for Educational Statistics and U.S. Bureau of the Census (cited in Au & Raphael, 2000) suggests a continuing growth of diverse students at U.S. schools. The possible mismatch in cultural and linguistic backgrounds between teachers and students presents a challenge for teachers to meet the needs of all students. Furthermore, the *No Child Left Behind Act* of 2001 has made schools and classroom teachers more accountable for students' academic achievements (Linn, Baker, & Betebenner, 2002). The challenge of educating all students is also reflected in teacher education programs (Hoffman & Pearson, 2000). Many pre-service teachers, like Joan, may be able to articulate their conceptual understandings of diversity. However, when working with diverse students, they find it hard to deal with many issues that have been discussed in a diversity course.

# BACKGROUND

There has been a growing body of research on preparing pre-service and in-service teachers for culturally responsive teaching (e.g., Chizhik, 2003; Cochran-Smith, 2000; Goodwin, 1997; Ladson-Billings, 1995, Sleeter, 1995) in various teacher education programs. A research focus on diversity issues, however, is relatively new in the literacy community in general (Garcia, Willis, & Harris, 1998) and in literacy teacher education community in particular. Some studies have investigated an integration of diversity issues into literacy teacher education courses. For example, Florio-Ruane (1994) used autobiographical writings as a tool to engage pre-service teachers in discussing diversity issues. Laframboise and Griffith (1997) asked pre-service teachers to examine diversity issues through reading and analyzing literary events and conflicts from children's literature. In a more recent study by Kidd, Sanchez, and Thorp (2002), pre-service teachers gathered family stories from the family members of case study students and learned through the stories about life experiences very different from their own.

Particularly relevant to this study was Schmidt's (1998a,b, 1999, 2001) study with the *ABC's model of Cultural Understanding and Communication*. She has used the model to help pre-service and in-service teachers to self-explore cultural values and experiences, get to know their students better academically and personally, and accordingly modify teaching to best support students' literacy learning. Nagel's (2002) study explored seven ways that the ABC model can be used to promote an awareness of and sensitivity to cultural and linguistic diversity between pre-service and in-service teachers, university professors, teachers, and children. Three out of the seven ways were particularly related to enhancing pre-service and in-service teachers' ability to get to know others who were different from themselves and to appreciate similarities and respect difference among themselves. In Germany, Finkbeiner and Koplin (2002) used the model with the students enrolled in English as a Foreign Language classes to promote their intercultural awareness. They discovered that the model helped the students develop cultural and language awareness, awareness of the subjectivity and relativity of culture and thinking, and a better understanding of and trust in others.

There, however, still seems to be few studies on exploring diversity issues in a literacy methods course for pre-service teachers, and in particular when the course has a component of field experiences. Inspired by Schmidt's work, I have used Schmidt's ABC's model to help pre-service teachers and teacher assistants enrolled in a literacy methods course to examine diversity issues during their field experiences with predominantly Latino students (Xu, 2000a,b, 2001). The findings of these studies indicated that the ABC model helped teachers self-examine their own roots and biases toward others from different cultures. More important, the model assisted the teachers as they modified their teaching in order to address diverse students' needs. After several years of implementing the ABC model with pre-service teachers who had field experiences in schools with predominantly Latino students, I became curious about the effect of the model on pre-service teachers when they were in a school with predominantly African American students. I wondered if the findings from my earlier studies would hold true for another group of pre-service teachers who were in a different field experience setting.

In this chapter, I will draw findings from Study 1 (Xu, 2000a,b, 2001) and from Study 2 (Xu, 2000c) to compare pre-service teachers' experiences with exploring diversity issues. The comparison will focus on two pre-service teachers, Betty from Study 1 and Pat from Study 2, who were in a different school setting for the field experiences. The chapter will conclude with discussions and implications for literacy teacher education and future research.

## PREVIOUS STUDIES

Both Study 1 and Study 2 were grounded in Au's theoretical framework of "diverse constructivist orientation" (Au, 1998). The "diverse constructivist orientation" situates diverse student empowerment in the context of literacy instruction. In particular, Au pointed out seven areas of literacy instruction in which teachers would enhance diverse students' literacy learning. They were:

1.  goal of instruction—literacy processes and attitudes, with an emphasis on ownership;
2.  role of the home language—additive approach, biliteracy;
3.  instructional materials—emphasis on multicultural literature plus other authentic materials;
4.  classroom management and interaction with students—teacher conducts lessons and organizes peer work groups in culturally responsive manner;
5.  relationship to the community—attention to community surrounding the school, greater parental involvement, instruction related to community issues and funds of knowledge;
6.  instructional methods—authentic literacy activities, skills taught in context, amount of explicit skill instruction may be considerable, and
7.  assessment—formal and informal assessment, consistent with constructivist views of literacy, with attention to sources of bias. (p. 307)

Au's theoretical framework was relevant to both studies because when pre-service teachers in these studies were teaching in the field experiences, they were dealing with these seven components of literacy instruction. I used these three research questions to guide both studies: (a) What were pre-service teachers' understanding of diversity before field experiences? (b) How did pre-service teachers teach diverse students during field experiences? and (c) What were pre-service teachers' understanding of diversity after field experiences?

## METHOD

### Participants and Setting

In Study 1, there were 20 pre-service teachers (1 male and 19 females) in their early 20s, four of whom identified themselves respectively as Mexican American, Korean and Mexican American, European and Mexican American, or European and Native American. Sixteen of the 20 teachers claimed to be from middle-class families, and four were from low socioeconomic status families. In Study 2, there were 17 middle class female pre-service teachers in their early 20s, one of whom was Mexican American.

The pre-service teachers in both studies had taken or were taking a diversity course while they were enrolled in my integrated field-based literacy methods course (reading and language arts). The literacy course focused on theories of literacy teaching and learning, strategies and materials for literacy instruction, and assessment administration and analysis. Throughout the course, we discussed readings and teachers' field experiences in relation to diversity issues. Beginning at the sixth week of the course, the pre-service teachers started their field experiences in a K-6th class, 3 hours per week for 10 weeks. The pre-service teachers also conducted a case study with an individual student. The teachers in Study 1 were in a school with predominantly Latino students while those in Study 2 were in a school with predominantly African American students.

## DATA COLLECTION

I adapted Schmidt's (1999) ABC's model to help the pre-service teachers explore diversity issues during their field experiences. The ABC's model includes: (a) *a*utobiography, (b) *b*iography, (c) *c*ross-cultural analysis, (d) *c*ross-cultural discussion, and (e) modification for classroom teaching (for details see *Introduction* by Schmidt and Finkbeiner). Before the field experiences, the pre-service teachers wrote their autobiography in which they described their cultural values and experiences, perceptions, and biases, shared their home and school learning experiences, and responded to my question, "How does your cultural background influence you as a future teacher?"

Next, the pre-service teachers formally and informally interviewed their case study students. The case study students shared their cultural and linguistic backgrounds as well as home and school learning experiences. Throughout field experiences, the pre-service teachers modified their knowledge about case study students, and the final version of such knowledge became the content for their case study students' biographies. Third, the pre-service teachers, based on their evolving knowledge of their case study students, developed a cross-cultural analysis chart. The chart listed similarities and differences between themselves and the students.

Fourth, the pre-service teachers, in class sessions and weekly reflections on each field experience, talked about their attitudes and feelings toward observed differences between themselves and their students, and those between what they believed about teaching and how literacy was actually taught in classrooms. During class discussions, I was a participant-observer and a facilitator, taking fieldnotes about the gist of discussions. The pre-service teachers also wrote a summative reflection on the whole field experiences.

Fifth, the pre-service teachers taught two lessons to a whole class and worked with case study students in a one-on-one setting. The two lessons were related to the cooperating teachers' planned content, but the pre-service teachers had the freedom to select instructional materials and strategies that they believed to be most appropriate for the lesson objectives. I observed at least part of each pre-service teacher's lesson teaching, took fieldnotes during my observations, and later discussed with the teacher about the teaching. The pre-service teachers reflected on each lesson. In lesson reflection, the pre-service teachers discussed teaching strengths, areas for improvement, and theory-to-practice connections in relation to diversity issues.

In working with case study students, the pre-service teachers first conducted informal assessment in reading, spelling, and writing, and took anecdotal records about case study students' participation in literacy activities. Then, the pre-service teachers used various instructional strategies and children's literature with case study students in supporting their strengths and addressing their needs. I briefly observed each pre-service teacher's sharing with his or her case study student at least once during each field experience and provided feedback to him or her. At the conclusion of the field experiences, each pre-service teacher wrote a case study report, which included: (a) the case study student's biography, (b) a description of the student's literacy development, (c) a description of the use of assessment tools, instructional strategies, and children's literature,

(d) reflection on the experiences with the student, and (e) a cross-cultural analysis chart and a discussion of cross-cultural differences.

## DATA SOURCES AND ANALYSIS

The data for both studies were from: (a) pre-service teachers' autobiographies, (b) their case study reports, (c) their lesson plans and lesson reflections, (d) reflections on each field experience and summative reflections, (e) observational fieldnotes of their teaching and of working with case study students, and (f) observational fieldnotes of on-campus class discussions.

I first categorized each data set based on the foci of the research questions: (a) understandings of diversity before field experiences, (b) teaching diverse students during field experiences, and (c) understandings of diversity after field experiences. Then, I used the constant comparison method (Bogdan & Biklen, 1994) to further analyze the data. I read and reread the data, categorized and subcategorized emerging themes, and cross-checked and then revised categories and subcategories to achieve consistencies across the whole data set.

For example, while analyzing a first data set in response to the first research question, I categorized one emerging theme as *relating one's experiences to diverse students*. Later, in analyzing the same data set in response to the second research question, I discovered two emerging themes and subcategorized them respectively as *relating one's experiences to understanding diverse students* and *relating one's experiences to teaching diverse students*. With these two subcategories, I went back to reread the data set and then to revise the category to reflect the consistency in subcategories. The category in the first data set thus became the subcategory—*relating to one's experiences to understanding diverse students*.

## FINDINGS

Betty from Study 1 and Pat from Study 2 were chosen for the case studies, because they shared some similarities in their own background and life experiences and in their sincere efforts for attempting to teach in culturally responsive ways at an upper elementary level. They, however, were also very different in their experiences with teaching. I have written about Betty's experience of learning to teach diverse students in comparison with other two pre-service teachers' (Xu, 2000b). She was the one among the three pre-service teachers who demonstrated the most positive changes in her conceptual understandings of her own cultural identity and values, in her perceptions of diverse students and of literacy teaching, and in her growing abilities to apply multicultural knowledge in teaching.

## Betty

*Understandings of diversity before field experiences.*   In her autobiography, Betty expressed her appreciation for an opportunity to write about her culture and values in the context of comparing them to a case study student's with whom she was going to work. "I did this in my multicultural education class. But this time, writing an autobiography seems to be more meaningful, because it can help me learn about students who are different from me." It was evident from her autobiography that Betty was aware of her own German and Irish heritage and of family values and work ethics. Her education with predominantly with European Americans; she was cognizant of her very limited exposure to other cultures, but held faith in her own abilities to learn about other cultures and to "try not to be biased and prejudiced."

In general, Betty believed that students from diverse backgrounds had a great deal of potential and were an important resource for the appreciation of differences. In particular, Betty considered using cooperative learning and encouraging the use of students' native language during her teaching. She specifically talked about building her teaching on students' "funds of knowledge" (Moll & Gonzalez, 1994). "My teaching should begin with what my students have known about a topic, not necessarily with what I am supposed to teach. After learning about students' prior knowledge on the topic, then I can build my lesson on their knowledge."

*Teaching diverse students during field experiences.*   Betty taught 2 whole class lessons to a fifth grade class (19 Latino/as and 1 African American) and worked with Alma for her case study. She also taught small group lessons with Alma being part of a group. Betty's teaching and in particular, her work with Alma were characterized as well planned with constant modifications in response to students' participation in and reaction to her teaching. For example, during a small group lesson on building students' prior knowledge on Marco Polo's adventure, Betty introduced the famous cities through which Marco Polo went and the concept of route. After reading aloud a few pages of the book, *City Maze* (Madgwick, 1984) that included some famous cities, Betty noted that Alma and some students in the group were not paying attention. Betty immediately stopped reading the book, realizing that the cities described in the book may hold little meaning and familiarity to the students. Betty thus concluded that the concept of route might be difficult for students to grasp. Betty then wrote a paragraph about students' neighborhood, presented it to Alma's group, and engaged them in discussing their routes to school, a park, and other places in the neighborhood. The students easily mastered the concept of route.

In other whole class and small group lessons, Betty often began a lesson or an activity with checking on or activating students' prior knowledge related to the lesson or activity. For example, before asking students to write about Marco Polo's adventure, Betty reviewed with Alma's group the genre of descriptive writing by asking the students to write about a trip to a place (e.g., a trip to a home country, a trip to a grocery store, and a trip to a mall). She specifically asked the students to describe what they saw and did during the trip and at the destination of the trip. After the students finished sharing their writing, Betty and the students did a graphic organizer to outline main ideas to be included in a descriptive writing on Marco Polo's adventure.

Betty's constant modification of her own teaching was also reflected in her efforts to learn about Alma. After reading Alma's writing (e.g., *My favorite vacation spot is my house because I could dance in my house like in a play, watch TV*) in the *My Favorite Book* that Betty suggested Alma to write, Betty not only learned about Alma's writing abilities, but more important, she was shocked to learn how insensitive she was to Alma's background. This incident helped Betty become "more of a listener than a teacher who must try his or her best to learn about students whose backgrounds and life experiences are different from the teacher's."

In my subsequent observations of her work with Alma, I noted that Betty spent at least one-fourth of her time with Alma on listening to Alma share her inside and outside-school literacy and life experiences. For example, knowing that Alma was a fluent Spanish-speaker, Betty suggested to Alma's teacher that Alma needed to read some texts written in Spanish. Betty also tried to locate, though unsuccessfully, books written in Spanish that focused on the topics that Alma was studying.

*Understandings of diversity after field experiences.* Teaching and working with Alma enhanced Betty's understandings of teaching diverse students. Perhaps the most important aspect of Betty's understandings of diversity was evident in her awareness that "a good intention for students" without knowing students' experiences and backgrounds will not lead to a successful lesson. Betty further came to understand that when a lesson did not go well, she should look into herself for reasons. During the lesson with Alma's group on building students' prior knowledge on Marco Polo's adventure, Betty learned the cities in the book *City Maze* did not make any meaningful sense to the group. She later changed to a paragraph written by her on students' neighborhood. Betty reflected on this valuable experience. "I had a good intention for students, then I forgot their prior knowledge and experiences. I was about to blame their low reading levels, when it dawned on me that the material I chose was the problem, not the children" (Xu, 2000b, p. 523).

In addition Betty noted the teacher did not seem to recognize the children's potential to succeed. In particular, Alma's achievements were essentially ignored. Betty further observed several barriers to Alma's achieving her potential. One barrier was Alma's no access to possible assistance in Spanish. Alma's school did not have any Spanish-English bilingual classes, and Alma's teacher who was a bilingual did not use Spanish to help Alma when Alma experienced difficulty in understanding a text written in English. Another barrier was the teacher's limited use of instructional strategies that may enhance students' literacy learning experiences. Betty attributed this barrier to Alma's teacher's limited professional development. She shared with me, in her summative reflections on her field experiences, that her teacher was not using any instructional strategies that the students and she enjoyed. "[These strategies] are not used in the classroom because her [Alma's] teacher has taught for many, many years and has gotten comfortable with the system that has worked for her for years" (Xu, 2000b, p. 521).

Furthermore, Betty, in her summative reflection on field experiences, stressed the importance of being a supportive teacher for students who may not have adequate family support for literacy learning. Betty appreciated her caring and supportive parents and teachers, and expressed that students like Alma, whose parents did not have time to help with homework and provide additional school-related activities, needed teachers who knew how to teach in response to students' linguistic and cultural backgrounds. Betty further advised her peers not to rely on what they have been told about the students, but to discover, through interactions and teaching, the abilities and potential of the students.

## Pat

*Understandings of diversity before field experiences.*   Pat did not talk much about her own cultural and linguistic backgrounds, but only to identify herself as a non-minority person with English and German heritage. "I don't remember much about my cultural background. And I have never asked my parents about it." She expressed her appreciation for her supportive parents and other family members, and teachers during her schooling who helped her lay a solid foundation for success. "I am thankful for my parents and for my teachers who supported me and challenged me."

She was also aware of her very little experience with students and people from other cultural and linguistic backgrounds, including African

Americans. She, however, did not express her interests in learning about other cultures. For Pat, teaching diverse students meant:

> to bring out [their] desire to excel and to challenge them in their learning. I only hope that I will be able to do this successfully as my teachers did for me. I think it is important for a teacher to have confidence in each student who can learn anything.

*Teaching diverse students during field experiences.*   Pat taught 2 whole class lessons, worked with a case study student, Dorla, and helped her cooperating teacher with group activities in a sixth grade classroom (20 African Americans and 5 Latino/as). Pat was one of a few students in her class who went the extra mile to gather materials for her lessons. Her lessons were often full of cooperative learning and hands-on activities. She modeled the teacher who believed that cooperative learning benefitted African American students. Pat also stressed activating students' prior knowledge on a subject in a lesson.

In her lesson on *Sound: Energy You Can Hear,* Pat used a KWL chart to help students become aware of their knowledge of sound and also to get them excited about learning more about sound. During the lesson, Pat brought many household items (e.g., rulers and pans) with which her students in small groups conducted sound experiments. She assigned one experiment to each group of students. At the conclusion of the sound experiments, she asked students in each group to explain the scientific concept that they had observed in the experiment. Later each group wrote about the definition of each concept related to sound and then compared their definition with the one written in their science textbook. Pat credited her students' engagement in the lesson to the interactive sound experiments that made the scientific concepts "easily understandable to the students." Pat, however, also speculated that her cooperating teacher might have told them [students] ahead of time that I was teaching, and it almost seemed as if they had been prepped prior to my getting there to act really good. Pat's conclusion about the students based on her experiences with the students was that they were "rowdy, loud, noisy, and behaving badly."

Pat's 2nd lesson on comparing life in France with life in USA (part of 6th grade social studies content) did not go so well, although she again used small group activities. She began the lesson with introducing the class to a Venn Diagram. "When I began to explain the Venn Diagram by using the comparison of a tomato and of a grapefruit, most of the students seemed interested." When each group of students started working on the Venn Diagram using one of the books on France that Pat had collected for the lesson, the students became "simply out of control." Based on my observations, the students did not seem to be interested in comparing life in France with life in the United States. Most of them were busy comparing something among themselves (e.g., clothes, sneakers, and even girlfriends). In her lesson reflection, Pat attributed her unsuccessful lesson to her possibly unclear and too general instruction, a large number of students in each group, and lack of "more specific rules like only one group member has the 'floor' to talk at a time."

Pat initially enjoyed working with Dorla, and was well prepared for each session with Dorla by gathering the instructional materials (e.g., books, charts) and by having a plan (e.g., working on Dorla's writing or vocabulary development). Dorla was very verbal and willing to share her interests in reading history stories, about slavery, and about her ancestors. Dorla's interests, however, were not supported during her time with Pat. Pat brought in books, like *The True Story of the Three Little Pigs* (Scieszka, 1989) and *Cinderella* (Galdone, 1978) for Dorla to read. Although Pat's performance on oral reading and retelling of the passages from the Informal Reading Inventory indicated her instructional reading level was at the 5th grade, throughout her time with Dorla, Pat often doubted about Dorla's abilities to read and write. "We also worked on correcting a writing sample that I had gotten from her teacher. She had many basic mistakes in her story that to me should not be made by a sixth grader." At times, Pat noted that Dorla was engaged in a book. For example, during the reading of *Fanny's Dream* (Buehner, 1996), Dorla pointed out for Pat the "secret pictures" hidden in the illustrations that Pat would otherwise have never noticed.

In her weekly reflective journals, Pat often mentioned that Dorla was unmotivated, and did not want to "do anything I brought for her." When I suggested that Pat ask Dorla for books that she liked, Pat again expressed her doubts, "I am not sure that she could read those history books." Toward the end of the field experiences, Pat expressed her growing frustration with Dorla's not wanting to work with her. "She remains distracted. I can't pinpoint the exact problem, so I'm having trouble correcting it." Pat did realize that Dorla chose easy books to read, and probably needed a boost in her self confidence. Pat, however, failed to praise Dorla and make her aware that she did something great, when Dorla noted the "secret pictures" hidden in the illustrations of the book, *Fanny's Dream*.

*Understandings of diversity after field experiences.* Pat did not consider her field experiences in a class with predominantly African-American students as successful, "I still don't know how to handle the discipline problems." She, however, admitted learning a little bit more about teaching diverse students. Pat realized the role that students' learning styles play in teaching. "I think that most of the students in this particular class are audio-visual learners. They may not learn by only doing worksheets or reading books." The power of cooperative learning was another thing that Pat learned about teaching. She acknowledged, "I honestly don't think that I could have taught lessons if I had not used group activities." Pat also believed that in order to teach African American students, "a teacher should first lay out the rules for students."

Pat further expressed her appreciation for her students who taught her "how challenging it is to teach African American students whose cultural and linguistic backgrounds were unfamiliar to me." Pat, on the other hand, expressed her contradictory view about teaching. She stated, "Students come from so many different backgrounds, and I have learned that not one formula will work for all the differences in a classroom." But she also mentioned, "whole language teaching was the best way for students of low-socioeconomic and different reading backgrounds to learn."

## DISCUSSION

The case studies of Betty and Pat indicated that field experiences had some effect on pre service teachers' enhanced understandings of diversity, although such effect varied between Betty and Pat. Before the field experiences, both teachers seemed to have limited, broad, and abstract views of diverse students and of teaching, although Betty's views were a little bit more specific than Pat's. After the field experiences, both Betty and Pat were able to state their views about diverse students and teaching. The field experiences provided the pre-service teachers with opportunities to observe how various diversity issues played a role in students' literacy learning. Such observations made it possible for the pre-service teachers to become aware of at least the presence of these issues in classrooms.

The case studies also suggested the complexity and multiplicity of pre-service teachers' exploring diversity issues in a literacy methods course. First of all, the issues of diversity that Betty observed were similar to, yet also, different from those that Pat noted. A common issue was related to students' abilities. Betty and Pat noted how students from different cultural and linguistic backgrounds possessed different strengths and needs related to literacy learning. The issue of diversity that Betty noted was students' native language and its role in literacy teaching and learning. Betty tried to find English and Spanish books for her case study student. Pat, on the other hand, seemed to be more aware of African American students' unique communicative styles, although such awareness was negatively presented in relation to discipline problems.

Additionally, the field experiences seemed to play multiple roles in pre-service teachers' developing understandings of diversity. It seems to be very beneficial for Pat to continue similar experiences with African American students and for Betty to continue interacting with Latino students so that they would have more opportunities to explore teaching diverse students. Pre-service teachers like Pat definitely need more experiences with African American students in order for them to become more familiar with students' linguistic and cultural backgrounds and to develop abilities to teach in a culturally responsive way. Equally importantly, Betty needs to have in-depth experiences with African American students, and Pat would benefit from her experiences with Latino students. In so doing, both of them would have a better chance to encounter, explore, reflect upon, and experience dealing with a wide range of diversity issues related to students from different cultural and linguistic backgrounds.

When I structured the field experiences, I wanted to use case study as a tool for the pre-service teachers to gain a deeper and holistic understanding of one student's literacy development. I also wanted the pre-service teachers to learn how to teach lessons, in a culturally responsive way, to a roomful of students whose backgrounds were different from the teachers. These two different types of experiences seemed to have allowed the pre-service teachers to observe and encounter diversity issues to varying degrees. Furthermore, the case study and teaching were meant to complement each other in that they together provided the pre-service teachers with relatively comprehensive experiences of learning about diverse students and about teaching.

The case studies of Betty and Pat illustrate this point. They seemed to gain more general insights about varying abilities from lesson teaching than from a case study. Their work with case study students offered one-on-one opportunities to learn from their students. Interesting enough, Pat seldom noticed in a one-on-one setting an African American student's unique communicative styles. She only focused on the discipline problems, which were obvious to her during lesson teaching.

As to pedagogical practices and materials, both Betty and Pat seemed to be knowledgeable of instructional strategies and children's books. I was glad to see neither of them asked their students to complete worksheets during teaching and during working with case study students. Most strategies promoted students' active engagement, but only a limited number of multicultural children's books were used during lesson teaching and during work with case study students. Furthermore, both Betty and Pat did not allow for students' self-selection of books. It is also interesting to note that Pat blamed her students for a "not so good lesson," whereas Betty looked into herself and, in particular her own teaching skills and knowledge of students, for a possible explanation of a "not so good lesson." Betty seemed to begin to situate self-examination within teaching and relating herself to diverse students. The field experiences have taught the pre-service teachers about the complexity of teaching. It has also helped me realize that pre-service teachers' knowledge of instructional strategies and materials would not guarantee their skillful teaching with students who are so different from themselves. Such a realization has made me think about refining the field experiences and about allocating more class time for discussions on field experiences and particularly on these diversity issues to which pre-service teachers failed to pay attention.

During both studies, I played multiple roles. First of all, my role as a member of a non-mainstream group (who immigrated to the United States more than a dozen years ago) has allowed me to personally experience various diversity issues. I, however, also acknowledge that my own cultural and linguistic experience may not be the same as diverse children have experienced. For example, I have limited knowledge about African American culture and languages. When the pre-service teachers, like Pat, had their field experience in a Title I school with predominantly African American, I considered their field experience as mine as well—I was learning along with the teachers. Another role I played was related to my profession. That is, I am a literacy teacher educator who is committed to preparing teachers for culturally responsive teaching of literacy. I am knowledgeable of theories and pedagogies related to teaching literacy, but I may not be equally well informed of theories and research related to addressing diversity issues. The last role I played was that of a researcher who has begun exploring how to help pre-service teachers become effective teachers for diverse teachers. This research focus has been relatively new (García et al., 1998).

My multiple roles intersected with one another, and they both enhanced my ability to conduct the studies, but also limited my perspectives and ability. For example, I wish that I had known better about African American cultures and languages and about culturally responsive teaching for African American children. I then would possibly have had a better chance to guide teachers like Pat in analyzing her teaching and in thinking of solutions to her frustrations with her case study student, Dorla. I felt that my limited personal and professional experiences with African Americans might have prevented me from becoming sensitive to diversity issues. After completing this chapter, I began thinking of how I would enhance my own ability to guide pre-service teachers while they are in a school setting with diverse students whose cultural and linguistic backgrounds are relatively unfamiliar to the pre-service teachers and me. It seems important to invite classroom teachers and members from children's community, who share diverse students' cultural and linguistic backgrounds, to participate in a similar study on exploring pre-service teachers' experiences with the ABC's model. Conducting a member check with classroom teachers and students themselves would be another way to bring other people's perspective to the study.

## CONCLUSION

This study explored pre-service teachers' understandings of diversity and of teaching diverse students. The results have suggested messiness and complexity of diversity and literacy (Smolkin, 2000). Such messiness and complexity have some implications for literacy teacher education and research. As evident in both studies, field experiences with diverse students in one literacy methods course can be very limited and, to some degree, superficial. Pre-service teachers need to have continuous experiences with diverse students during which they repeatedly self-examine cultural beliefs and experiences and explore diversity issues in the context of learning to teach in a culturally responsive way. Literacy teacher educators need to make the effort to provide pre-service teachers with experiences with diverse students throughout their teacher education program. A wide range of experiences with *different* diverse students (e.g., Latinos, African Americans, and Asian Americans) would allow pre-service teachers to learn to teach effectively with diverse students and to encounter various diversity issues, some of which may be more relevant to one group of diverse students than to another group. Secondly, a majority of literacy teacher educators and researchers, including myself, are from middle-class and privileged backgrounds and have had limited experiences with people from other cultural and linguistic backgrounds (Merryfield, 2000). In order for us to better prepare pre-service teachers, we should begin, along with pre-service teachers, self-exploring our own cultural beliefs, values, biases, identity, and examining diversity issues such as white privilege, power relationships, and social injustice of which we may not be conscious. We need to conduct constant self-reflections on our own teaching of literacy teacher education courses and particularly on our pre-service teachers' learning experiences with teaching diverse students in classrooms (Sleeter, 1995). It is my hope that more literacy teacher educators and researchers in our community would be part of this important and challenging endeavor to better prepare pre-service teachers for cultural and linguistic diversity.

## REFERENCES

Au, K.H. (1998). Social constructivism and the school literacy learning of students of diverse backgrounds. *Journal of Literacy Research, 30,* 297-319.

Au, K.H., & Raphael, T.E. (2000). Equity and literacy in the next millennium. *Reading Research Quarterly, 35*, 170-188.

Bogdan, R.C., & Biklen, S.K. (1994). *Qualitative research for education: An introduction to theory and method*. Boston: Allyn & Bacon.

Buehner, C. (1996). *Fanny's dream*. New York: Dial Books for Young Readers.

Chizhik, E.W. (2003). Reflecting on the challenges of preparing suburban teachers for urban schools. *Education & Urban Society, 35*, 443-459.

Cochran-Smith, M. (2000). Blind vision: Unlearning racism in teacher education. *Harvard Education Review, 70*, 157-190.

Finkbeiner, C., & Koplin, C. (2002, October). A cooperative approach for facilitating intercultural education. *Reading Online, 6*(3). Available: http://www.readingonline.org/newliteracies/lit_index.asp?HREF=finkbeiner/index.html

Florio-Ruane, S. (1994). The future teachers' autobiography club. *English Education, 26*, 52-66.

Galdone, P. (1978). *Cinderella*. New York: McGraw-Hill.

García, G.E., Willis, A.I., & Harris, V. (1998). Introduction: Appropriating the creating space of difference in literacy research. *Journal of Literacy Research, 30*, 181-186.

Goodwin, L. (1997). Multicultural stories. *Urban Education, 32*, 117-145.

Hoffman, J., & Pearson, P.D. (2000). Reading teacher education in the next millennium: What your grandmother's teacher didn't know that your granddaughter's teacher should. *Reading Research Quarterly, 35*, 28-44.

Kidd, J.K., Sanchez, S.Y., & Thorp, E.K. (2002). A focus on family stories: Enhancing preservice teachers' cultural awareness. In D.L. Schallert, C.M. Fairbanks, J. Worthy, B. Maloch, & J.V. Hoffman (Eds.), *51st yearbook of the National Reading Conference* (pp. 242-252). Oak Creek, WI: National Reading Conference, Inc.

Ladson-Billings, G. (1995). Toward a theory of culturally relevant pedagogy. *American Educational Research Journal, 32*, 465-491.

Ladson-Billings, G. (2000). Fighting for our lives: Preparing teachers to teach African American students. *Journal of Teacher Education, 52*, 206-214.

Laframboise, K., & Griffith, P. L. (1997). Using literature cases to examine diversity issues with preservice teachers. *Teaching and Teacher Education, 13*, 369-382.

Lewis, A. (2001). There is no "race" in the school yard: Color-blind ideology in an (almost) all-white school. *American Education Research Journal, 38*(4), 781-811.

Linn, R.L., Baker, E.L., & Betebenner, D.W. (2002). Accountability systems: Implications of requirements of the No Child Left Behind Act of 2001. *Educational Researcher, 31*(6), 3-16.

Madgwick, W. (1984). *City maze*. New York: Millbrook Press.

Merryfield, M.M. (2000). Why aren't teachers being prepared to teach for diversity, equity, and global interconnectedness? *Teaching and Teacher Education, 16*, 429-443.

Moll, L.C., & Gonzalez, N. (1994). Critical issue: Lessons from research with language-minority children. *Journal of Reading Behavior, 26*, 439-456.

Nagel, G.K. (2002, November). Building cultural understanding and communication: A model in seven situations. *Reading Online, 6*(4). Available: http://www.readingonline.org/newliteracies/lit_index.asp?HREF=nagel/index.html

Nieto, S. (2000). Placing equity front and center. *Journal of Teacher Education, 52*, 180-187.

Nieto, S. (2002). *Language, culture, and teaching: Critical perspectives for a new century.* Mahwah, NJ: Lawrence Erlbaum Associates.

Raschka, C. (1993). Yo! Yes? New York: Orchard Books.

Schmidt, P.R. (1998a). The ABC's of cultural understanding and communication. *Equity & Excellence in Education, 31*(2), 28-38.

Schmidt, P.R. (1998b). The ABC's Model: Teachers connect home and school. In T. Shanahan & F. Rodriguez-Brown (Eds.), *47th yearbook of the National Reading Conference* (pp. 194-208). Chicago: National Reading Conference.

Schmidt, P.R. (1999). Know thyself and understand others. *Language Arts, 76*, 332-340.

Schmidt, P.R. (2001). The power to empower. In P.R. Schmidt & P.B. Mosenthal (Eds.), *Reconceptualizing literacy in the new age of multiculturalism and pluralism.* Greenwich, CT: Information Age Publishing.

Scieszka, J. (1989). *The true story of the three little pigs.* New York: Puffins Books.

Sleeter, C.E. (1995). White preservice students and multicultural education coursework. In J.M. Larkin & C.E. Sleeter (Eds.), *Developing multicultural teacher education curriculum* (pp. 17-29). Albany: State University of New York Press.

Smolkin, L. (2000). RRQ Snippet: How will diversity affect literacy in the next millennium? *Reading Research Quarterly, 35*, 548-552.

Xu, H. (2000a). Preservice teachers integrate understandings of diversity into literacy instruction: An adaptation of the ABC's model. *Journal of Teacher Education, 51*, 135-142.

Xu, S.H. (2000b). Preservice teachers in a literacy methods course consider issues of diversity. *Journal of Literacy Research, 32*, 505-531.

Xu, S.H. (2000c, December). *Preservice teachers' developing understandings of diversity: The ABC's model and teaching African American students.* Paper presented at 50th National Reading Conference, Scottsdale, AZ.

Xu, S. H. (2001). Preservice teachers connect multicultural knowledge and perspectives with literacy instruction for minority students. In P.R. Schmidt & P.B. Mosenthal (Eds.), *A volume in language, literacy, and learning: Reconceptualizing literacy in the new age of multiculturalism and pluralism* (pp. 323-340). Greenwich, CT: Information Age.

# CHAPTER 8

# A SUCCESSFUL ABC'S IN-SERVICE PROJECT

## Supporting Culturally Responsive Teaching

### Andrea Izzo and Patricia Ruggiano Schmidt

## ABSTRACT

This chapter reports a study of successful in-service learning that used the *ABC's of Cultural Understanding and Communication* (Schmidt, 2001) as the foundation for developing culturally relevant pedagogy in urban schools. During *two* years, after school, teachers experienced the *ABC's Model*, studied ways to communicate and connect with family and community members, and designed and implemented culturally relevant or culturally responsive literacy lesson plans across the curriculum. As a result, their home/school/community collaboration and their professional collaboration permitted them to change their pedagogy. The teachers concluded that this in-service program had supported their professional development and benefitted their students.

*ABC's of Cultural Understanding and Communication:*
*National and International Adaptations,* 161–187

7

## INTRODUCTION

The teachers in this study began their program by participating in a year-long in-service (30 hours) to learn about culturally relevant pedagogy as part of a *New York State Systemic Change Grant*. They were given in-service credit by the school district and paid by the grant for the additional hours necessary to write lesson plans, record interviews, complete surveys, and communicate with families and community members. Toward the end of the school year, they began to design lessons that connected home, school, and community for literacy development. However, they soon realized that they needed additional support to continue their work. Upon their request, the professional development professors applied for a second *New York State Systemic Change Grant*. It paid the teachers for after school support meetings to continue designing lesson plans. Thus, an opportunity emerged to study the results of the in-service program over two years.

At the end of the second year of the ABC's in-service program, participants completed a survey regarding their professional development experience. The following excerpted comments indicated that the follow-up support for in-service was essential for their success.

> In the past, we have had professional development programs for a day or two, and then we're on our own.

> I like trying new ideas. But, I start out ready to change my teaching, and then, after a little time, I seem to go back to my old ways. Working together changes that behavior.

> After our in-service work about connecting with families and community for literacy learning, I think it was good to have time to share and help each other keep doing what we've learned.

> This in-service project called culturally relevant pedagogy was different. We got the support we needed to keep going.

> We benefitted, our students benefitted and their families benefitted. We learned new way to teach and motivate our kids.

These statements reflect what researchers suggest-that professional development need reflection, time, and support (Banks & Banks, 1995; Fullan, 1999, 2004;Goodlad, 1998; Schon, 1983; Watson & Fullan, 1992) for the adaptation and implementation of new instructional practices.

The purpose of this chapter is to report on the teachers' changes in home/school/community collaboration, the changes in lesson plans from year one to year two, and the changes in teachers' perceptions concerning culturally relevant teaching. Data collected were analyzed to discover answers to the following questions: (1) How did teachers make use of the "funds of knowledge" brought to the classroom by children, families, and community members during the first and second years? (2) How did the lesson plans change during the two years? (3) How did the teachers define culturally responsive teaching? (4) How did the teachers evaluate the in-service project?

Answers to these questions not only help us understand the power of supporting teachers as they try new ideas, but also contribute to our understanding of the research and practice around strong home, school, and community connections that promote students' literacy development and understanding of the curriculum (Au, 1993; Edwards, 1999, 2003; Faltis, 1993; Goldenberg, 1987; Heath, 1983; Leftwich, 2002; McCaleb, 1994; Moll, 1992; Reyhner & Gracia, 1989; Schmidt, 1998a, 2000, 2001, 2002 Xu, 2000).

## SOCIOCULTURAL PERSPECTIVE

The *ABC's of Cultural Understanding and Communication* (Schmidt, 1998b, 1999, 2001), explained in the introduction and in other chapters in this book, served as the guide for the in-service program. This model is based on sociocultural research that focuses on the complexity of developing literacy within cultures of home, school, and community (Cummins, 1986; Heath, 1983; Rogoff, 1990; Purcell Gates, L' Allier, & Smith, 1995; Trueba, Jacobs & Kirton, 1990; Vygotsky, 1978). Such a literacy perspective on classroom life is determined by students and teachers who elect to bring the home cultures into social interactions, and therefore, contribute to the definitions of language and literacy (Bloome & Green, 1982; Green, Kantor, & Rogers, 1990; Kantor, Miller, & Fernie, 1992). In other words, classrooms embracing this perspective encourage children to make meaning through social interactions across and within cultural settings. The belief is that children become literate within the cultures of home, school, and community as they construct the classroom culture (Dyson, 1989; Heath, 1983; Moll, 1992; Schiefflin & Cochran-Smith, 1984; Taylor, 1983; Taylor & Dorsey-Gaines, 1988; Wells, 1986).

With these ideas in mind, culturally relevant pedagogy or culturally responsive teaching can be defined as teachers making connections with the curriculum based on a student's family, culture, and community (Au, 1993; Ladson-Billings, 1994). When these connections are made, a student's prior knowledge and schemata are stimulated and validated; the student has a better chance of making meaning (Wells, 1986) and relating school learning to his or her life.

## HOME/SCHOOL/COMMUNITY CONNECTIONS AND CULTURALLY RELEVANT PEDAGOGY

Families and children from diverse ethnic and cultural backgrounds and lower socioeconomic levels often feel a discontinuity between home and school. When teachers reach out to connect with family members and use them as resources for learning, there is often a narrowing of the academic gap and an increase in positive attitudes toward school (Boykin, 1978; Edwards et al., 1999; Faltis, 1993; Goldenberg, 1987; Heath, 1983; Moll, 1992). The teachers who make this effort and create meaningful literacy lesson plans are actually implementing culturally relevant pedagogy or culturally responsive teaching. These teachers connect the curriculum to the knowledge and experiences of diverse cultures in their classrooms by validating family backgrounds, and using the literacies found in the children's cultures.

Previous studies by Reyhner and Garcia (1989) showed a significant decrease in cultural discontinuity between home and school when teachers from European American backgrounds and families of Polynesian, Hispanic, and Native American students in Southwestern schools gathered resources to engage the children in classroom literacy activities that reflected their cultures. Within months, literacy performance significantly improved. Similarly, studies of African American males indicate that learning by doing rather than emulation of "White Talk" allows them to gain conceptual understandings (Gordon, 1988; Murrel Jr., 1994). Furthermore, connecting learning to African American students' community, family interests, and values produces students who are enthusiastic, engaged, and ready to learn (Boykin 1978, 1984; Howard, 2001; Lee, 1991; Levine, 1994; Tatum, 2000).

However, due to many educators' lack of knowledge and understanding of the literacies related to particular cultures, they are frequently unable to connect school and community literacies. For example, Moll's (1992) concept regarding "funds of knowledge" might demonstrate that many Latino students have mechanical abilities involving literacy skills related to their community's needs that usually go unrecognized in schools. Similarly, African American community literacies, such as oral storytelling, recitation, song, and poetry may also be ignored (Delpit, 1995; Edwards, Dandridge, McMillon, & Pleasant, 2001; Walker-Dalhouse & Dalhouse, 2001). Additionally, cultural conflict and struggles seem to be common occurrences for children from Asian backgrounds. Unfortunately, ethnographic research (Pang & Cheng, 1998; Schmidt, 2003; Trueba et al., 1990) has demonstrated that family knowledge and traditions are typically ignored by teachers from European American backgrounds.

## TEACHER EDUCATION PROGRAMS

To counteract the insensitivity to community funds of knowledge, teacher education programs are attempting to prepare professionals who are responsive to diverse groups of children in their classrooms and make culturally compatible and dynamic connections between home and school (Cochran-Smith, 1995; Florio-Ruane, 1994; Noordhoff & Kleinfield, 1993; Schmidt, 1998b; Spindler & Spindler, 1987; Tatum, 1992; Willis & Meacham, 1997). However, lifelong emotions and attitudes of present and future teachers regarding cultural and ethnic diversity and poverty often deter the preparation process (Florio-Ruane, 1994; Lalik & Hinchman, 2001; Schmidt, 1998a/2002). In light of this information, there is evidence that teacher self-knowledge may be the first and foremost consideration when attempting to help teachers understand diverse groups of students (Banks, 1994; Britzman, 1986; Osborne, 1996). And for these reasons, we used the *ABC's of Cultural Understanding and Communication* as the basis for the in-service program.

## ABC's of Cultural Understanding and Communication

The following is a brief explanation of the ABC's Model that has been explicitly detailed in previous chapters.

1.  Teachers write their autobiographies starting with their earliest memories of family traditions, religion, education, victories, defeats et al. The life stories are only shared with the instructor so personal information may be confidentially included.

2.  Teachers interview parents or family members of students who are culturally different from themselves. This occurs on neutral ground, usually not school. The interviews at a local coffee shop, park or community center. The student's home is also acceptable if the teacher is willing to visit. The teacher begins by asking the family member what she would like to see happen in school for the student. The teacher attempts to discover student interests and routines outside of school. The teacher also shares his or her own life experiences at appropriate times during the interview.

3.  The teacher then creates a chart comparing and contrasting similarities and differences between the life of the family member and the life of the teacher.

4.  Next, the teacher analyzes the differences. He or she writes why certain differences are admired and why certain differences make

one feel uncomfortable. The purpose of this exercise is to examine one's own culture in relation to the culture of the person interviewed. This helps develop an awareness of ethnocentricity.

5. Finally, the teacher begins to make connections by studying the curriculum and exploring ways to make studies meaningful to specific students and their families and communities. Inviting mother and a new baby into the classroom to discuss human development may be one way to bring relevance to learning. Inviting a new arrival from Puerto Rico to teach a song or dance to the class and discuss the Island's geography is another way to include differences. After experiencing the *ABC's Model's* first four steps, teachers design lesson plans for connecting home, school, and community for children's reading, writing, listening, speaking, and viewing based on numerous modifications of the model. They see ways to develop collaborative relationships with families in an atmosphere of mutual respect, so that students gain the most from their education.

There have been numerous studies examining teacher attitudes and behaviors during the ABC's process (Finkbeiner & Koplin, 2002; Leftwich, 2002; Nagel, 2002; Schmidt, 1998b, 1999, 2000), but few studies during the year or years after (Schmidt, 2000, 2001). There is little understanding of what happens with a group of teachers during the years following focused study of the *ABC's Model*. Those studies concerning the year after have been individual case studies and have demonstrated successful implementation, but no studies have looked at a group of teachers during the following year after their in-service program. Therefore, this chapter describes the two years of in-service guided by the *ABC's Model*. It contributes to our understanding of the in-service needed for the implementation of culturally responsive teaching.

## METHODOLOGY

### Setting and Participants

Ninety percent of the students in this high poverty, urban school in the Northeastern United States were from African American and Latino origins and 10% were of European American origins. Ninety-five percent of the children received free or reduced breakfasts and lunch. Six teachers from European American origins, and a librarian and community assistant from African American origins volunteered to meet a total of 30 hours after school during the fall and spring 2002/2003 academic year for the culturally relevant pedagogy professional development program. All teachers were tenured with 5-20 years experience. Four pre-service teachers joined the group as part of their practicum before their professional teaching block. Two participated during the first year and another two during the second year.

We, the two literacy professors of European American origins, in the education department of a small, liberal arts, religious affiliated college initiated and facilitated the in service program. One of us had worked in the school during the previous 4 years, teaching an early literacy course to undergraduate students during the school day. The pre-service teachers tutored first grade students, helping them write their names, reading multicultural children's literature and playing phonics and sight word games.

**Procedures**

The city school district teachers and professors met weekly and biweekly during the 2002/2003 school year to discuss and implement practical applications of home/school communication and create and teach culturally relevant literacy lessons to improve reading and writing achievement. The following outline lists the topics of study.

Schedule of Topics for the 2002/2003 School Year

- ABC's of Cultural Understanding and Communication—Why know thyself and understand others? Cultural analyses between and among participants.
- Why home/school/community connections for literacy development? Study of research.
- Know the community: Learning the realities of cultural funds of knowledge.
- Community leaders and community power.
- How to begin to talk … to share … to listen.
- Examining parent conferences, curriculum nights, e-mail, newsletters, phone calls, and home visits.
- Meeting on neutral ground.
- Family/teacher/student dialogue-Collaboration.
- Culturally relevant pedagogy and motivation.
- Culturally relevant pedagogy and academic achievement.
- Planning relevant pedagogy with families and community.
- Implementing and assessing lesson plans.

The teachers actively participated in the *ABC's of Cultural Understanding and Communication* (Schmidt, 1998b) to develop their communication skills and working relationships with families. They interviewed numerous parents and family members in homes, recreation centers, and local fast food sites and asked *for* help *from* the families to learn more about the children's interests and academic needs. They also shared personal stories to begin building the trust *for* working relationships. As a result, teachers heard about family problems and joys and students' home lives. From these meetings, teachers completed cross-cultural analyses. This helped them see their own attitudes and biases regarding teaching and learning. The process, not only developed a greater understanding of their students' families, but also allowed the teachers to discover family, community, and school resources to encourage collaborative literacy learning.

In the spring of 2003, teachers created culturally relevant literacy lessons across the curriculum. Their lessons were observed, videotaped, and analyzed. Being pleased with their successes, a proposal was submitted to present a workshop at the International Reading Association 2004 Annual Convention. It was accepted and the school district found finances to help support travel and housing for the teachers and their principal.

## Support Meetings

During the following school year, as part of a *New York State Systemic Change Grant*, five of the teachers, 2 pre-service teachers, the librarian and community assistant met, again, in after school support meetings for 16 hours to create and discuss culturally relevant lessons that they planned to implement in their classrooms. From the 2002/2003 year's in-service work, lesson plans were analyzed on videotape and in field notes from participant observations, by the professors. A series of characteristics appeared in teachers' successfully implemented culturally relevant literacy lessons. They discussed and evaluated the list and agreed to use it as their guide for future lessons. They were:

Characteristics of Successful Culturally Relevant Literacy Lesson Plans

1. High Expectations.
2. Positive relationships with families and community.
3. Cultural sensitivity-reshaped curriculum-mediated for culturally valued knowledge.
4. Active teaching methods.
5. Teacher as facilitator.

6.  Student control of portions of the lesson--lots of talk--"healthy hum."

7.  Instruction around group and pairs-low anxiety.

The 2003/2004 support meetings began with a discussion of ideas around the presentation of readings related to culturally relevant pedagogy collected by one of the professors. Next, each member of the group shared ideas about the implementation of their classroom literacy lessons. They talked about problems and accomplishments related to home, school, and community connections. Then, all went off in pairs to design new culturally responsive literacy lesson plans. The last 15 minutes of each meeting was set aside for sharing accomplishments *of* the sessions. Additionally, several Saturday morning meetings occurred to prepare materials for the 2004 IRA Convention.

## Data Collection and Analysis

Data sources for this study were the written lessons and teacher reflections, records of family communication, videotapes *of* lessons, interviews, surveys *of* teacher attitudes, and researcher participant observations. Reflections from after school meetings were recorded by one professor in order to capture key comments and evaluate sessions.

Data were collected and analyzed by researchers and participants (Wasser & Bresler, 1996). Teachers and researchers viewed videos, lessons, and reflections, separately and together. Surveys were given to the participants throughout the two years to evaluate process and progress. Teachers also systematically recorded all family and community contacts during the academic year. These multiple data sets were triangulated to enhance the validity and reliability of the study (Merriam, 1998).

In the qualitative research tradition (Lincoln & Guba, 1995), data were coded and categorized from the beginning of data collection (Strauss, 1987). The categories for each were merged to form themes grounded in the record of parental contacts and the implementation of culturally relevant literacy lesson plans.

## FINDINGS

There were three major themes that answered the initial research questions and gave us new insights into professional development. They were, (1) a significantly greater number of home/school/community connections were made during spring 2004 than spring 2003. Perceptions appeared to change. (2) The teachers collaborated to create many more culturally relevant literacy lesson plans. They systematically and easily wrote lessons that developed into units of study, sharing across grade levels and content areas and making use of the community assistant's and librarian's expertise. (3) The teachers claimed to be empowered to share their work with pre-service teachers, during workshops in the school district, and at the 2004 International Reading Association Convention.

## Changes in Home/School/Community Connections

During the fall of the 2002 school year, when participants were asked individually how they ranked their home/school/community connections, all gave answers from very good to excellent. Most participants initially believed they were doing quite well with home/school/community connections. They appeared confident and were enrolled in this course to learn a few new ideas for communication. Most believed they knew enough about their students and their families to teach effectively in their classrooms.

At the end of the year, when asked to rank themselves on home/school/community connections, no one selected "excellent." Four ranked themselves as "very good" and three ranked themselves as "good," and two ranked themselves as "fair." These dramatic changes indicate that the teachers became aware of the potential depth and authenticity of home/school/community connections and the realization that they had previously been considering just the "tip of the iceberg" when they evaluated themselves. Their comments follow with the first comment from September 2002 and the second, from June 2003.

**Teacher 1**:   I know my students and the social worker keeps us informed concerning family problems.

> I have a good relationship with many families. I am learning. I see the need for more personal contacts and hope I can make the time to do that. I am calling more and writing individual, positive notes. Some parents even write back!

**Teacher 2**:   We send home a weekly newsletter. Parents can tell what's going on in the classroom.

> My weekly newsletter is a good start, but I need much more. I have made three home visits this year. I would never have done this before. I think word is out that I care. The parents are picking up their kids after school and stopping to talk to me.

**Teacher 3**:   We have parent conferences twice a year and our community liaison person keeps us current.

I never realized how close I could get with parents. This is good! I have visited two homes and I call often, asking them to contribute to our class. They all have said "Yes," to any of my requests. A mother brought her baby to class as part of our nutrition unit. A father, who is a carpenter, brought in his tools as part of the simple machine unit.

**Teacher 4**:   I know this community. I have taught here for many years. The children are so needy but I talk to parents all the time. They feel comfortable with me.

I have good communication with my children's parents, but I can see how much I can use their ideas in my class. When teaching the health unit about smoking, I invited a parent who discovered had quit three months ago to share his ideas about smoking. He was amazing with the kids! I never would have done this before.

**Teacher 5**:   I call parents whenever I need to. I get my point across about a child. I then get them to come to school to talk.

I realize now that school is not neutral ground. I need to talk to parents, in person, in places that are safe for both of us. I realize how much I need to communicate with parents if my children are going to buy into school. And I can't be telling them … I have to ask them. We need to work together for the children.

**Teacher 6**:   The children have very difficult home situations. I am constantly talking with them.

I am from the upper middle class and highly educated. I am Black, but have great difficulties with the poverty issues in this community. I am learning how to communicate and empathize with the African American and Latino families. They have to learn to trust me, and that won't happen if I don't develop trusting relationships with them. This course has helped me see this.

**Teacher 7**:   I am always trying to connect with the community, but it's hard to parents involved.

Parents are very busy, but they want to be involved. I can see so many ways I can work with teachers and families. I am in a position to bring them together and this course has helped me see how to do it.

**Teacher 8**:   I just don't have time to get to know my parents; I'm too busy working with their children, but when I need to I can connect with the parents very well.

> It is absolutely important for me to get to know my children and their families. It is the best use of my time. The payoff is phenomenal in terms of motivation to learn.

**Teacher 9**:   I wish we could get more parents involved, but I try. They need to understand that their kids won't go anywhere if they aren't given a chance in school.

> I am in the position to get more parents involved. As the librarian, I can bring resources to teachers and help them make plans to connect home and school for literacy learning. I hope we can get more parents to come in on a regular basis and listen to children read or read to our children. I think I could make that happen.

The participants recorded the number of parent/family contacts from the beginning of the project to the end of the school year. Dates, times, places, and topics of discussion were written on a sheet provided by investigators. During the fall semester, 25% of the parents had been personally contacted by phone or were sent notes in addition to the required fall conferences. These were the parents of the children who have serious academic or emotional problems. Much more contact occurred second semester; records showed that teacher participants talked with all of their parents by phone, in school, in home or in the neighborhood, at least twice, outside of the regularly scheduled parent conferences. Most meetings were positive and productive for the children. Additionally, notes became a two-way experience between parents and teachers.

A significantly greater number of home/ school/ community connections were made during 2003/2004. Each participant recorded daily contacts by phone, in school or in the neighborhood. Teachers studied children's school registration cards to discover family occupations, personal interests, and community information. All teachers personally talked with parents at least twice in the fall and twice in the spring outside of the usual required parent conferences. Most experienced positive exchanges ... something never previously accomplished with so many. As usual, teachers followed the New York State Curriculum for their grade levels and content areas, but additionally, they systematically contacted family and community members in order to bring their knowledge to the curriculum. Then they made phone contacts and personal visits to homes and neutral ground (Denny's, Recreation Centers, Church Centers, etc.). At least weekly, there were family and community members in classrooms, something that had never occurred in the past. Finally, teachers observed videotapes of their lessons from the previous spring 2003. They critically analyzed their work privately or with a trusted colleague, talking about student time on task, student interest and classroom management. They saw changes in their children and their teaching. This helped them design lessons during the 2003/2004 school year that they believed were culturally responsive following the *Seven Characteristics* they found in successful lessons from the previous year.

## SUCCESSFUL CULTURALLY RELEVANT LITERACY LESSON PLANS AND CHANGES

The following are brief descriptions of several culturally relevant units from each grade level. A few other examples of lesson topics are included to give an idea of additional literacy lessons across the curriculum. After these examples, the changes in lesson plans over two years will be presented.

*Kindergarten.* A *Community Helpers Unit,* included visits from local police, firefighter, and trash collector. The students began an in depth study of their immediate neighborhood with an enlarged map of the community placed on the floor of the classroom with the main streets ane locations of their homes. Digital pictures were taken of neighborhood houses, shops, and significant landmarks. Children pasted these on the map; all were labeled and discussed. The students then went on a field trip visiting the local establishments near the school. A fish store, pizza shop, Chinese Restaurant, gas station, hair salon, drug store, laundry, and day care center were on the list. At each site, the proprietors contributed to community soup with a can of vegetables or broth given to them the day before by the teacher. The proprietor or worker briefly told about the business and what it did for the neighborhood. The students returned to the school to write thank you notes and invitations to the Community Soup Luncheon held in their classroom. These were sent and the following week, children surveyed the ingredients and charted the recipe. The students also wrote alphabet poems about the community helpers they had studied and the shops they'd visited. Each child read a poem at the luncheon. Each guest received a place mat decorated for their shop. The soup was cooked in the cafeteria and served in the kindergarten room by parents of the children.

Not only did these children experience a great deal of relevant reading, writing, listening, speaking, and viewing, but they were introduced to and used compasses in coordination with their community map and community field trip. This lead to study of the globe and land forms. The teacher explained that the world has many people who live in many different locations. Children's literature, videos, and posters helped the children learn about different homes, food, and clothing. From these viewing experiences, students read, wrote, drew, and talked. They also decided to design their special dream homes and tell about the parts of the world they would live if dreams came true. Last, they focused on their own family celebrations, sharing again with literacy activities.

Other units throughout the spring included culturally relevant literature activities. One dealt with Cinderella stories from around the world. Murals were created and were compared and contrasted with Venn Diagrams. Story elements were emphasized. Skin color was also an important focus in the study of similarities and differences.

*Third grade.*   In the Third Grade inclusive classroom, the teachers began with family belief systems, such as mottos. What can you tell about a family with the motto, "Pull together?" Children concentrated on this activity by creating family mottos and explaining what they meant. The class discussed why certain mottos help people think. The teacher then turned to Kenya and Japan. The class discussed geography and guessed possible mottos for these nations. They researched both nations using the globe and literature. The teacher read *Sadako and the Thousand Paper Cranes (l993), Jambo Means Hello: Swahili Alphabet Book (1981), Hiroshima, Non Pika (1980). Grandfather's Journey (1993), NdUo Runs (l996),* and many more stories related to Kenya and Japan. Peace and the ravages of war became important topics of discussion. Students wrote haiku and shared and studied greetings and important phrases in both languages. Language and geography were initially analyzed and math was related to distances, latitude and longitude. Then students prepared questions for the community visitors from Kenya and Japan and compared and contrasted the cities and homes of these countries with their own, using bubble mapping. Three languages labeled much of this classroom: English, Swahili, and Japanese.

Comparing and contrasting prior knowledge and experiences with new topics, and ideas occurred regularly in every subject. Students talked, read, wrote, drew and reflected with a critical ear toward diverse perspectives.

*Fifth grade.*   The fifth grade inclusive classroom studied the Caribbean through music, drama, and literature. The children read *The Cay* (2002) as historical fiction in the World War II era. They read *Coconut Kind of Day (1990), How Many Days to America? (1994), The Golden Flower (1998), Caribbean Dream (2002), Island in the Sun (2001),* and many others. They learned the geography, and flora and fauna of the region while plotting as many islands as possible. During class activities, various forms of Caribbean music could be heard along with videos showing the geography of the islands. They perused atlases in pairs to learn about scale of miles and complete related activities regarding their hemisphere. They created salt maps and were ready to ask many questions when two musicians from the Caribbean (Jamaica and Montseratt) arrived to perform for their class.

Many of the children had relatives and friends from the Caribbean who lived in their neighborhoods. Several students mentioned that they had family in Harlem. Of course, *Harlem (1997)* by Walter Dean Myers became a favorite picture book. This led to student interviews of family members shared in class for more authentic connections. The third grade teachers learned that contacting community and families gave depth to the curriculum and enlivened their classroom.

## Changes in Lesson Plans

Lesson plans designed and implemented during the two school years, 2002/2003 and 2003/2004, were collected from all participants and evaluated according to criteria based on the seven characteristics of culturally relevant lesson plans (Izzo & Schmidt, 2005). The seven characteristics, described earlier in the chapter are: high expectations, positive relationships with families and community, cultural sensitivity, active teaching methods, teacher as facilitator, student control over portions of the lesson, and instruction around groups and pairs (Izzo & Schmidt, 2003; Schmidt & Izzo, 2004). These criteria were rated on a scale of 0-3 and a total score was calculated for each lesson plan. Lesson plans were rated by the researchers separately and minor discrepancies were discussed and reconciled. There were no significant discrepancies.

We found that individual lesson plan scores varied over both years, but the average scores were higher in the second year. This growth indicates that in the second year teachers were writing lesson plans that reflected the seven characteristics of culturally relevant pedagogy more closely than they did in the first year. We wanted to learn more about the variations that occurred, particularly, which characteristics were evident and which were lacking. So, in addition to calculating the total scores, we looked at all lesson plans for each specific grade level and found the average score for each characteristic, one year at a time. Then we compared scores from the first year to scores from the second year, noting differences.

The lesson plans developed for kindergarten showed substantial gains in the scores for all characteristics. As you look at Figure 8.1, notice that all of the second year scores are well above the first year scores. The greatest increase was found in teacher as facilitator and student control over portions of the lesson. These findings suggest that the teachers began to move toward student-centered learning experiences, releasing some of

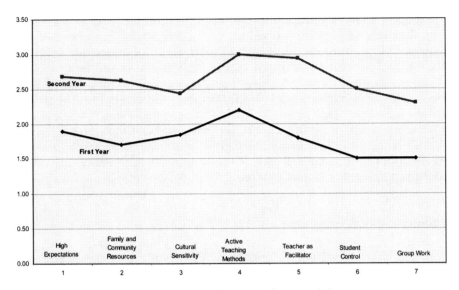

Figure 8.1.   Grade K: Average scores for seven characteristics.

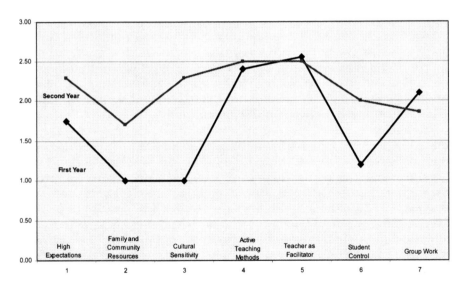

Figure 8.2.   Grade 3: Average score for seven characteristics.

the control they had previously maintained. This type of shift requires increased self-confidence in their own abilities as teachers and trust in students' abilities to be active participants in learning.

In grade three, we noted that in the first year, active teaching methods and teacher as facilitator were already firmly established and the most substantial gains were made in the following three areas: cultural sensitivity, student control over portions of the lesson, and use of community resources. These findings suggest that the teachers were sensitive to the importance of encouraging active engagement in a curriculum-based approach. The gains in cultural sensitivity and use community resources indicate their increased knowledge and skills in making the content relevant to the culture and use of community of the students. The gains also reflected the same growth we detected in the kindergarten teachers regarding the release of control over some portions of the lessons. (See Figure 8.2.)

In grade five, lesson plans demonstrated strong use of community resources and teacher as facilitator in the first year with substantial growth in student control over some portions of the lesson, cultural sensitivity, and group work in the second year. These findings suggest that the use of community resources was enhanced when the curriculum was reshaped and mediated for culturally valued knowledge. Further, activities requiring group work may have served as a bridge between teacher as a facilitator and releasing some control over the learning experience. (See Figure 8.3.)

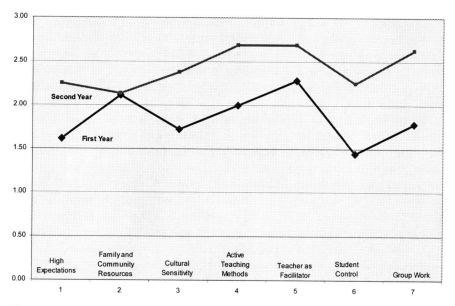

Figure 8.3.    Grade 5: Average score for seven characteristics.

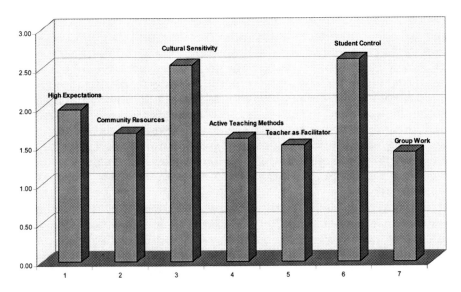

Figure 8.4.   Overall growth.

In order to determine overall growth for the group of teachers, we averaged the gains for each characteristic and found that as a group the teachers wrote lesson plans that demonstrated an increase in scores for all seven characteristics. The results of the lesson plan analyses were supported by the analyses of videotaped lessons, indicating that the lesson plans designed and implemented with culturally relevant pedagogy as a priority. The most substantial growth overall was found in student control over portions of the lesson, cultural sensitivity, and high expectations. (See Figure 8.4.)

These findings were particularly enlightening. The increase in cultural sensitivity was expected because the foundation and focus of the in-service were the *ABC's of Cultural Understanding and Communication.* The increase in student control over portions of the lesson and high expectations suggests that understanding who students are as individuals and members of a community illuminates their strengths. When teachers begin to plan learning experiences based on this understanding, their confidence in students' abilities to learn and to manage learning experiences increases exponentially (Izzo & Schmidt, 2005). They come to realize that, ultimately, they are teaching the students rather than just teaching the curriculum and the benefits of this approach is far-reaching. Their self-efficacy related to teaching increased, thus empowering them to take more academic risks and encourage their students to do the same.

## EVALUATION OF THE IN-SERVICE:
## COLLABORATION AND EMPOWERMENT

The teachers collaborated in and out of support meetings to create many more culturally relevant literacy lessons across the curriculum. They systematically and easily wrote lessons, sharing across grade levels and content areas making use of the community assistant's and librarian's expertise (Izzo & Schmidt, 2003). The teachers repeatedly expressed gratitude for the opportunities to plan and share together. They often stated, "We've bonded." "We've learned so much from each other." "We have so many great ideas, but now we have the time to share them."

The teachers went from creating individual lessons during the first year to thematic units the second year, and they attempted to integrate reading writing, listening, speaking, and viewing in all content areas. The students used learning logs, read many more pieces of fiction, nonfiction, and picture books, wrote/drew, and talked more than ever before. The classrooms were more active, physically and verbally, but students were on task. Many more culturally relevant picture books were read to students at all grade levels, since many served to motivate the students at the beginning of lessons. All genre of literature were available at learning centers for research and independent study. Teachers did not rely only on teachers' manuals. They asked help from each other and talked to each other about ideas. Every new unit or lesson began with,

> Who can we call to come into the classroom? We have to make sure they are getting reading, writing, listening, speaking, and viewing. Do you think our students can see some connection to themselves in this lesson?

Last but not least, there seemed to be much less fear or hesitation about contacting families. They were beginning to see family members as people who can contribute to the classroom, not people you call when there is trouble with learning. They saw families as resources for understanding and assisting the children to become academically successful.

Furthermore, teachers bonded and were empowered to share their work with pre-service teachers during student teaching, and during the in-service workshops. Teachers invited their student teachers to the workshops and encouraged them to bring ideas and materials. Education students, who were observing in their classrooms, were also invited. Pre-service teachers actively shared in the design of lessons as well as contributing materials and resources. All of the pre-service teachers expressed the desire to attend IRA 2004, but unfortunately, funding was not available.

In preparation for the two and one-half hour workshop for IRA, the teachers planned to the minute. They decided order of presentation and suggested ways that seemed effective. We discussed that visuals would be essential. So the teachers outlined their presentations, designed posters of their children's work, prepared photos of significant lessons, and typed handouts of lessons, materials, and resources. Last on the agenda, they selected literature to take with them for modeled portions of lessons. Their workshop at IRA proved worthwhile and interesting. The audience of 60 stayed almost the entire time, giving the group confidence to submit another proposal for 2005. Notice of acceptance was received in September 2004. For this presentation, the group studied the evolution of their culturally relevant lessons for the last three years.

## Videotape

Additionally, the teachers asked that a video of their latest classroom lessons be created. I was assigned the task, and with volunteer film editors from *Time Warner,* a 7 minute video was created from the classroom lessons. While observing the videotaped lessons, and reading field notes from participant observations, student responses in all of these classrooms were notable. Students could be seen participating in a variety of reading writing, listening, speaking, and viewing activities related to personal experiences. They met adults from their community, talented people, with new information, and interesting stories to share. Some of the adults were actually friends and/or family. During these lessons, according to teacher surveys and interviews, classroom management issues lost their significance with more time on task and differentiated instruction. Students had many more questions and comments, because they were actively learning to inquire and respond. Students practiced reading, writing, listening speaking, and viewing in ways that were thematic and connected, as well as, interesting and relevant.

Finally, preliminary analyses of district pre and post tests demonstrated that students in these three classes out performed similar classes in the same school. The kindergarten children in this study, not only out performed the two other classes in the school, but also out performed a suburban district's kindergarten classes on phonemic awareness, sight words, initial consonant sounds, and writing stories with temporary spelling. The third grade inclusive classroom children in this study performed as well as one of the self-contained third grades and out performed the other self-contained classroom. Students in the fifth grade, inclusive classroom outperformed students in one of the self-contained classes and were slightly below the other self-contained class on the district reading and writing tests. The teachers claimed that these results were significant and were a testament to all of their in-service work.

## DISCUSSION

The support meetings following the in-service seemed to make a difference. A few weeks after they ended, teachers were interviewed and asked to define culturally relevant pedagogy. All responses were positive, but one teacher seemed to articulate the definition with particular clarity,

> It's nice to have a Multicultural Day, but that isn't culturally relevant pedagogy. It is about a lot, but mainly about the kids we teach. It's about their families and communities and how we ask them to share their lives to educate the children. It's about getting to know them and letting them get to know me so we can respect each other for the good of the children.{\ex}

As the teachers were interviewed, we formulated a group definition to guide us as we prepared for the future.

### Defining Culturally Relevant Pedagogy

- Teaching to and valuing the children's home and community experiences.
- Participation in the ABC's of Cultural Understanding and Communication helps you get started.
- Teachers talk frequently with family members in positive ways and reach out for family participation.
- Teachers share portions of their personal lives with families and share working relationships with families.
- Teachers learn about community resources.
- Shares information for the child's education on a neutral or equal playing field to develop trust and gets family members involved as partners in their children's education.
- Encourages family involvement in the creation and implementation of in-service programs.
- Creates lessons that include reading, writing, listening, speaking, and viewing and connect home, school, and community.
- Everybody benefits when there is culturally relevant pedagogy: children, families, teachers, and community.

With this depth of understanding, our hope is that these teachers will continue their good work.

Due to the collaborative support, teachers in the second year automatically began drawing upon home and community and making connections to the mainstream curriculum, developing patterns of behavior for creating lessons, and creating working relationships with families (Izzo & Schmidt, 2003). Family members were now systematically called upon to support learning in and out of the classrooms.

However, there are many limitations in this study. The teachers were volunteers who were willing to learn new ideas. They were given 3 hours of school district in-service credit for their 30 hours of participation, they were paid for the time spent in support meetings by a New York State mini-grant, and they were recognized by the IRA with acceptance to present a workshop at the 2004 Convention. These factors all played a part in the successful implementation of culturally relevant pedagogy. So the questions, now, are:

- Is the literacy improvement in all the classes only temporary?
- Will these teachers make a significant difference in their children's literacy performance every year?
- Was the in-service realistic?
- Was the support during the year after, realistic?
- Is in-service around culturally relevant pedagogy too expensive?
- Will the teachers continue to collaborate?

Time will tell us if this in-service has lasting benefits. Similar studies are being conducted in the same urban school district in other elementary schools with small groups of teachers. Furthermore, longitudinal studies need to be instituted to answer questions about the lasting effects of this in-service work.

Unfortunately, over the years, teachers across our nation have experienced day long or week-long workshops with no support to follow (Fullan, 1999). These expensive workshops only fulfill state mandates; their significance is rarely measured. Therefore, it is our belief that the time has come to give culturally relevant pedagogy a real chance to make a difference. And that chance should be supported with intense in-service and intense support and assessment to follow. It is time to realize that support is necessary if teachers are expected to implement and adapt their in-service learning.

In Conclusion, we believe that no matter what the educational program or reading program, culturally relevant pedagogy has the potential for closing the academic gap. This small study brings us information that begs to be explored. Culturally relevant pedagogy isn't easy to accomplish, because it requires attitude changes about race, ethnicity, culture, language, and poverty. Since most present and future teachers are of European American origins, and the curriculum they teach represents their cultural perspectives, they have the extraordinary challenge of recognizing their own ethnocentrisms (Sleeter, 2001; Spindler & Spindler, 1987). When this is accomplished, they can begin to understand and develop an appreciation for differences as well as an ability to connect curriculum to community and family funds of knowledge (Moll, 1992).

## ACKNOWLEDGMENT

Funding for this project came from the U.S. Department of Education awarded to Syracuse University's New York State Higher Education Support Center for Systems Change Grant #H027 A020 1 04, CFDA #R40n to the New York State Education Department.

## REFERENCES

Au, K. (1993). *Literacy instruction in multicultural settings*. New York: Harcourt, Brace Javanovich College Publishers.

Banks, 1. (1994). *An introduction to multicultural education*. Boston: Allyn & Bacon.

Banks, J., & Banks, C.A. (1995). *Handbook of research on multicultural education*. New York: Macmillan.

Bloome, D., & Green, J. (1982). The social contexts of reading: A multidisciplinary perspective. In B. A. Hutson (Ed.), *Advances in reading language research* (Vol. 1, pp. 309-338). Greenwich, CT: JAI Press.

Boykin, A,W. (1984). Reading achievement and the social-cultural frame of reference of Afro-American children. *Journal of Negro Education 53*(4), 464-473.

Boykin, A,W. (1978). Psychologicallbehavioral verve in academic/task performance: Pre-theoretical considerations. *Journal of Negro Education, 47*(4), 343-354.

Britzman, D. (1986). Cultural myths in the making of a teacher: Biography and social structure in teacher education. *Harvard Educational Review, 56*, 442-456.

Cochran-Smith, M. (1995). Uncertain allies: Understanding the boundaries of race and teaching. *Harvard Educational Review, 65*(4), 541-570.

Cummins, J. (1986). Empowering minority students: A framework for intervention. *Harvard Educational Review, 56*(1), 18-36.

Delpit, L.(1995). *Other people's children*. New York: The New Press.

Dyson, A.H. (1989). *Multiple worlds of child writers: Friends learning to write*. New York: Teachers College Press.

Edwards, P.A., Pleasants, H., & Franklin, S. (1999). *A path to follow: Learning to listen to parents*. Portsmouth, NH: Heinemann.

Edwards, P.A., Dandridge, J., McMillon, G.T., & Pleasants, H.M. (2001). Taking ownership of literacy: Who has the power? In P.R. Schmidt & P.B. Mosenthal (Eds.), *Reconceptualizing literacy in the new age of multiculturalism and pluralism* (pp. 111-134). Greenwich, CT: Information Age Press.

Edwards, P. (2004). *Children's literacy development: Making it happen through school, family, and community involvement.* Boston: Allyn & Bacon.

Faltis, C.J. (1993; 2000). *Joinfostering: Adapting teaching strategies for the multilingual classroom.* New York: Maxwell Macmillan International.

Finkbeiner, C., & Koplin, C. (2002). A cooperative approach for facilitating intercultural education. *Reading Online, 6*(3). Newark, DE: International Reading Association.

Florio-Ruane, S. (1994). The future teachers' autobiography club: Preparing educators to support learning in culturally diverse classrooms. *English Education, 26*(1), 52-56.

Fullan, M. (1999). *Change forces: The sequel.* Philadelphia: Falmer.

Fullan, M. (2004). *Leading in a culture of change: Personal action guide and workbook.* New York: Corwin Press.

Goldenberg, C.N. (1987). Low-income Hispanic parents' contributions to their first grade children's word-recognition skills. *Anthropology and Education Quarterly, 18*, 149-179.

Goodlad, J. (1998). *Educational Renewal: Better teachers, better schools.* New York: Jossey-Bass.

Gordon, B. (1988). Implicit assumptions of the Holmes and Carnegie Reports: A view from an African American perspective. *Journal of Negro Education, 57*(2), 141-158.

Green, J., Kantor, R., & Rogers, T. (1990). Exploring the complexity of language and learning in the classroom. In B. Jones & L. Idol (Eds.), *Educational values and cognitive instruction: Implications for reform* (Vol. 3, pp. 333-364). Hillsdale, NJ: Erlbaum.

Guba, E., & Lincoln, Y.S. (1989). *Fourth generation evaluation.* Newbury Park, CA: Sage.

Heath, S.B. (1983). *Ways with words: Language life and work in communities and classrooms.* Cambridge: Cambridge University Press.

Howard, T. (2001). Telling their side of the story: African American students' perceptions of culturally relevant teaching. *The Urban Review, 33*(2), 131-149.

Izzo, A., & Schmidt, P.R. (2003, December). *Collaboration at work: Teachers engage in a multifaceted project to increase literacy learning.* Paper presented at the 53rd National Reading Conference. Scottsdale, AZ.

Izzo, A., & Schmidt, P.R. (2005, May). *Creating culturally relevant literacy lessons: A developmental approach.* Paper presented at the International Reading Association 50th Annual Convention, San Antonio, TX.

Kantor, R., Miller, S., & Fernie, D.(1992). Diverse paths to literacy in a preschool classroom: A sociocultural perspective. *Reading Research Quarterly, 27*(3), 185-201.

Ladson-Billings, G. (1994). *The dreamkeepers: Successful teachers of African American children.* San Francisco: Jossey-Bass.

Lalik, R., & Hinchman, K. (2001). Critical issues: Examining constructions of race in literacy research: Beyond silence and other oppressions of white liberalism. *Journal of Literacy Research, 33*(3),529-561.

Lee, C. (1991). Big picture talkers/words walking without masters: The instructional implications of ethnic voices for an expanded literacy. *Journal of Negro Education, 60*(3), 291-304.

Leftwich, S. (2002). Learning to use diverse children's literature in the classroom: A model for preservice teacher education. *Reading Online, 6*(2). www.readingonline.org: International Reading Association.

Levine, D.D. (1994). Instructional approaches and interventions that can improve the Academic performance of African American students. *Journal of Negro Education, 63*(1),46-63.

Lincoln, Y.S., & Guba, E. (1985). *Naturalistic inquiry.* Beverly Hills, CA: Sage.

McCaleb, S.P. (1994). *Building communities of learners.* New York: St. Martin's Press.

Merriam, S.B. (1998). *Qualitative research and case study applications in education.* San Francisco: Jossey-Bass.

Moll, L.C. (1992). Bilingual classroom studies and community analysis: Recent trends. *Educational Researcher, 21*(2), 20-24.

Murrell, P.C. Jr. (1994). In search of responsive teaching for African American Males: An investigation of students' experiences of middle school mathematics curriculum. *Journal of Negro Education, 63*(4),556-569.

Nagel, G. (2002). Building cultural understanding and communication: A model in seven situations. *Reading Online, 6*(4). www.readingonline.org: International Reading Association.

Nieto, S.(1999). *The light in their eyes.* New York: Teachers College Press.

Noordhoff, K., & Kleinfield, J. (1993). Preparing teachers for multicultural classrooms. *Teaching and Teacher Education, 9*(1),27-39.

Osborne, A.B. (1996). Practice into theory into practice: Culturally relevant pedagogy for students we have marginalized and normalized. *Anthropology and Education Quarterly, 27*(3), 285-314.

Pang, V.O., & Cheng, L.L. (Eds.). (1998). *Struggling to be heard: The unmet needs of Asian Pacific American children.* Albany: SUNY Press.

Purcell-Gates, V., L'Allier, S., & Smith, D. (1995). Literacy at the Harts' and the Larsons': Diversity among poor inner-city families. *The Reading Teacher, 48*(7), 572-578.

Rogoff, B. (1990). *Apprenticeship in thinking.* New York: Oxford Press.

Reyhner, J., & Garcia, R. L. (1989). Helping minorities read better: Problems and promises. *Reading Research and Instruction, 28*(3), 84-91.

Schiefflin, B., & Cochran-Smith, M. (1984). Learning to read culturally: Literacy before schooling. In H. Goelman, A.Oberg, & F.Smith (Eds.), *Awakening to literacy* (pp. 3-23). Portsmouth, NH: Heinemann.

Schmidt, P.R. (1998a/2002). *Cultural conflict and struggle: Literacy learning in a kindergarten program.* New York: Peter Lang

Schmidt, P.R. (1998b). The ABC's Model: Teachers connect home and school. In T. Shanahan & F.V. Rodriguez-Brown (Eds.), *National reading conference yearbook* (Vol. 4, pp. 194-208.) Chicago: National Reading Conference.

Schmidt, P.R. (1999). Know thyself and understand others. *Language Arts, 76*(4), 332-340.

Schmidt, P.R. (2000). Emphasizing differences to build cultural understandings. In V. Risko & K. Bromley (Eds.), *Collaboration for diverse learners: Viewpoints and practices.* Newark, DE: IRA.

Schmidt, P.R. (2001). The power to empower. In P.R. Schmidt & P.B. Mosenthal (Eds.), *Reconceptualizing literacy in the new age of multiculturalism and pluralism.* Greenwich,CT: Information Age Press.

Schmidt, P.R. (2005). *Preparing educators to communicate and connect with families and communities.* Greenwich, CT: Information Age Publishing.

Schmidt, P.R., & Izzo, A. (2004, May). *Creating culturally relevant literacy lessons with k-5 urban teachers.* Workshop presented at the International Reading Association 49th Annual Convention, Reno-Tahoe, Nevada.

Schon, D. (1983). *The reflective practitioner.* New York: Basic Books.

Sleeter, C.E. (2001). Preparing teachers for culturally diverse schools. *Journal of Teacher Education, 52*(2),94-106.

Spindler, G., & Spindler, L. (1987). *The interpretive ethnography of education: At home and abroad.* Hillsdale, NJ: Lawrence Erlbaum Associates.

Strauss, A.L.(1987). *Qualitative analysis for social scientists.* New York: Cambridge University Press.

Tatum, A. (2000). Breaking down barriers that disenfranchise African American adolescent readers in low-level tracks. In P. Mason & J.S. Schumm (Eds.), *Promising practices for urban reading instruction* (pp. 98-118). Newark, DE: International Reading Association.

Tatum, B. (1992). Talking about race, learning about racism: The application of racial identity theory in the classroom. *Harvard Educational Review, 62*(1), 1-24.

Taylor, D. (1983). *Family literacy: Young children learning to read and write.* Exeter, NH: Heinemann.

Taylor, D., & Dorsey-Gaines, (1988). *Growing up literate.* Portsmouth, NH: Heinemann.

Trueba, H.T., Jacobs, L., & Kirton, E. (1990). *Cultural conflict and adaptation: The case of the Hmong children in American society.* New York: The Falmer Press.

Vygotsky, L.S. (1978). *Mind in society: The development of higher mental process.* Cambridge, MA: Harvard University Press.

Walker-Dalhouse, D., & Dalhouse, A.D. (2001). Parent-school relations: Communicating more effectively with African American parents. *Young Children,* 75-80.

Wasser, J.D., & Bresler, L. (1996). Working in the interpretive zone: Conceptualizing collaboration in qualitative research teams. *Educational Researcher, 25*(5),5-15.

Watson, N., & Fullan, M.G. (1992). Beyond school district-university partnerships. In M. Fullan & A. Hargreaves (Eds.) *Teacher development & educational change.* London: Falmer Press.

Wells, G. (1986). *The meaning makers: Children learning language and using language to learn.* Portsmouth, NH: Heinemann.

Willis, A.I., & Meacham, SJ. (1997). Break point: The challenges of teaching multicultural education courses. *JAEPL, 2,* 40-49.

Xu, H. (2000). Preservice teachers in a literacy methods course consider issues of diversity. *Journal of Literacy Research, 32*(4), 505-531.

## YOUTH LITERATURE CITED

Anderson, H. (1996). *Ndito runs.* New York: Henry Holt & Company.

Belafonte, H., & L. Burgess. (2001). *Island in the sun.* New York: Penguin Press.

Bunting, E. (1994). *How many days to America?* New York: Clarion

Climo, S. (1989). *Egyptian cinderella,* New York: Thomas Crowell.

Climo, S. (1993)., *The Korean cinderella* New York: Thomas Crowell.

Climo, S. (1996). *The Irish cinderlad.* New York: Harpercollins.

Climo, S. (1999). *The Persian cinderella.* New York: Harpercollins.

Coburn, J. (1998). *Angkat: The Cambodian cinderella.* Arcadia,CA: Shen's Books.

Coerr, E. (1993). *Sadako and the thousand paper cranes.* New York: GP Putnam's Sons.

Feelings, T. & M. (1981). *Jamb means hello: Swahili Alphabet book.* New York: Puffin Books.

Isadora, R. (2002). *Caribbean dream.* New York: Scholastic Books, Inc.

Jaffe, N.(1998). *The golden flower.* New York: McGraw Hill.

Joseph, L. (1990). *Coconut kind of day.* New York: HarperCollins.

Maruki, T. (1980). *Hiroshima, No Pika.* New York: Lothrop, Lee & Shepard Books.

Myers, W.D. (1997). *Harlem.* New York: Scholastic Books.

Say, A. (1993). *Grandfather's journey.* New York: Houghton Mifflin.

Steptoe, J. (1987). *Mufaro's beautiful daughters: An African tale.* New York: Scholastic.

Taylor. T. (2002). *The cay.* New York: Yearling.

CHAPTER 9

# THE ABC'S ONLINE

## Using Voice Chats in a Transnational Foreign Language Teacher Exchange

### Eva Wilden

**ABSTRACT**

The ABC's model of cultural understanding and communication (Schmidt, 1998a) has been successfully implemented in various face-to-face educational settings (Finkbeiner & Koplin, 2001, 2002), but little research exists on whether the model can be effectively implemented in online learning and teaching environments, as well. This chapter reports on an ABC's Online project in which the model was implemented in a transnational online exchange between European foreign language teachers. The paper addresses the following issues: The first part sets out to discuss the significance of intercultural competence as educational goal in Europe today. Secondly, the implementation of the ABC's model in a transnational online exchange between foreign language teachers from Germany and Great Britain will be illustrated. Finally, using tentative results of a qualitative content analysis, this study outlines how the teachers benefitted from the

*ABC's of Cultural Understanding and Communication:*
*National and International Adaptations,* 189–211
189

ABC's Online exchange with regard to their personal and professional development.

## INTRODUCTION

The *ABC's of Cultural Understanding and Communication* (Schmidt, 1998b,c, 1999, 2001) has been successfully implemented in various classrooms around the world (cf. Finkbeiner & Koplin, 2001, 2002; Leftwich, 2002; Xu, 2000a,b, 2001). So far, it has been used almost exclusively in face-to-face educational settings from kindergarten to university levels, thereby requiring both ABC's partners to be physically present. Recently, attempts have been made in the field of foreign language learning and teaching to also use the model across distance by means of using synchronous and asynchronous online communication tools (Knierim, Wade & Wilden, 2004; Masterson, in progress). Other intercultural online projects (Furstenberg et al., 2001; O'Dowd, 2003) have shown that language learners can benefit from such a project with regard to their linguistic and intercultural competence. However, experience with the ABC's Online is still rather limited.

This chapter reports on a project in which the ABC's Model was implemented in a transnational online exchange between foreign language teachers from Germany and Great Britain. The goals of the project were to promote the teachers' professional and personal development with regard to their intercultural competence, to familiarize them with the ABC's Model as a successful method they could use in their own teaching and to further develop their computer literacy. The exchange between the participants in Germany and Great Britain was carried out exclusively online by using both synchronous and asynchronous online communication tools, such as voice chats, text chats, and online forums.

The chapter addresses the following issues: The first part sets out to discuss why intercultural competence is such a significant educational goal in Europe today. Furthermore, the benefits of learning and teaching foreign languages in reaching this goal will be discussed as well as the teachers' role in this context. The second part explains how the ABC's Model was implemented in the transnational online exchange between foreign language teachers in Germany and Great Britain. Finally, in the third part some examples will be presented of how the teachers benefited from the exchange with regard to their personal and professional development.

### Learning and Teaching in Europe Today

In classrooms around the world, we are witnessing an increasing linguistic and cultural diversity. At the moment, this phenomenon is especially noticeable in Europe following the growth of the European Union and the increasing mobility of people (Finkbeiner, 1995; Finkbeiner & Koplin, 2001, 2002; see also the survey article by Finkbeiner, in this volume). The effects of this social development are apparent in our classrooms, as well. The multicultural and heterogeneous population of schools in the German federal state of Hesse are illustrative: According to statistics of the academic year 2002/2003, by the Hessian Ministry of Education, 17% of all pupils at Hessian schools had an international background (Hessisches Kultusministerium, 2003, p. 87).[1] In conurbations such as Frankfurt/Main, as much as 39% of all pupils had an international background. In addition to this, the group of international pupils at Hessian schools is in itself very diverse since the pupils originate from various countries. On the one hand, it is imperative to integrate these international pupils in order to empower them to actively take part and contribute to the society. On the other hand, this heterogeneous and multicultural situation in an increasing number of German schools offers the chance to provide *all* pupils with opportunities to develop their intercultural competence.

Other factors that increase the contact across cultures and languages are the advancement of infrastructure and transportation as well as the development and ubiquity (at least in industrialized countries) of information and communication technologies. Especially, the latter greatly facilitate instant communication with people around the globe and allow for constant access to otherwise remote information. As a result of the developments depicted above, a growing number of people encounter cultural diversity and need to develop strategies and competencies to successfully cope with multicultural situations.

## Intercultural Learning and Foreign Languages

Fostering intercultural competence is one of the key goals of modern foreign language teaching today and is even considered a general educational goal (cf. Bach, 1998; Baron, 2002; Bundeszentrale für politische Bildung, 1998; Finkbeiner, 1995; Finkbeiner & Koplin, 2001, 2002; Gogolin, 2003; Kramsch, 1995). For example, let us take a look at the curricula relevant for the teacher participants in this project. In the case of Germany, the Standing Conference of the Ministers of Education and Cultural Affairs of the Länder (Kultusministerkonferenz, 1996) issued a recommendation proclaiming intercultural competence as a key competence that should be developed in every child and young adult in Germany. In the German federal state of Hesse, the curriculum for teaching English as a foreign language in secondary schools (*Gymnasium*) claims that by learning a foreign language, students acquire insights into the target culture as well as their own culture. It says that "assumptions, values and norms which were formerly taken for granted are now being challenged and prove to be socially and culturally determined" (Hessisches Kultusministerium, 2002, p. 2; orig. in German, translation by author). Similarly, the English National Curriculum for modern foreign languages promotes cultural development across the curriculum "through providing pupils with insights into cultural differences and opportunities to relate these to their own experience and to consider different cultural and linguistic traditions, attitudes and behaviors." (Department for Education and Employment, 1999, p. 8). Furthermore, it makes suggestions on how to implement cultural development in the foreign language classroom. These examples illustrate the potential of learning and teaching foreign languages to foster intercultural competence: Ideally, both learners and teachers of the foreign language, not only master the structural aspects of the target language, but at the same time, gain insights into the target culture. Moreover, by learning about, experiencing, and possibly understanding the foreign culture they might also see their own culture in a different light. This means that they might change their perspective on the foreign and at the same time on their own culture and in doing so reach a third perspective or, as Kramsch (1993) called it, the third domain.

> The only way to start building a more complete and less partial understanding of both C1 [one's own culture] and C2 [foreign or target culture] is to develop a third perspective, that would enable learners to take both an insider's and outsider's view on C1 and C2. (Kramsch, 1993, p. 210)

In a later publication, Kramsch (2004) refers to language learners and teachers as "go-betweens," a term usually used for mediators.

> [...] in a more general sense, one could say that learning a foreign language is a mediating endeavor between two or more languages and cultures because it requires interpreting, translating, explaining, and negotiating the meaning of statements and points of view that sometimes conflict with one's own. (Kramsch, 2004, p. 107)

Similarly, Bredella (1995) points out that understanding the *Other* (people from the foreign or target culture) is only possible in a reciprocal interplay between the native and foreign culture in the process by which one would reach the third domain. Fischer (1994) suggests that the main responsibility of teachers is

> to help build bridges for their students, bridges whose footings are set in both culture and language. [...] Students from both cultures can meet on the bridge and view both the target culture and their own native culture

from a different perspective. (Fischer, 1994, p. 75; cited in Bach, 1998, p. 196)

Thus, learning and teaching foreign languages is a way of fostering and supporting the development of those skills and attitudes needed in intercultural encounters.

### Intercultural Learning and the Role of Foreign Language Teachers

Teachers need to have the experience of going through learning processes in order to be able to facilitate their pupils' learning processes. Good teachers are always learners themselves (Finkbeiner, 2004; Krumm, 2003). The same applies to intercultural learning processes in the sense that teachers have to undergo intercultural learning processes themselves to be able to initiate and foster intercultural learning processes in their pupils. Legutke (2000) claims that only those teachers who cross borders themselves can help others to do the same and to understand the *Other*. Therefore, Finkbeiner (2004) proposes the LMR plus model for teacher education in which the "plus" refers to intercultural learning and computer literacy.

In this context, the professional development of teachers refers to the development of their personality, the extension of their experiences and the ability to reflect on their own teaching (Krumm, 2003, p. 354). In contrast to this, foreign language research in the 1960s and 1970s, was mainly concerned with developing new teaching methods, and since the 1980s research, has focused on the learners and their language acquisition processes (Krumm, 2003). In such research, teachers are taken into consideration as external factors, but they are not at the center of attention. Therefore, this project focuses on the experiences teachers make in an intercultural exchange and how these might promote their personal and professional development. Furthermore, the project looks at teacher tandems in order to gain new insights into the reciprocal perception of cultures and their representatives among foreign language teachers. According to Bredella (1995), Kramsch (1993, 1995) and others, the reciprocal perception of the *Self* and the *Other* bears crucial importance in intercultural discourses (see above).

### Doing the ABC's Online: Adapting the ABC's Model to the Demands of Online Communication

In the ABC's Online exchange the adaptation of Schmidt's ABC's Model (1998a, b, 1999, 2001) by Finkbeiner and Koplin (2001, 2002) was further adapted to meet the particular demands of online communication. However, the basic elements of the ABC's Model remained the same (Schmidt, 1998a). The following changes were made (cf. Knierim et al., 2004):

1.  Before the actual start of the ABC's exchange, the participants completed an introductory phase to familiarize themselves with the online communication tools available in the project (see below). In addition, they got in touch with each other and introduced themselves without touching on the very personal topics of the ABC's right from the start. Because of the lack of face-to-face interaction, this phase is of crucial importance to any online project. It facilitates the development of confidence and a sense of community. Furthermore, it is advisable to thoroughly acquaint participants with the online communication tools to eliminate any inhibitions or insecurities which might arise in those who have no experience in using these kind of tools (Salmon, 2000, 2002).

2.  The autobiographies were composed using a word-processing software. They were then uploaded onto the exchange website in a protected non-public area or were e-mailed to the moderator. Just as in any other ABC's project, the autobiographies remained private and were not shared with anyone else apart from the moderator (Schmidt, 1998a).

3.  The reciprocal interviews with the ABC's partners (Finkbeiner & Koplin, 2002) were conducted using online communication tools, namely voice chats and online forums. On the basis of these network-based interviews the participants composed their biographies of the partner and exchanged those biographies again through the online forum. The partners then took part in another voice chat (or communicated in the online forum) to reciprocally validate their biographies.

4.  The comparisons were composed on the basis of the autobiography and biography and once again exchanged via the online forum, as was the feedback on the comparisons.

In comparison to the original face-to-face ABC's, the exchange in an online ABC's project generally requires more structuring by the moderator of such a project. According to Salmon (2000) and Stencel (2004) this applies especially to the early stages of an online project. This is because of the particular demands of online communication and collaboration which for most participants is still a novelty. In the course of time participants become increasingly independent from the moderator (cf. Salmon's model of teaching and learning online through computer-mediated conferencing; Salmon, 2000, 2002).

## Doing the ABC's Online: Schedule of a Transnational Online ABC's Exchange with Foreign Language Teachers

The schedule for the ABC's Online project was devised to match the following criteria: (1) To set out a practicable time-frame for teacher participants as well as the moderator of the exchange with regard to the limits of the academic year in both countries and the overall workload of everyone involved. (2) To allow for ample time and opportunities for participants to familiarize themselves with the online communication tools and to gradually increase their autonomy with respect to online communication and collaboration (cf. Salmon, 2000, 2002; Stencel, 2004). (3) To provide sufficient time and opportunities to foster an in-depth ABC's exchange with the partner.

In addition to these considerations, it is important to note that the schedule had to be adapted to the individual needs and workloads of each teacher tandem doing the exchange. In some cases, the schedule proved to be too tight and the teachers had to continue the exchange into the following month. Especially the two different schedules of the academic years in Great Britain and Germany caused a few delays. Furthermore, in some cases technical challenges with the voice chat and also other extra-curricular activities impeded the continuation of the exchange.

The overall duration of the exchange was ten weeks, from October to December 2004 (not including two extra weeks of vacation between weeks 2 and 3). Three weeks before the actual start of the project, in October, the exchange web site was available for registration: From that point on, participants were encouraged to chit-chat with everyone, browse through the available information and resources and in general to familiarize themselves with the online environment. They were asked to write their first message in the general forum (see below) in which they were to introduce themselves by sharing who they are, describing their schools, writing about their motivation to participate in the project, and sharing personal partialities, such as their favorite food or drink (Salmon, 2002). Then they were encouraged to respond to at least two introductions by other participants. Additionally, prior to the actual start of the exchange, there was a poll on which form of address[2] should be used when communicating in German (the participants agreed on the less formal address). Furthermore, participants were asked to start composing their autobiographies as early as possible. The moderator made short sample excerpts of autobiographies by teachers from earlier ABC's projects available on the exchange website (Schmidt, 1998a, p. 29) so as to provide the participants with a model. (See Table 9.1.)

**Table 9.1.**

| Week | Activity |
|------|----------|
| 1 & 2 | • teachers are matched with their ABC's partner and get in touch with their partners<br>• tasks in the partner forum (see below):<br>  1. post five telling words about yourself and respond to your partner's five words (cf. Salmon, 2002)<br>  2. share your earliest experience as a foreign language learner and tell each other about your first lesson as foreign language teacher<br>  3. ask your partner at least three questions about things you are interested in<br>• teachers finish the autobiographies<br>• teachers attend one of several introductory sessions in the voice chat (introduction to using the voice chat and discussion of any questions related to the exchange project) |
| 3 & 4 | • teachers conduct 1st voice chat interview (approximately one hour) with partner (proposed topics: The first time you met someone from England or Germany / Family: Who are the members of your family? Is your family important to you? / Friends: A true friend is someone who . . . Who is your most important friend? Why? / Your first lesson as a foreign language teacher).<br>• teachers conduct 2nd voice chat interview with partner (proposed topics: One of your earliest memories . . . / A difficult experience in your life . . . / Are you religious? What do you believe in? / Your most important teachers . . . / What do you look like?) |
| 5 | • teachers write biography about their partner and send it to their partner through the partner forum (again moderator provides short sample excerpts of biographies by teachers from earlier ABC's projects)<br>• in the partner forum: teachers give each other feedback on biographies |
| 6 | • teachers conduct 3rd voice chat interview with partner to validate biographies (moderator encourages to discuss biographies with respect to what the teachers liked, what they found surprising and to dissolve any possible misunderstandings) |
| 7 & 8 | • teachers do the comparisons by:<br>  1. charting a list of differences and similarities<br>  2. writing an analysis of their self-image and their image of the partner in which they relate and compare images (again moderator provides short sample excerpts of comparisons by teachers about someone else from earlier ABC's projects)<br>• teachers send their comparison to the partner in the partner forum |
| 9 & 10 | • teachers conduct an optional follow-up voice chat interview to discuss comparisons<br>• teachers plan further cooperation<br>• teachers wrap up exchange |

## Doing the ABC's Online: Participants

The participants in this project were foreign language teachers in Germany and Great Britain. There were thirteen participants, ten female and three male. The teachers from Germany were between the ages of 30 and 51 with an average age of 44.2 years. The teachers from Great Britain were between the ages of 22 and 29 with an average age of 24.6 years (two participants did not specify their age). The teaching experience of the teachers from Germany ranged from 0 to 27 years (one teacher had just finished teacher training) with an average experience of 15 years. The teaching experience of the teachers from Great Britain ranged from 0 till 1 year (most participants from Great Britain were doing their teacher training while taking part in the project).

All participants in the project were teachers of modern foreign languages. The teachers in Great Britain were all teachers of German as a foreign language (except for one who taught French) and most of them also taught one other modem foreign language (Russian or French). The teachers in Germany were all teachers of English as a foreign language and also taught at least one other subject such as maths, biology, German, arts or social sciences.

Since communication in the project was mainly done with online communication tools it is necessary to look at the participants' prior knowledge about and experience with computers. The picture is very diverse:[3] All participants in the project had their own personal computer (two did not have an internet connection at home), however, the experience of using computers ranged between 2 and 24 years with an average of 13.7 years. In a questionnaire at the beginning of the project the statement "I know a lot about computers" was rated as follows: Four teachers fully agreed with the statement, two teachers somewhat agreed, four somewhat disagreed and one fully disagreed. Except for one, they did not have any experience using voice chats prior to the ABC's Online project. Five of them had used text chats before the project and seven had experience using online forums.

## Doing the ABC's Online: Language Use

In this project the ABC's Model was used with foreign language teachers of German and English working together in bilingual tandems[4] (and one group of three teachers). Therefore, language use in general and the question of which language should be used was a big issue in the project. The foreign language teachers of German live in Great Britain and with one exception are native speakers of English (one teacher is a native speaker of French living in Great Britain). The foreign language teachers of English live in Germany and are all native speakers of German (one teacher grew up bilingually with English and German). Each tandem consisted of one native speaker of English (in one case a native speaker of French with a near-native competence in English) and one native speaker of German. In this way, all the teachers worked together with expert speakers of their foreign language, and at the same time, acted as expert speakers of their partner's foreign language (cf. Finkbeiner's LMR plus model; Finkbeiner, 2004).

In order to give everyone equal opportunities to practice and use their foreign language and gain control over bias that might have been created by power of language (Fehling, 2005), it was agreed to alternate between English and German as the language of communication on a weekly basis beginning with German in week 1.[5] At the beginning of each week, the moderator posted a message in the general forum announcing the language of communication in the forums and voice chats for that week. With regard to the ABC's texts, the moderator asked the participants to write their autobiographies in their native language and the biographies in the foreign language. They could choose for themselves in which language to write the comparison. The teachers were asked to compose the autobiography in their native language because of arguments proposed by Finkbeiner and Koplin (2002). They argue that "it can be difficult (and, for some, off-putting) to express life stories in a language different from the one in which the life stories themselves are situated" (2002, The language issue, para. 2); schemata and scripts differ between languages and cultures and are often difficult to translate into another language. In keeping with this, the biographies about the partner were written in the foreign language in order to express the life-story in the language in which they are situated in. Moreover, this procedure satisfied the participants' wish to practice their foreign language skills in the project. This wish was explicitly expressed by some participants in the questionnaire preceding the exchange and can also be seen in the fact that a few of them decided to do the comparison in their foreign language.

## Doing the ABC's Online: Using Voice Chat, Online Forums and Text Chat

The further adaptation of the ABC's Model to the needs of online communication has been illustrated above. By using various online communication tools the ABC's partners living in two different countries were enabled to bridge the geographical gap and were able to communicate both synchronously and asynchronously and collaborate across distance.

The main online communication tools used in the project were the exchange website[6] with online forums (based on the course management system *Moodle*[7]) and a voice chatting software (*CentraOne*; this kind of software is also referred to as audio-graphic conferencing: Hampel, 2003; Hampel & Hauck, 2004). In a voice chat, participants can speak with each other in real time across distance using a standard computer, an internet connection and a headset (earphones with a microphone). Furthermore, the voice chat software used in this project provided a presentation area with whiteboard which was used by the moderator to suggest possible topics for the reciprocal interviews (see Figure 9.1).

Additionally, a simple text chat software was occasionally used as a substitute for the voice chat due to technical challenges. In an online forum, participants asynchronously exchange written messages which are presented in various topical discussion threads. In this project, two kinds of online forums were used, both of which were accessible on the exchange website: (1) A general forum which was accessible to everyone in the project and which was used for communication among all participants, e.g., for general announcements or initial introduction to the project.

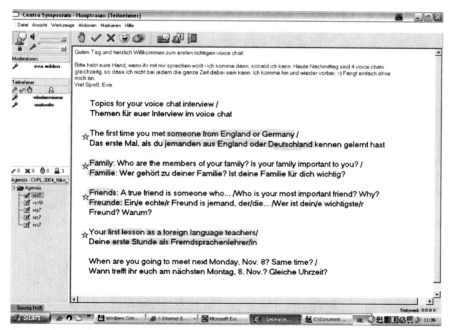

*Source:*   Screenshot courtesey of Centra Software, Inc.

Figure 9.1.   Voice chat.

(2) A private partner forum accessible only to the ABC's partners in which they communicated and collaborated in addition to the voice chat interviews. Every pair had their own private partner forum which was only accessible to them (and to the moderator) but not to other participants. In this way the privacy and confidentiality were guaranteed as integral parts of the ABC's Model (Schmidt, 1998a).

## Foreign Language Teachers Experiencing the ABC's Online: Some Examples

The results of the ABC's Online exchange between foreign language teachers in Germany and Great Britain will be discussed with these guiding questions:

- How did the teacher participants in this project define the term "culture?"
- How did the participants together with their partners in this project negotiate cultural schemata?
- How did the ABC's Online project help the teacher participants to change perspectives?
- What are the technological implications of doing the ABC's with online communication tools?

These questions will be discussed on the basis of the data collected throughout the ABC's Online project and in the interviews[8] after the project, i.e., voice chat[9] recordings, text chats, online forum entries, texts written by participants in the ABC's process (autobiography, biography and comparisons), and interview recordings. The voice chat and interview recordings were transcribed so that all data could be analyzed following the qualitative content analysis approach (Mayring, 2003). The results of the analysis will be discussed and exemplified with the help of excerpts from the voice chat transcriptions, interview transcriptions, and comparisons.

### How Did the Teacher Participants in This Project Define the Term "Culture?"

Since the curricula for teaching modern foreign languages require teachers to facilitate their pupils' intercultural learning processes (see above) and all the teachers in this project explicitly expressed their wish to do so, it is worthwhile to look at the teachers' notion of "culture." In other words, what do they understand by the term "culture" and how do they explain the phenomenon? The answers to this question are very revealing since they influence how the teachers will go about the business of raising intercultural awareness in their students. These are some of the explanations[10] given by two teachers in the project:

> Culture is a lot of different things which you can both see and experience, so the way people talk and what they say. I think it is a mixture of your personal values which you obviously get from your parents or your carers, they are kind of passed down. But then you also, your external environment. So, that would be, people do not really agree when I say this, but religion, I think, is a huge cultural difference.[...] It would be food, it would be language, experiences probably, I would say as well. I would say the experiences you have had. And what, your history.[...] And I do find that if somebody tried to explain culture, if somebody said to me "What is English culture?" then I would go "I do not know." Because the thing is quite difficult. I do not feel as if we actually have culture in the sense of, you know kind of, if you said "What do you see as culture in Britain?" I would say "Roast beef and Yorkshire pudding and fish and chips and drunken football hooligans." Which is not the only thing at all. But that is the, that is how I feel culture has gone, our culture has gone. Which is really sad because it is not the whole at all.[...] But is such a difficult, culture is such kind of abstract thing, isn't it? It is not just one thing. And the other thing is, the fact that we are such a multicultural society now. A bit like Germany. The Indian stuff is kind of coming and, you know, the Italians came as well and then we have got the Afro-Caribbean. Yeah, it is this kind of melting pot of different kinds of cultures that have all slightly changed everything.[...] (Teacher A from Great Britain)

> It is shared experience, shared history, sort of a way of living that is informed by history, or shared history or shared identity. It can also be education, sort of how people in that culture are educated, which develops the way that they identify themselves.[...] it depends, because culture can be the group in which you live but it can also be, you can say someone is, has culture or is cultured which means they are educated and well informed and they know things and that sort of thing, enlightened. There is sort of a difference I think in English.[...] So you can say you live in a culture and that could be a word that is used to describe a group of people with shared interest, shared history etc. But you can also say someone is cultured or has culture. So therefore they can be cultured and live in a culture. That means it is different things really, depending on the context. (Teacher C from Great Britain)

Both teachers, in their attempts to explain their understanding of culture, either implicitly or explicitly distinguish between what has been referred to as culture with a big "C" and culture with a little "c" (cf. Baron, 2002, p. 39). Culture with a big "C" refers to "high culture," e.g., the arts and literature, while culture with a little "c" refers to everyday culture (Teacher C: "someone is cultured or has culture" vs. "you live in a culture"). As Baron (2002) points out "those interested in intercultural learning will search for the answers to their questions" (p. 39) in culture with a little "c," as seems to be the case with both teachers A and C.

Another striking aspect of culture mentioned by teacher A is the distinction between things "which you can both see and experience." This notion corresponds to the Weaver's (1993) iceberg analogy of culture in which he distinguishes between external (visible, conscious) parts of culture "above water level" and internal (invisible, unconscious) elements of culture "below water level" (Weaver's analogy will be further discussed below). The fact that teacher A seems to be aware of this distinction can support her in her endeavor to foster intercultural learning in her pupils, for Weaver stresses that intercultural misunderstandings occur below water level, i.e., when invisible and potentially unconscious beliefs, values and thought patterns clash. It is necessary to prevent or solve such misunderstandings by effectively applying intercultural communication strategies (Finkbeiner & Koplin, 2002) and by trying to understand behavior, a statement or an event.

Also, both teachers A and C seem to see "culture" as a very complex, fuzzy and dynamic phenomenon. Both mention a number of elements which belong to their understanding of culture and find it difficult to specify what culture is (teacher A: "It is not just one thing."). Moreover, teacher C stresses the collective nature of culture by pointing out that it "could be a word that is used to describe a group of people with shared interest, shared history, etc." This understanding resembles Hofstede's (1997; cited in Baron, 2002, p. 39) notion of culture as collective programming of the mind that distinguishes one group of people from another.

### How Did the Participants Together with Their Partners in This Project Negotiate Cultural Schemata?

The following is an excerpt from one of the voice chat interviews between teachers A and B. In this passage, teacher A explains her family situation to her partner. She explains her blood relationship to her half-brother:

A:   Our mums are the same but (-)
A:   Our mum is the same but our dads are different.
A:   But he calls my dad, dad.
A:   And he calls his father his father, so his biological father he calls [name].

A:   And sees him very, very rarely now because he is a bit of a ( ... ) (laughs)

A:   If I can be so harsh.

A:   So, yeah, it is a bit of a strange family really because of the number of grannies I have had and grandparents and stuff.

A:   So not your average family.

B:   Oh, I would not say so.

B:   Isn't that what they call the patchwork family? (interruption)

B:   I do not know if you heard the last thing I said.

B:   Was that I think our kind of family is quite common.

B:   And it is (-)

B:   They have a word for it.

B:   It is called the patchwork family.

B:   And lots of my friends, I know they have children with different grandparents.

B:   It seems to be the trend.

B:   So I do not know your family that uncommon.

This passage demonstrates how according to Weaver's (1993) iceberg analogy, teachers A and B in their interaction touch upon both the visible and invisible parts of culture. A concludes her explanation with the comment that her family situation is "strange" and "not the average." In doing so she refers to the Western Euorpean schema of "family." In the interview, after the exchange, she explicitly explains this schema of a "normal" family:

> Two children, same parents. And this is, this is I am sure not the case now. I know it is not the case now. But in kind of the average kind of nuclear family, mum and dad, have been married since they were twenty, with two children. Dog, three-bedroom house.

In her remark, teacher A shows that she is aware of a possible difference between prototypical schema and reality. Her own situation demonstrates that today families often have a different structure compared to traditional societies. This awareness is also to be seen in the statement of her partner teacher B who offers the term "patchwork family" to denote the modern concept of "family." This concept says that a family can be a group of people with children living together, even if they do not agree with the traditional concept of "family" with mother, father, and children. In doing so, both teachers go to the "under water level" to explore a cultural concept and implicitly negotiate the value of family bonds.

A similar example is the following excerpt, which is again from one of the voice chat interviews between teachers A and B. In this passage, A and B talk about the different forms of address in their languages (first or family names, the personal "du" and the more formal "Sie" in German). A lives with a Danish partner and her partner's brother is a teacher in Denmark. A talks about an experience she had with regard to Danish schools where pupils call their teachers by their first names:

A:   That is just something that I find really strange, because it is just so, it is so different to here [in Great Britain] where you are always called Miss or Sir.

A:   And then, and then [first name; her partner's brother] is called [first name].

A:   And I am just going, "Wow that is a bit weird."

B:   Well, we do not have that in Germany.

B:   They call the teachers by their second name.

B:   But I still think it is more informal than in England.

B:   In England I think they believe more in hierarchy and it is more a formal system.

B:   I just think that is a culture thing, probably.

A:   That is interesting, because I would see the German system as being more hierarchical and more formal than the UK.

A:   So maybe schools are different to work environments, because [name of a large Germany-based company A used to work for] was very, very hierarchical, very male dominated and very, very, very formal.

In this example, A and B negotiate their perceptions of the level of formality in each others' countries, especially with regard to schools. Again they touch upon both the external and internal elements of culture according to Weaver: visible behavior on the one hand (people saying "du" and using first names) and invisible values, beliefs or thought patterns on the other (level of formality, hierarchy). It is interesting to note the discrepancy between their respective perception of each others countries where each has the impression that the level of formality is higher in the other country. In this instance, teacher A's perception of her own culture does not correspond to teacher B's perception of A's cultural background. And likewise, in this example teacher B's self-perception of her own culture does not fall in line with A's perception of B's cultural background. This phenomenon—the incongruity of the self-perception of one's culture and the perception of one's culture through representatives of another culture—has been extensively described by Kramsch (1993, pp. 207-210; see also Finkbeiner's model of autostereotypes and hetero-stereotypes; Finkbeiner, 2005, pp. 273-275). It demonstrates the necessity of negotiation of meaning and changing perspectives in intercultural communication in order to reach a common understanding.

### How Did the Abc's Online Project Help the Teacher Participants to Change Perspectives?

Comments by teachers about the ABC's Online project illustrate how they assess their experiences in terms of changing perspectives. Teacher C (from Great Britain) wrote in his comparison about his exchange with teacher D and about having to reflect his own life-story:

> I find it very strange to read about myself, and I found it equally strange to have written about my life and my personal history for the Autobiography [sic]. Generally speaking, I am not the kind of person to spend lots of time reflecting upon my life and my own personality and history. Doing the auto-biography and helping D to prepare the biography caused me to have to think about these things.

Likewise he said in an interview[11] after the exchange:

> I mean sitting there and describing myself and my personality was quite strange for me. I mean, it wasn't a, it isn't necessarily a negative thing. It makes me aware of things to improve and things I can sort of say I am not good at and what is one of my strong points.

In general, Teacher C commented on the project and on reflecting his own as well as the target culture:

> I enjoyed taking part. And it was interesting chatting to someone who obviously has experiences of England and seeing it from a different perspective identity.

And further:

> But I mean interculturally, you are both reflecting on your individual cultures and sort of an outside view, and so sharing a positive sort of role model of how a German person really is. And not a stereotype. And how an English person really is. You hold stereotypical views. And you would hope by the point of which you have done a language degree and you are graduating, you are being a teacher, you would hope you did not still hold stereotypical views. Because that would be, therefore, influencing the next generation.

The first two quotations show C's uneasiness with having to reflect on his own person, history and background. Yet, in the two subsequent statements he emphasizes the benefits he experienced in the process. Similarly, teacher A writes in her comparison about the experience of reading about herself from a different perspective:

> It is strange to read what someone has written about you. This is especially the case when B gave views on what I look like and what kind of person I am. The general facts are okay as you know those yourself[,] it is the interpretation that is worrying, because ahs [sic] the other person got a nice view of you or does she think that you are selfish and someone who is not pleasant to be with or talk to. I need to have the feeling that people want to spend time with me and enjoy it. Even if you have lots of friends and people tell you that you are a good person[,] you still feel a little apprehensive when someone new gets to know you and you hear their views and thoughts about you without holding anything back. So when I first started reading the comparison[,] that is what worried me the most.

Likewise, teacher B concludes in her comparison:

> Never would I have considered sitting down and writing about my life. Reading my life through the words of another person makes me appreciate my curriculum vitae in a different perspective that I have [sic] before.

Even though the process of reflecting the *Self* and reading what someone else had to say about themselves caused moments of uneasiness for the participants these comments illustrate that the teachers in the ABC's Online exchange appreciated the experience of changing perspectives, which was one of the outcomes of the ABC's project.

### What Are the Technological Implications of Doing the ABC's With Online Communication Tools?

The changes that had to be made to adapt the ABC's Model to the needs of online communication have been described above. In spite of their overall positive feedback on the ABC's Online project, the teachers pointed out a few shortcomings with regard to the online communication within the project. One aspect mentioned was the lack of visual impression, because the ABC's partners had never seen each other. Due to this, the feeling prevailed in some cases to have only an incomplete picture of the partner. This request could be met through exchanging pictures, short video clips, or through setting up one or more videoconferences instead of a voice chat.

The frequency of the online exchange was another aspect mentioned by some participants who felt they had not had enough opportunities to converse with their partners. This was due to their general workload which sometimes did not leave a satisfactory amount of time for the project. Also, in some cases, technical problems with the internet access or installing the voice chat delayed the exchange. As this aspect has impact on the intensity of an online project, a more frequent exchange would have been beneficial in some cases. However, this enthusiastic passage from the comparison written by teacher A mentions this aspect in a positive manner:

> It is amazing how similar B and I are. We have only spoken four times and made contact my [sic] email every now and again, but it has been enjoyable and also interesting that we have so many things in common and have spoken so much on such a range of topics.[...] I like her a lot and would really like to get to know her better after the project comes to an end. There is a lot more to learn that is something I have felt through out [sic] the project you can't learn a whole life story in such as short space of time; there is lots more I want to know about, but also, there is a lot of day to day stuff that makes someone a friend who you enjoy spending time with.

## CONCLUSION

This chapter set out to report on a project in which the ABC's Model was implemented in a transnational online exchange between foreign language teachers from Germany and Great Britain. The ABC's Online exchange seems to have been effective with regard to the following aspects of the participants' professional and personal development: (1) They gained new insights into the target culture by conducting an intensive exchange with a representative of that culture. In addition, they reflected on their own cultural backgrounds and discussed them with their partners. (2) Comparing life-stories and reading about themselves in somebody else's words helped them to change perspectives. In general the teachers felt that this experience was beneficial, as well as revealing. (3) They further developed their computer literacy with respect to new online communication tools. (4) They gained first-hand experiences with the ABC's Model as a method to foster their pupils' intercultural learning processes and discussed how to adapt the model to their own teaching. (5) Through the professional as well as personal exchange with a colleague from another country they expanded their knowledge of educational systems and were able to discuss and compare their everyday vocational experiences. One teacher from Great Britain commented on this aspect in her comparison as follows:

> In addition, it is great to have met someone who can hopefully become a friend and a colleague; this will be advantageous for both of us. I have also learned more about the German school system which has been informative as well as useful.

In summary, the ABC's Online appears to be a successful approach to promoting teachers' personal and professional development with regard to their intercultural competence and computer literacy. In spite of the overall positive feedback and results of the ABC's Online project, a few shortcomings were identified in reference to the online communication tools that were used in the project and which need reconsideration. However, the ABC's Online seems to be effective with respect to (1) promoting cultural awareness and intercultural communication strategies, (2) acquiring new perspectives on the *Self* and the *Other*, as well as new insights into the target culture, and (3) further developing computer literacy.

## NOTES

1.  The Hessian statistics on international pupils only account for those pupils who do not dispose of German citizenship. As a result those pupils who possess a German passport but have a different cultural background, e.g., second- or third-generation-migrants, appear in these statistics as "Germans." However, due to their international background they contribute to the multicultural situation of Germany today.

2.  In German there are two forms of address in the second person singular: Depending on degree of formality and informality either the more formal "Sie" or the less formal "du" will be used.

3.  Two of the thirteen participants in the project concluded the exchange early and did not hand in all questionnaires. Therefore, the following specifications only apply to eleven participants (n = 11).

4.  In the context of foreign language learning the word "tandem" refers to co-operative and autonomous learning partnerships of two learners. In a tandem learners with different native languages work together to improve their language skills and learn more about each others cultures. For more information on "Language Learning in Tandem" see: http://www.slf.ruhr-uni-bochum.de/(Last access: July 11, 2005)

5.  The tandem with the French native attempted to do a trilingual English-French-German exchange.

6.  http://www.occo-unik.de (last access: July 11, 2005)

7.  For more information on *Moodle* see: http://moodle.org/(last access: July 11, 2005)

8.  The semi-structured interviews with the teachers after the ABC's Online exchange were conducted in February and April 2005. The interviews were tape-recorded.

9.  The voice chats between the teachers and their ABC's partners took place in November and December 2004.

10.  Both from interviews with the teachers after the ABC's Online project.

11.  This and the following two comments are from the interview the moderator conducted with teacher C after the project.

# REFERENCES

Bach, G. (1998). Interkulturelles Lernen. In J.-P. Timm (Ed.), *Englisch lernen und lehren. Didaktik des Englischunterrichts* (pp. 192-200). Berlin: Cornelsen.

Baron, R. (2002). *Interculturally speaking: "Landeskunde", intercultural learning and teacher training in Germany from an American perspective.* München: Langenscheidt-Longman.

Bredella, L. (1995). Verstehen und Verständigung als Grundbegriffe und Zielvorstellungen des Fremdsprachenlehrens und -lernens? In L. Bredella (Ed.), *Verstehen und Verständigung durch Sprachenlernen? Dokumentation des 15. Kongresses für Fremdsprachendidaktik, veranstaltet von der Deutschen Gesellschaft für Fremdsprachenforschung (DGFF), Gießen, 4.-6. Oktober 1993* (pp. 1-34). Bochum: Brockmeyer.

Bundeszentrale für politische Bildung (Ed.). (1998). *Interkulturelles Lernen. Arbeitshilfen für die politische Bildung.* Bonn: Bundeszentrale für politische Bildung.

Department for Education and Employment & Qualifications and Curriculum Authority. (1999). *Modern foreign languages. The National Curriculum for England.* London: DfEE & QCA.

Fehling, S. (2005). *Language Awareness und bilingualer Unterricht. Eine komparative Studie.* Frankfurt/Main: Peter Lang.

Finkbeiner, C. (1995). *Englischunterricht in europäischer Dimension: Zwischen Qualifikationserwartungen der Gesellschaft und Schülereinstellungen und Schülerinteressen. Berichte und Kontexte zweier empirischer Untersuchungen.* Bochum: Brockmeyer.

Finkbeiner, C. (2004). Cooperation and collaboration in a foreign language teacher training program: The LMR plus model. In E. Cohen, C. Brody, & M. Sapon-Shevin (Eds.), *Learning to teach with cooperative learning: Challenges in teacher education* (pp. 111-127). Albany: State University of New York Press.

Finkbeiner, C. (2005). *Interessen und Strategien beim fremdsprachlichen Lesen. Wie Schülerinnen und Schüler englische Texte lesen und verstehen.* Tübingen: Gunter Narr.

Finkbeiner, C., & Koplin, C. (2001). Fremdverstehensprozesse und interkulturelle Prozesse als Forschungsgegenstand. In A. Müller-Hartmann & M. Schocker-v. Ditfurth (Eds.), *Qualitative Forschung im Bereich Fremdsprachen lehren und lernen* (pp. 114-136). Tübingen: Gunter Narr.

Finkbeiner, C., & Koplin, C. (2002). A cooperative approach for facilitating intercultural education. *Reading Online*, 6 (3). Retrieved July 11, 2005, from http://www.readingonline.org/newliteracies/lit_index.asp?HREF=/newliteracies/finkbeiner

Furstenberg, G., Levet, S., English, K., & Maillet, K. (2001). Giving a virtual voice to the silent language of culture: the CULTURA project. *Language Learning & Technology*, 5 (1), 55-102. Retrieved April 25, 2005, from http://llt.msu.edu/vol5num1/furstenberg/default.html

Gogolin, I. (2003). Interkulturelle Erziehung und das Lehren und Lernen fremder Sprachen. In K.-R. Bausch, H. Christ, & H.-J. Krumm (Eds.), *Handbuch Fremdsprachenunterricht* (pp. 96-102). Tübingen: A. Francke.

Hampel, R. (2003). Theoretical perspectives and new practises in audio-graphic conferencing for language learning. *ReCALL, 15* (1), 21-36.

Hampel, R., & Hauck, M. (2004). Towards an effective use of audio conferencing in distance language courses. *Language Learning & Technology, 8*(1), 66-82. Retrieved April 25, 2005, from http://llt.msu.edu/vol8num1/hampel/

Hessisches Kultusministerium. (2002). *Lehrplan Englisch. Bildungsgang Gymnasium.* Wiesbaden: Hessisches Kultusministerium.

Hessisches Kultusministerium. (2003). *Bildungspolitik in Zahlen. Daten aus dem Schulbereich 2003.* Wiesbaden: Hessisches Kultusministerium.

Knierim, M., Wade, E., & Wilden, E. (2004). *Intercultural learning online with the ABC's of intercultural understanding and communication.* Paper presented at the EuroCALL-Conference 2004 of the European Association for Computer-Assisted Language Learning, Vienna/Austria, September 1-4.

Kramsch, C. (1993). *Context and culture in language teaching.* Oxford: Oxford University Press.

Kramsch, C. (1995). Andere Worte – andere Werte: Zum Verhältnis von Sprache und Kultur. In L. Bredella (Ed.), *Verstehen und Verständigung durch Sprachenlernen? Dokumentation des 15. Kongresses für Fremdsprachendidaktik, veranstaltet von der Deutschen Gesellschaft für Fremdsprachenforschung (DGFF), Gießen, 4.-6. Oktober 1993* (pp. 51-66). Bochum: Brockmeyer.

Kramsch, C. (2004). The go-between. In J. Quetz & G. Solmecke (Eds.), *Brücken schlagen. Fächer – Sprachen – Institutionen. Dokumentation zum 20. Kongress für Fremdsprachendidaktik der Deutschen Gessellschaft für Fremdsprachenforschung (DGFF), Frankfurt am Main, Oktober 2003* (pp. 107-131). Berlin: Pädagogischer Zeitschriftenverlag.

Krumm, H.-J. (2003). Fremdsprachenlehrer. In K.-R. Bausch, H. Christ, & H.-J. Krumm (Eds.), *Handbuch Fremdsprachenunterricht* (pp. 352-358). Tübingen: Francke.

Kultusministerkonferenz. (1996). *Empfehlung „Interkulturelle Bildung und Erziehung in der Schule". Beschluss der KMK vom 25. Oktober 1996.* Bonn: Kultusministerkonferenz.

Leftwich, S. (2002). Learning to use diverse children's literature in the classroom: A model for preservice teacher education. *Reading Online, 6* (2). Retrieved July 11, 2005, from http://www.readingonline.org/newliteracies/lit_index .asp?HREF=leftwich/index.html

Legutke, M. K. (2000). Lehrer als Lerner. Fremdverstehen durch »entdeckende und erlebte Landeskunde« in der Lehrerfortbildung. In L. Bredella, F.-J. Meißner, A. Nünning, & D. Rösler (Eds.), *Wie ist Fremdverstehen lehr- und lernbar? Vorträge aus dem Graduiertenkolleg „Didaktik des Fremdverstehens"* (pp. 18-42). Tübingen: Gunter Narr.

Masterson, M. (in progress). *A European adaptation of the ABC's of cultural understanding and communication for the foreign language classroom: Promoting intercultural learning in an Irish context.* Doctoral dissertation, University of Kassel, Germany.

Mayring, P. (2003). *Qualitative Inhaltsanalyse. Grundlagen und Techniken.* Weinheim: Beltz.

O'Dowd, R. (2003). Understanding the "other side": Intercultural learning in Spanish-English e-mail exchange. *Language Learning & Technology, 7*(2), 118-144. Retrieved April 25, 2005, from http://llt.msu.edu/vol7num2/odowd/default.html

Salmon, G. (2000). *E-moderating. The key to teaching and learning online*. London: Kogan Page.

Salmon, G. (2002). *E-tivities. The key to online teaching, training and learning*. London: Kogan Page.

Schmidt, P. R. (1998a). The ABC's of cultural understanding and communication. *Equity and Excellence, 31*(2), 28-38.

Schmidt, P. R. (1998b). The ABC's model: Teachers connect home and school. *National Reading Conference Yearbook, 47*, 194-208.

Schmidt, P. R. (1999). Focus on research. Know thyself and understand others. *Language Arts, 76*(4), 332-340.

Schmidt, P. R. (2001). The power to empower. Creating home/school relationships with the ABC's of cultural understanding and communication. In P. R. Schmidt & P. B. Mosenthal (Eds.), *Reconceptualizing literacy in the new age of multiculturalism and pluralism* (pp. 389-433). Greenwich, CT: Information Age.

Stencel, P. (2004). Moderating discussions in online courses. Paper presented at the EuroCALL-Conference 2004 of the European Association for Computer-Assisted Language Learning, Vienna/Austria, September 1-4.

Weaver, G. R. (1993). Understanding and coping with cross-cultural adjustment stress. In M. Paige (Ed.), *Education for the intercultural experience* (pp. 137-167). Yarmouth, ME: Intercultural Press.

Xu, S. H. (2000a). Preservice teachers integrate understandings of diversity into literacy instruction: An adaptation of the ABC's model. *Journal of Teacher Education, 51*, 135-142.

Xu, S. H. (2000b). Preservice teachers in a literacy methods course consider issues of diversity. *Journal of Literacy Research, 32*, 505-531.

Xu, S. H. (2001). The ABC's of cultural understanding and communication: Teacher assistants learn to respect, appreciate, and apply differences in literacy instruction. In P. R. Schmidt & A. Watts (Eds.), *Exploring values through literature, multimedia, and literacy events. Making connections* (pp. 48-63). Newark, DE: International Reading Association.

CHAPTER 10

# THE ABC'S AS A
# STARTING POINT AND GOAL

## The Online
## Intercultural Exchange Project (ICE)

Claudia Finkbeiner and Markus Knierim

### ABSTRACT

This chapter reports on three subsequent implementations of the Intercultural Exchange Project (ICE). The ICE is a web-based intercultural learning project which is situated in the university setting in Germany and in the United States. Undergraduate students in the United States collaborated online with their partners in Germany, who were students in three and four-year foreign language teacher education programs. The ICE project originated with the idea of transferring our experiences in previous face-to-face ABC's projects to an online learning environment so that it would allow for cooperative transatlantic intercultural learning and exchange. As the ABC's had not been used online, at the time we started, and the Cultura project (Furstenberg et al., 2001) had already been proven to be a very successful online intercultural learning project, we decided to first collect ideas by fol-

*ABC's of Cultural Understanding and Communication:*
*National and International Adaptations,* 213–244

lowing and adapting the Cultura design, then develop the ICE project and adapt it to our specific needs in qualifying future foreign language teachers. This helped us gain highly valuable insights into intercultural learning online, which now allows for the implementation of an ABC's into a web-based learning design.

## INTRODUCTION

We would like to start our chapter on intercultural learning online with the metaphor of a vehicle. We have chosen this metaphor deliberately as vehicles bring us from one place to the other; they help us interconnect and they stand for modern technology. Sometimes they break down; this is why we need to take care of them by watching the board instruments, replacing parts, and getting regular inspections. These are the requirements also for online intercultural learning.

In this chapter, we will maneuver our vehicle along a multi-lane *Autobahn*, an interstate highway, *auto strata, or* a *valtakatu*—whatever it is called. Just as in real life, we will have to continuously cross and switch lanes: (a) We start from the first lane with the ABC's (Finkbeiner & Koplin, 2000, 2001, 2002; Schmidt, 1998, 2001), (b) Next, we move to the center lane, ICE, (c) Then we maneuver to the right lane, Cultura (Furstenberg et al., 2001). And, of course, there is an extra lane for unexpected events, for sudden stops, for emergencies as well as for new and further developments.

The fuel that we need for our vehicle to work and keep running is the intercultural learning fuel. The motor that makes the machinery work in a transnational context, among others, are the computer and the online learning environment. On the *Autobahn* or highway you will see vehicles with license plates from many different countries and states and in order to keep the traffic moving and to avoid accidents, all drivers, no matter where they come from, need to agree on certain basic rules and the meaning of signs. However, unlike the traffic signs that have been agreed upon and are composed of a finite, reliable and stable set of symbols, language and culture have to be constantly renegotiated as they consist of infinite, non-reliable and dynamic sets of signs and symbols. Thus, steering our vehicles in language and culture traffic is even more challenging.

The scenario of the *Autobahn* or highway implies that we will sometimes move fast and make quick progress. Sometimes there will be bumper-to-bumper traffic, and we will have to stand still and be patient. Some cars might stall and break down for no obvious reason. Then, we need to look inside and go deeper, under the surface of the iceberg (Weaver, 1993) to see and understand what went wrong. Generally speaking, we need to be aware of the fact that if we go too fast or if the motor is idling at a stand-still, we will waste fuel. This is why we advocate—staying with the *Autobahn* or highway analogy for intercultural learning—an environmentally friendly, that is, educationally sound approach to intercultural learning. Such an approach will pace the learning process according to the learn-ers' needs.

We believe that projects such as the ABC's, Cultura, and the ICE—the latter being the focal point of this chapter—as well as other projects presented in this volume, such as MOBIDIC (Finkbeiner & Fehling, this volume), comply with this approach to intercultural learning, because they all take into account the following principles (Finkbeiner, this vol-ume):

- they consider each individual with his or her "self" as a very impor-tant factor in intercultural learning (Finkbeiner & Koplin, 2000, 2001, 2002)
- they define the self in relation to the other (Finkbeiner, 2005)
- they make intercultural learning feasible for the students by turn-ing it into clearly defined literacy events
- they consider intercultural learning a cooperative, reciprocal, and constructive process.

The trigger for our Intercultural Exchange Project (ICE) can be seen in the success we have had with several face-to-face ABC's projects in our university classes (Finkbeiner & Koplin, 2000, 2001, 2002). This encour-aged us to start working on an online intercultural learning project.

Particularly for foreign language learners and teachers, the computer offers huge potential as it opens the door into a world usually hidden and only accessible for world travelers. In our project we did not only make the world accessible to our participants, but we defined ourselves through and in this world: "We are the world," was a statement from one of our students during one of our online intercultural projects.

Taking this statement as the opener for this chapter, we will first high-light reasons for intercultural learning in online environments. We will start quite provocatively with a focus on globalization, technology, and culture. We will then put special emphasis on intercultural learning online and refer to some interesting examples of Internet-based activities for intercultural learning. However, we will also talk about the challenges we need to deal with when facing intercultural learning in an online envi-ronment. We will conclude this part with a survey of the Cultura project and move on to the ICE project, which will be at the core of this chapter. We will not only describe this project, but also give insight into the tools we developed and used. The project evaluation will focus on important events that occurred in our online learning and issues that came up, such as the right to privacy, the dilemma of public vs. private interaction as well as the impact of different electronic tools. Furthermore, in the evaluation, we will elaborate on the accompanying feelings of the participants. These have to be taken seriously, since feelings largely influence all learning processes (Finkbeiner, 2005). As intercultural learning is most closely connected to the self-image, this is even more crucial (Finkbeiner, 2005, pp. 272-276). Finally, we will conclude with some lessons learned and recommendations derived on the implementation of an online ABC's.

## GLOBALIZATION—TECHNOLOGY—CULTURE

Traditional dress has been replaced by suits in business settings in every country in the world; young people in urban areas everywhere watch films made in Hollywood, listen to rock and roll, play video games, talk on cell phones, wear jeans, drink Coke, eat pizza (or McDonald's hamburgers), speak English, and increasingly, frequent cybercafes. (Herring, 2001, p. vii)

Herring's characterization of the impact of globalization on the development of the world's everyday and popular cultures emphasizes only one side of the story: Alongside an increasingly globalized and universalized world, there are movements of fragmentation as well (Clark, 1997; Menzel, 1998), which entail cultural diversification and ethnocentrism. Developments of this kind have surfaced, for instance, after the breakups of the former Soviet Union and former Yugoslavia (Finkbeiner, 1995, pp. 8-9). In the case of former Yugoslavia, for example, the different dialects of Serbo-Croatian spoken in what are now Bosnia & Herzegovina, Croatia, and Serbia & Montenegro, are now claimed to represent three distinct languages, "in line" with the political changes.

Herring's remarks also vividly illustrate the power of the Western (especially the United States) socioeconomic model and its associated cultural practices, which increasingly permeate people's lives in many regions of the world. Since the mid-1990s, this development has gained even stronger momentum through the massive expansion of the Internet and the widespread availability of time and space-independent communication technologies. Even though the World Wide Web is not yet—literally speaking—"worldwide," it has become a medium of global reach, being accessible from (geographically) remote places such as Vanuatu (7,500 Internet users; Internet World Stats, 2005a) or Swaziland (27,000 Internet users; Internet World Stats, 2005b).

Nine years ago, it was felt that the Internet represented a quantum leap as far as availability of information and ease of communication were concerned:

> the introduction of the international electronic network constitutes a revolution as far-reaching in its way as the invention of printing. Printing democratized the written word by making it accessible quickly and to constantly growing circles of readers. The Internet has extended access to knowledge beyond the universities, and into a much wider sphere of professional and amateur consumers. (Sussex & White, 1996, p. 200)

At the time, the Internet was just about to become part of people's everyday lives, a development which has accelerated exponentially since then. At present, we are witnessing changes similar to the first worldwide literacy revolution, which was launched by Gutenberg in 1457.

The information highway has been "transforming our learning culture and daily life as dramatically as Gutenberg's press did in the middle ages" (Finkbeiner, 2001, p. 131). Today, access to the Internet is almost as ubiquitous as cable television; more and more people are not merely "amateur consumers" (Sussex & White, 1996, p. 200), but have turned into amateur and semi-professional producers and disseminators of information by publishing their own websites. These developments did not stop in front of classroom doors in many areas of the world, and countless publications have appeared, showing evidence of teachers' highly creative and imaginative efforts—across all disciplines and teaching contexts—to utilize the Internet in order to make a difference in their students' learning experience.

However, educators also need to be aware of the following: Not only does the Internet store and present information, it also conveys a new form of cultural meaning. This implies that Internet users do not only need to learn how to interpret this cultural meaning, but also learn how to express their own cultural or sub-cultural message online. Of course, the command of foreign languages is crucial if we want to rely on first-hand interpretation as well as first-hand messaging of these cultural meanings. In this respect, foreign language learning and competence are necessary for critical language awareness (Fehling, 2005; James & Garrett, 1991).

## Intercultural Learning Online

As the Internet became more widely available, educators around the world began to embrace the opportunities offered by the new technology, namely access to a huge variety of up-to-date information via the World

Wide Web as well as fast and convenient electronic communication with people close by and far away. Early on, second and foreign language educators set out to harness this potential for the benefit of their students' foreign language and culture learning processes, and some even envisioned a new era of more authentic and culturally relevant classroom activities and projects. This kind of enthusiasm is reflected in Herring's (2001, p. vii) retrospective statement: "Some people believe that the increased cross-cultural contact facilitated by computer networks will reduce cultural distances, transforming the world into an electronic global village."

To make this optimistic outlook happen, however, remains a challenging task: Opening up new avenues, as facilitated by the Internet, in this case, is one thing, but actually walking down the path and reaching your aim, such as intercultural learning, can be quite another. Even though the Internet has the power to reduce geographical distances as well as temporal differences to zero, personal and cultural distances may actually be enlarged (Finkbeiner, 2001, p. 131). As this phenomenon might not always be perceived by learners nor by their teachers, intercultural online projects as the one reported upon here are important preconditions for becoming culturally and linguistically aware Internet users.

As the issues of language and culture in Internet usage are at the center of our interest, we will give a brief overview of (a) how the Internet has been incorporated into foreign language and culture education thus far, and (b) to what extent the various activities and projects have addressed the complex and dynamic nature of intercultural learning.

## Internet-based Activities for Intercultural Learning

Basically, one can distinguish two general categories of Internet use in the foreign language classroom: (1) activities within a single classroom based on authentic target-language/culture materials, and (2) activities involving online communication and cooperation. Activities of the latter type can take place:

- between foreign language learners and members of the target language culture(s) (e.g., learners of English in Germany cooperating with native speakers of English)
- between learners of the same target language coming from different source cultures (e.g., students in Poland and students in Germany using English as a *lingua franca* in a joint project).

Activities of the first category generally take a "virtual realia" approach. Smith (1997, ¶ 1) defines virtual realia as "digitized objects and items from the target culture which are brought into the classroom as examples or aids and used to stimulate spoken or written language production." In other words, teachers choose materials available on the World Wide Web, which are culturally relevant and appropriate for their learners, as the starting point or springboard for various kinds of classroom activities (see Table 10.1 for examples). Activities of the second category, on the other hand, are typically more challenging in that they require learners to engage in real, authentic interaction using the target language. If planned and implemented with care, projects of this kind may turn out to be the most motivating and memorable experiences for language learners; this is especially true for foreign language education settings, where contact with native speakers would otherwise be very difficult to realize. Table 10.2 presents some activities of this kind which involve learners in online intercultural communication and cooperation.

**Table 10.1.   Internet-Based Activities for Intercultural Learning Within a Single Classroom**

| General Idea | Example |
|---|---|
| Students take virtual tours of cities, museums, a country's tourist attractions, etc. to plan their own, imaginary trips to the country where the target language is spoken. | Learners of English may use the information provided at http://www.mustseenewyork.com in conjunction with the current subway schedule (available at http://www.mta.nyc.ny.us/nyct/subway) to plan their itinerary for a trip to New York City (Knierim, 2004). |
| Students examine video and audio clips of interviews with representatives of the target culture in order to discover and analyze culturally appropriate discourse strategies and kinesic behavior. | The CNN Learning Resources website (http://literacynet.org/cnnsf/archives.html) provides a great variety of video clips, complete with transcripts, and simple vocabulary and comprehension activities, which can serve as pre-tasks to an examination of cross-cultural differences (O'Dowd, 2002, p. 8). |
| Students search the Web for specific information on a holiday celebrated in an anglophone country and compare it to one from their own culture. | Learners explore the symbols used to represent St. Patrick's Day and compare those with symbols used for holidays in their own culture(s) (Feyten et al., 2002, pp. 141-144). |
| Students make use of online databases specifically designed to foster language and cultural awareness in cross-cultural communication. | The website of the Interculture Project (http://www.lancs.ac.uk/users/interculture/cat4.htm) presents learners with "an example of communication breakdown or misunderstanding between people from different countries, gives them some options to choose from in relation to the situation and then informs learners of the consequences of their choice" (O'Dowd, 2002, p. 11). |

**Table 10.2.   Internet-Based Activities for
Intercultural Communication and Cooperation Between
Students From Different Classrooms**

| General idea | Example |
| --- | --- |
| Students cooperate with a partner class from the target culture by exchanging emails on a specified, culturally relevant topic. | Learners of German in the USA corresponded via email with learners of English in Germany to compare a series of parallel texts (i.e., texts written by authors from each culture on the same topic, e.g., racism or beauty) (Belz, 2003). |
| Students join the discussions in online chat rooms and online forums (or bulletin boards) on websites from the target language and culture. | Learners of French visit the forums offered on the *Le Monde* newspaper's homepage to exchange their views on topical issues with people from France and, potentially, many other countries (Hanna & Nooy, 2003). |
| Students meet with a partner class from the target culture in online video-conferences to discuss orally, in real time, their findings from other parts of a larger intercultural project. | Learners of English in Spain and learners of Spanish in the USA conduct several video-conferences to discuss cultural questionnaires and certain movies from each culture (O'Dowd, 2000). |

Even though this overview of Internet-based activities for intercultural learning in foreign language education contexts cannot claim to be exhaustive, it does nevertheless illustrate the scope of activities and projects imaginable.

## Challenges of Intercultural Learning Online

The sample activities and projects described in Tables 10.1 and 10.2 above are typical ways of how the Internet is currently used in an increasing number of foreign language classrooms. They address various aspects of informational, behavioral, and achievement culture (Omaggio Hadley, 1993) and can thus facilitate intercultural learning. However, the degree to which these activities emphasize cultural attitudes, values, beliefs and the dialogic nature of intercultural learning is often limited:

- Single-classroom activities may allow for cross-cultural comparisons as far as they are observable, but beyond that, the learners have to rely on their teacher for explanations of cultural phenomena and their underlying values and beliefs (Weaver, 1993; Finkbeiner, this volume). This is an extremely challenging task for the individual teacher, especially in foreign language teaching contexts where the teacher may not be a native speaker (Smith, 1997).

- Even many online projects involving the cooperation between language learners and native speakers of the target language do not succeed in engaging the students in reflective, focused discussions about culturally determined phenomena. It can be argued that this is primarily due to the lack of a coherent and stringent methodological framework in which the acquisition of intercultural competence takes center stage.

- The language factor is another important issue that has to be taken into account (Finkbeiner, this volume). Even though English is used as the foreign language and *lingua franca*, there is often a large number of native languages present in ESL and EFL classes. English proficiency can vary considerably among students. Underlying schemata and scripts often differ to a large extent, and values as well as attributions are not comparable. The language issue has to be considered even more in the secondary-school setting. Proficiency levels in English as a second, foreign, or other language are generally lower among these students than among those in the university setting, and the challenges even greater (Finkbeiner & Koplin, 2002).

Particularly the first two of these issues were borne in mind when Furstenberg et al. (2001) developed the Cultura project, "which is considered by many to be the state of the art in on-line approaches to culture learning" (O'Dowd, 2002, p. 10). As the Cultura project served as the springboard for our own ICE (Intercultural Exchange) projects and accompanied prior ABC's studies (Finkbeiner & Koplin, 2000, 2001, 2002), we will describe it in some detail in the following.

## THE CULTURA PROJECT

The Cultura project represents a "web-based, cross-cultural, curricular initiative ..., designed to develop foreign language students' understanding of foreign cultural attitudes, concepts, beliefs, and ways of interacting and looking at the world" (Furstenberg et al., 2001, p. 55). Cultura distinguishes itself from the majority of approaches to intercultural learning, both web-based and "traditional," in that it attempts to explicitly address the portion of the iceberg—to stay with Weaver's (1993, p. 160) metaphor—that is hidden below the surface of the water. To tackle this challenge, Cultura relies on web-based activities intended to raise the students' cultural awareness as well as various forms of electronic communication, as the following brief description of the project illustrates.

Cultura was first developed in 1997 and emerged from an online cooperation between students of French at the Massachusetts Institute of Technology in Cambridge, USA, and students of English at the Institut National des Télécommunications in Evry, France. It is worth mentioning that the basic methodological framework of Cultura is similar to that of the ABC's Model. Both models use texts generated by the learners for cross-cultural analyses of differences and similarities (Schmidt, 2001, p. 390).

Cultura consists of five steps (Furstenberg et al., 2001):

1.  The American and French students filled in a series of online questionnaires highlighting issues and topic areas that lend themselves to cultural comparisons (e.g., work, leisure, race, gender, family, education, individualism) (Furstenberg et al., 2001, p. 60). The questionnaires included word associations (with words such as "school," "police," "suburb," "individualism"), sentence completions (e.g., "A good neighbor is someone who …"), and situation reactions (e.g., "A mother slaps her child in the supermarket") (pp. 60-65). The students responded to the questionnaires in their respective native languages (or in the language of the country where the students were studying), since "only then can one hope to access the hidden cultural values, which are intrinsically language-bound" (p. 97). The American and French students' responses were posted on the project website, appearing vis-à-vis to facilitate the subsequent cross-cultural comparisons and analyses.

2.  During their regular face-to-face class meetings, the students then shared their observations based on the questionnaire responses and started to form hypotheses as to the underlying reasons for the cultural differences they noticed.

3.  During the next phase of the project, the American and French students "(a) share[d] their observations and hypotheses; (b) sen[t] queries for more details, clarification, and more in-depth understanding of the differences they observed; and (c) respond[ed] to whatever question was posed to them" (Furstenberg et al., 2001, p. 61). This exchange took place in an online forum, which allowed for asynchronous (i.e., time-independent), text-based electronic communication between the partners (see also below).

4.  In order to put their own findings into a broader perspective, the students then examined additional resources, chiefly French and American opinion polls which were related to the issues raised in the questionnaires.

5. Finally, the students' cross-cultural analyses were even further broadened by investigating French films and their American remakes, articles from online newspapers or magazines dealing with similar topics from a French and an American point of view, and text excerpts (from fields such as anthropology, history, literature, and philosophy) that revealed the author's view about the other culture (p. 61). The students' discussions continued in the online forum and during a series of videoconferences, which allowed for synchronous (i.e., real-time), oral interaction between the partners.

Overall, the Cultura project made a significant contribution to raising the students' intercultural awareness, as Furstenberg et al.'s (2001) in-depth analysis of the students' online discussions illustrates. Moreover, the students' commitment to the project turned out to be extraordinary, particularly because Cultura, just like the ABC's, uses a "hands-on approach, [requiring the] students [to] produce and analyze *their own* data" (p. 56; emphasis added).

## THE ABC'S AND CULTURA: A SYNOPSIS

We believe that the success of projects such as Cultura, the ABC's, and the ICE as described in the following lies in the fact they are firmly grounded in constructivist pedagogy. This means, that the students are put in the driver's seat to take charge of their learning themselves, scaffolded by the clear methodological framework of each project. Thus, the framework serves as a "guide rope for discovering another culture" (Furstenberg et al., 2001, p. 91).

Another strength of the projects described here lies in the fact that they emphasize the dialogic nature of intercultural learning—following Schmidt's (1999) motto "Know thyself and understand others"—and the appreciation of differences. Last but not least, the "third domain" as proposed by Kramsch (1993), or the "third space" as suggested by O'Connor (2000), can be grasped better in a hands-on approach, for it then becomes a dynamic construct created in a collaborative effort by those engaged in the process (Finkbeiner, this volume).

This reciprocal approach to intercultural learning enables the participants to jointly construct their understandings of the values, attitudes, and beliefs inherent in one's own and each other's culture. The biggest difference between the projects can be seen in their communication modes: While the ABC's was originally conceived as a face-to-face project, Cultura was an online project right from the beginning. Yet, as our considerations here taken together with Wilden's account (this volume) demonstrate, the ABC's can be implemented in an online environment as well.

## FROM THE ABC'S AND CULTURA TO THE ICE PROJECT

Extracts of a few questions used in the Cultura project served as an additional catalyst for raising cultural and language awareness when conducting our ABC's projects between 1999 and 2002 on the University of Kassel campus, Germany (Finkbeiner & Koplin, 2000, 2001, 2002). The most interesting result was that these questions helped us and our students put a strong emphasis on language and the huge difference it can make when expressing the "same" thing in different languages (Finkbeiner, this volume). As we are dealing with future foreign language teachers, the language issue has always been of major importance to us. This is why we saw the chance of learning from Cultura in order to be able to answer our questions raised earlier in the context of the ABC's. The results were so promising that we wanted to gain a deeper insight into specific effects caused by the Cultura methodology.

Another factor was that the ABC's alone is a wonderful cultural learning experience for learners, yet it puts high emphasis on the learners' commitment to the literacy tasks. The ABC's and the Cultura methodology taken together are too time-consuming for our classes. This is why (a) from a research point of view and (b) for pragmatic reasons, we separated both approaches and examined the effects in different groups.

After having implemented parts of the Cultura project into our ABC's classes, we further developed and adapted our approach and integrated it into an intercultural learning approach in an online environment. The adaptations we came up with were our own Intercultural Exchange (ICE) projects, which we introduce in the next section.

## THE ICE PROJECT: TIME FRAME, PARTICIPANTS, AND SETTING

Between 2002 and 2004, students from different English as a Foreign Language (EFL) teacher education classes at the University of Kassel (UNIK), Germany, embarked on the path of intercultural explorations together with intermediate German as a Foreign Language classes at the University of California at Santa Barbara (UCSB).

The UNIK students were enrolled in courses in the field of Applied Linguistics, Foreign Language Research, and Intercultural Communication in the Department of English & Romance Languages, where they were pursuing three- and four-year EFL teaching degrees for the primary, secondary, or vocational school level. The specific contexts and subject matter at UNIK, in which our ICE projects took place, varied from semester to semester:

- The first time, the project was part of a class on intercultural learning.
- The second time, we implemented it as a component of a class on computer-assisted language learning.
- The third time, it involved students taking a class on holistic and action-oriented EFL learning and teaching.[1]

All courses were at the undergraduate level (*Proseminare*), and the majority of the students were 20-23 years old, although we had a few students pursuing a second degree and in-service teachers seeking additional qualification, who were in their thirties and early forties. The instructors of the courses varied as well.[2]

The students at UCSB were second-year learners of German, taking Intermediate German classes at their university. The courses were taught by our project partners.[3] To match the larger number of students in the classes at UNIK, each semester, two German classes in Santa Barbara cooperated with one class in Kassel. As far as age was concerned, the students in California were comparable with their exchange partners in Germany. However, there were three notable differences between the two groups of participants: (1) While all of the UNIK students were pursuing EFL teaching degrees,[4] the students at UCSB came from a variety of backgrounds, majoring in different subjects. (2) The classes at UCSB focused on language learning, incorporating the ICE as the culture component. The classes at UNIK, on the other hand, were essentially content-oriented (see above), and the foreign language (i.e., English) served as the vehicle of functional classroom communication (Finkbeiner, 2001, 2004). That is, no formal language instruction or practice was part of the course. (3) The students in Kassel were more advanced foreign language learners. On average, the students in Kassel were at the Advanced-Low to Advanced-High levels according to the ACTFL (American Council on the Teaching of Foreign Languages) proficiency guidelines (ACTFL, 2001), whereas the students in Santa Barbara were at the Intermediate-Low to Intermediate-High levels.

Overall, the heterogeneity between the groups of students—as far as their academic background, educational goals, and foreign language proficiency are concerned—as well as the varying contexts in which our ICE projects were situated, challenged us to adjust and fine-tune the ICE project to the needs of our students and our particular learning objectives.

## THE ICE PROJECT: DESIGN AND PROCEDURES

Basically, each of the ICE project implementations involved the following steps:

1. A pre-questionnaire on the notion of culture.
2. A warm-up phase for the students to get to know each other (via email or in an online forum).
3. Two or more cycles (depending on the time available) of:
   (a) filling in web-based questionnaires on culturally relevant topics (using word associations, sentence completions, and situation reactions similar to the ones used in Cultura as well as more open-ended, personal questions designed specifically for the ICE project);
   (b) discussing the responses to the questionnaire online (in small groups, via e-mail or in an online forum) as well as in class.
4. An online chat session toward the end of the project to further expand on the most controversial topics discussed previously.
5. A project evaluation (in an online forum and in class).

The following sections focus on steps 1, 3a, and 5 to illustrate some of the intercultural learning processes as they surfaced in our ICE projects. Furthermore, the analysis of the data obtained at these stages is highly relevant with regard to our endeavor to integrate the Cultura and ABC's Models in an online environment for foreign language learners.

### The ICE Pre-Questionnaire

In order to introduce and sensitize our students to the notion of culture, we developed a questionnaire (as shown in Table 10.3) together with our UCSB partners, which we used at the beginning of all ICE projects. As in Cultura, the questionnaire is administered in the students' respective native language as cultural schemata are intricately bound to language (see above; Finkbeiner & Fehling, 2002; Finkbeiner, this volume).

Discussing the responses to the questionnaire in class helped the students as well as the instructors, to establish some common ground for

**Table 10.3.   The ICE Pre-Questionnaire**

| *Questions for the Students in the USA* | *Questions for the Students in Germany* |
| --- | --- |
| 1. What does the word/concept "culture" mean to you? | 1. Was verstehen Sie unter dem Wort/ Konzept "Kultur"? |
| 2. What do you think people need to know in order to belong to a particular culture? | 2. Was müssen – Ihrer Meinung nach – Menschen wissen, um zu einer bestimmten Kultur zu gehören? |
| 3. Which culture(s) do you belong to? How do you know? | 3. Zu welcher Kultur bzw. welchen Kulturen gehören Sie? Woran machen Sie das fest? |
| 4. What do you know about people in Germany? Where did you gain this knowledge from? | 4. Was wissen Sie über Menschen in den USA? Wo haben Sie dieses Wissen erworben? |
| 5. What do you think people in Germany think of people in the U.S.? | 5. Was denken – Ihrer Meinung nach – Menschen in den USA über Menschen in Deutschland? |

negotiating culture-related issues and for coming to terms with the multi-faceted nature of culture. It was only by pooling together all students' answers and discussing them, that many of the participating students gradually became aware of the fact that there is more to culture than tangible artifacts and behaviors: that there may be an underlying driving force—ideas, attitudes, beliefs, that one cannot grasp by careful observation alone (see Finkbeiner & Koplin, 2002, who liken the process of intercultural learning to a hermeneutic circle).

In other words, this rather simple questionnaire did not only elicit our students' initial assumptions about the notion of culture, but piqued their curiosity and helped trigger a process crucial to the success of the project: to engage in intercultural, collaborative dialog to discover hidden meanings.

Furthermore, the students began to realize that, even though culture is rooted in social norms, beliefs, and attitudes, it is constantly in flux. The changing faces of culture and how perceptions can change over time became very obvious to our students when they realized, for example, that their associating of "Krieg" ("war") with the United States was very much context-dependent: The war in Iraq was still in full swing at the time, and the images of American troops struggling to maintain order in the streets of Kabul, Afghanistan, were ever so present on the news.

The discussions on the questionnaire responses—both face-to-face with their fellow students in Kassel and online with the students in Santa Barbara—helped them in many cases to distinguish blunt stereotype from the many shades reality can take.

**Table 10.4.   Stated, Assumed, and Desired Auto-Stereotype: One American Student's Perspective on Being American**

| Stated Auto-Stereotype | Assumed Auto-Stereotype | Desired Auto-Stereotype |
| --- | --- | --- |
| We are the exception to the rule, I swear. | average, everyday, over-weight, stupid, insensitive, burger-eating, buffalo kill-ing, green-house gas pro-ducing, UN ignoring, gun toting, tv worshipping, tab-loid believing, war monger-ing, wool-over-the-eyes Americans | I want you to believe we are the exception to the rule. |

Our students were quite aware of possible, assumed stereotypes and how these might affect the communication with their project partners on the other side of the Atlantic. For example, one of the students in Santa Barbara introduced himself in his online bio-sketch with the following message:

> I'm excited to be involved in an exchange with all you fine Germans. Hope-fully we can learn a lot from each other and make friends (I'm coming to Germany over the summer). I can tell you this: we aren't your average, everyday, overweight, stupid, insensitive, burger-eating, buffalo killing, greenhouse gas producing, UN ignoring, gun toting, tv worshiping, tabloid believing, war mongering, wool-over-the-eyes Americans ... we're the exception to the rule, I swear.

This example demonstrates how the different tools we used contrib-uted to meta-reflection on auto-stereotypes and hetero-stereotypes (Fink-beiner, 1995, 2005). In this respect, it turned out to be helpful to distinguish between the different levels of auto-stereotype as shown in Finkbeiner's (2005) model. The student's forum entry quoted above shows the discrepancy of auto-stereotype and assumed as well as desired auto-stereotype (see Table 10.4).

## Word Associations, Sentence Completions, and Situation Reactions

Just as in Cultura, we used word associations, sentence completions, and situation reactions to trigger the students' primary associations on certain important issues. Yet, in contrast to Cultura we left out more gen-eral topics and selected topics directly related to the university and stu-dent life. Because of the importance of the topics to our students, we

## UCSB Intercultural Exchange    UNI KASSEL VERSITÄT

Home    Questionnaires    Tools    About ICE    Contact

| An educated person is ... | Eine gebildete Person ist ... |
|---|---|
| not always university educated, open-minded and progressive, and one who reads more than the sports page in the paper | jemand, der anderen sein Wissen/Meinung auf eine angenehme Art und Weise mitteilt ohne dabei überheblich/eingebildet zu wirken |
| someone who uses their knowledge to make a difference in the community. | |
| Someone who realises that what they know is only a construct of learned material, but that real education comes from experience. | jemand, der sehr belesen ist und sich in vielen Bereichen auskennt. Wo verstecken sich diese Leute denn nur in Kassel? Irgendwo müssen die doch auch sein. |
| | jemand der sehr belesen ist und ein breites Allgemeinwissen hat. |
| An educated person is one who has studied many different subjects and has realized that they actually know very little and do not act like they know everything. | eine Person, die sich nicht nur in einem Bereich intensiv auskennt, sondern in verschieden gebieten, die zum allgemeinwissen gehören. |
| someone who keeps themselves informed about the world around them. | klug. |

Figure 10.1.   Sentence completions: American and German students' responses.

hoped for their commitment and motivation. This was necessary as the project constituted but one part of the course, next to other class assignments.

   To illustrate the Cultura-style question types, Figure 1 shows a few student reactions to the trigger "An educated person is . . . "/"Eine gebildete Person ist...."[5] The UNIK and UCSB students' responses to questions like this one, displayed side by side on the screen, prompted intense discussions in the online forums and contributed to an awareness of the strong ties of both language and culture. Due to space constraints, we cannot address the forum discussions in any more detail in this chapter.

## Moving Toward the ABC's Model in an Online Environment

In our third implementation of the ICE, we moved beyond the narrowly focused activities adapted from Cultura (i.e., the word associations, sentence completions, and situation reactions) by adding more open-ended and also more personal questions. Our decision to do so was founded in our students' express desire—voiced in a previous ICE project—to add a somewhat more personal "flavor" to the exchange right from the beginning; apparently, our students had felt that the questionnaire activities, which we used to generate the data for the cross-cultural comparisons afterwards, lacked a context that was sufficiently relevant to them. This is exactly the context that would usually be provided by the ABC's.

Therefore we closed the circle by relating back to where we had started, the *ABC's of Cultural Understanding and Communication*. We added questions which allowed the students to address the issues raised in the questionnaires by sharing part of their life stories. It was at this point that we realized that adapting Schmidt's (1998, 2001) ABC's Model, which we had already used in our face-to-face classes (see Finkbeiner, this volume; Finkbeiner & Koplin, 2001, 2002), might prove a valuable addition to our online ICE projects.

Seen against this background, we present and discuss the data obtained from one of the open-ended, personal questions to illustrate our first steps toward an adaptation of the ABC's model in an online environment.

## "How Important Is Religion in the United States, Your City, Your University, Your Family?" ["Welche Bedeutung hat Religion in Deutschland, in Ihrer Stadt, Ihrer Universität, Ihrer Familie?"]

We had our students first answer this question on an (anonymous) online questionnaire in the mother tongue—the students in Kassel answering in German, the students in Santa Barbara answering in English—and then compare and discuss their answers in an online forum. With regard to an online ABC's, it is, obviously, the final focus on "family" within this question that is of primary concern here. That is, we were especially interested in how our students would describe the importance of religion for their family or themselves personally. To what extent would they share rather personal information on this issue? And would they be willing to share these personal issues in an online environment and with partners they had only "met" online? These are the pivotal questions that guided our analysis of the data in the following questionnaire responses.

The scope of detail the students decided to reveal in their question-naire responses varied considerably, ranging from not addressing the importance of religion in their family or personal life, to quite detailed accounts of how religion has influenced or influences their life. According to the levels of detailed information provided, we categorized the students' answers into four levels:

*Level 0: The response does not address the importance of religion in the student's family or personal life.*

Responses at this level of detail simply omit the personal sphere alto-gether, even though they usually address the non-personal sphere (coun-try, city, university) in quite some detail. It should be noted, however, that we cannot say with any certainty whether a student deliberately avoided to address the personal sphere.

*Level 1: The response merely states that religion is of (no) importance in the student's family or personal life.*

Examples:

In my family religion is not that important. I would say that spirituality is important but we do not subscribe to one organized religion.

My family is a very odd religious mix. There are individuals who are Catho-lic, New Age, Liberal Ecumenical (part Catholic and Protestant), Conserva-tive Evangelical/Reformed. No one is an atheist.

Religion hat in meiner Familie (hauptsächlich bei meinen Eltern) einen hohen Stellenwert (Religion plays an important role in my family, especially for my parents].

Ich persönlich lege großen Wert darauf [d.h., auf Religion]. Obwohl ich nicht oft zur Kirche gehe, ehre ich Gott und fühle mich von ihm beschützt und gesegnet (Personally, I highly value it [i.e., religion]. Although I do not often go to church, I do honor God and feel protected and blessed by him).

Even though answers at this level may contain some interesting infor-mation about the religious aspects of a student's life (as, for example, in the second answer quoted above), they lack references to events or devel-opments in his/her life, which might trigger a further exchange of views, as would be crucial in our reciprocal version of the ABC's Model (see Finkbeiner, this volume).

*Level 2: The response states that religion is of (no) importance in the student's family or personal life and mentions one detail (underlined in the quotations below) from the student's life story.*

Examples:

I attended a Catholic school and received all the sacraments. I attend church every Sunday and am involved in my faith, as is the rest of my family.

Personally, I'm not religious. I used to be vehemently nonreligious, but I've settled into a sort of mellow agnosticism.

In meiner Familie sind fast alle aus der Kirche ausgetreten, allerdings glauben fast alle an Gott (In my family, almost everyone left their church, yet almost all of them believe in God).

Answers at this level refer to one specific detail, event or development in the person's biography that might lend itself to further exploration.

*Level 3: The response states that religion is of (no) importance in the student's family or personal life and mentions two or more details from the student's life story.*

Examples:

Both of my parents were raised Protestant, and they are still very spiritual. Although they never took me or my brothers to church, my mom frequently calls me with prayer requests. My boyfriend is Jewish, and my parents accept him, but they would prefer that I date a Christian guy.

Perhaps my view of religion is obscured by my personal opinions and the attitude of my family toward religion. Both my parents grew up as Catholics church goers but stopped going to church upon gaining independence from their parents and have actually gone on to explore other religions, particularly eastern religions such as Buddhism. Even my younger sister takes part in these explorations of other religions. She is fascinated by ancient Egyptians and their beliefs and has gone to Buddhist gatherings with my father.

Ich bin nicht christlich erzogen worden, obwohl ich getauft und konfirmiert bin. Meine Eltern haben mich nie zu irgendeinem Glauben gezwungen. Andererseits habe ich viel vom buddhistischen Glauben mitbekommen, dem meine Mutter angehört (I haven't been raised Christian, although I was baptized and received Confirmation. My parents never forced me into any belief. On the other hand, I'm quite familiar with Buddhism, which my mother practices).

Answers at this level refer to two or more specific details, events or developments in the person's biography that might lend themselves to further exploration.

**Table 10.5.  Levels of Detail in Students' Questionnaire Responses Addressing the Importance of Religion in Their Family or Personal Life**

| Group of students | Level of Detail* | | | | |
|---|---|---|---|---|---|
| | 0 | 1 | 2 | 3 | Mean |
| German students ( n = 41 ) | 19.5% | 36.6% | 24.4% | 19.5% | 1.44 |
| American students ( n = 22 ) | 18.2% | 40.9% | 31.8% | 9.1% | 1.32 |

*The levels of detail are defined as follows (examples of each level are given in the text):
0 = The response does not address the importance of religion in the student's family or personal life.
1 = The response merely states that religion is of (no) importance in the student's family or personal life.
2 = The response states that religion is of (no) importance in the student's family or personal life and mentions one detail from the student's life story.
3 = The response states that religion is of (no) importance in the student's family or personal life and mentions two or more details from the student's life story.

An overall picture of the amount of detailed personal information that the students shared through their questionnaire responses can be gleaned from Table 10.5. More than half of the German students, as well as more than half of the American students did not refer to the importance of religion in their family or personal lives (level 0), or merely stated that religion was (or was not) important for them without giving any further details (level 1).

This finding is of major relevance for our ultimate goal, the implementation of a full-fledged online ABC's: If our students refrained from sharing personal experiences and parts of their life stories in an online environment, the success of an online ABC's would be at stake, at least when following a format akin to the one we adopted here (i.e., using anonymous questionnaires, the responses to which were visible to all project participants; the issues of anonymity and privacy will be taken up in the evaluation of the ICE, below). However, the crux of the issue may lie in the format itself, which forced the instructors to use a preselected question presented in a questionnaire. Thus, the topics were not agreed upon by the participants. In this respect, a most basic principle of the ABC's as well as of autonomous constructivist learning had not been considered, which is, that all participants have to feel comfortable with the topic they talk about and explore.

On another, maybe surprising note, we observed that more German than American students supplemented their statements with specific details or references to events and experiences in their lives (see Table 10.5). This is a somewhat unexpected result in the light of earlier research which emphasizes the openness of Americans as far as conversing about their personal lives is concerned (see, for example, Furstenberg et al.,

2001). However, the figures presented in Table 10.5 cannot tell the full story, as we do not know if some of the students, who did not address this part of the question, skipped it incidentally or deliberately (for whatever reason). This may have skewed the results as presented in Table 10.5. In fact, two of the German students clearly stated their concerns as to sharing personal issues in an online environment:

> In meiner Familie spielt Religion eine kontroverse Rolle, die ich nicht im Internet verbreiten möchte (In my family, religion is a controversial issue, which I would not like to discuss on the Internet).

> Angaben über meine Familie verbreite ich definitiv nicht über das Netz! (I don't share information about my family on the web, that's for sure!).

Despite the already acknowledged problem that the question on religion had been preselected and not jointly agreed upon by the participants, these statements by some individual students as well as the overall picture, as summarized in Table 10.5, clearly show that it is of critical importance to further investigate issues of privacy, trust, and anonymity if an online ABC's is to succeed (see also Wilden, this volume). Our first step toward tackling this matter is represented in the ICE project evaluation.

## Evaluating the ICE

We conducted three ICE projects with our partners in Santa Barbara over two years, based on (a) our prior experiences with face-to-face ABC's projects (Finkbeiner & Koplin, 2002) and (b) Cultura as a "guide rope" for an online intercultural exchange. By building on the ABC's and Cultura models, we aimed at providing a well-structured framework, which we consider crucial—particularly at the beginning of any online exchange project—to keep the motivation up and the vehicles running, to return to the automobile metaphor.

In comparison with Cultura, we introduced new topics, which we felt would be interesting and stimulating for our students, in the online questionnaires and discussions; we employed different communication channels for the online discussions, including email, online forums (or bulletin boards), and online chat; and, finally, we experimented with a "new" type of question that would potentially lend itself to more open-ended, contextualized, personal, and at the same time sophisticated intercultural exchanges, as proposed by the ABC's Model (Schmidt, 1998, 2001).

In this chapter, we have not been able to deal in depth with all of these issues but have chosen to illustrate two major points: (1) the opportunities for intercultural learning provided to our students by the ICE pre-questionnaire as well as the word associations, sentence completions, and situation reactions; (2) the students' and our own initial experiences with questions of a more personal nature. Since we have now reached a stage where we, the instructors, feel ready to try a full-fledged online ABC's, we considered it paramount to ask our students for their feedback on how they felt about writing on the web and using different channels of electronic communication. In the following, we summarize and discuss our students' feedback and focus on those issues that may influence our way of shaping an online ABC's.

## How Did the Students Feel About Writing on the Web?

When confronted with this question, there was general agreement among both the students in Germany and the United States that the Internet and, in particular, the ICE project provided a great way of interacting with people thousands of miles away and learning more about each other's cultures. Here are some of the students' reactions:

> It was fun discussing cultural differences and practicing a second language with the use of internet technology. (Student on the U.S. campus)

> I think that this project is a very good experience because at the same time that you get to practice the language that you're learning you get to learn the culture. (Student on the U.S. campus)

> I actually like this internet-project in some ways. It's a good way of exchanging ideas and I had to think about some of the questions for a long time, because I never really thought about some things before. (Student on the German campus)

> I think it is just great to be able to communicate over long distances in the blink of a moment. (Student on the German campus)

However, one issue that actually resulted in an outpour of messages and interesting follow-up comments was that of anonymity, trust, honesty and seriousness in an educational online environment such as the ICE project website. All threads in the online forum on this topic were started by the German students, and overall there were 26 German students (but no American students) expressing some degree of concern regarding the anonymity of one's forum postings or the "intimate" character of some of the questionnaires:

> I'm a little bit afraid of the net. I don't trust it.... I'm careful to give personal information. (Student on the German campus)

It is very unusual to tell about your life and your thoughts somebody you don't know and you have never seen. (Student on the German campus)

One student said that she does not answer the questions like she really feels, because she gets influenced by the project's public forum. But what is the sense of a project in which the participants do not give access to their true initiate opinions, thoughts, ideas? If everyone just writes what he thinks will most please the profs or the project, than the whole online communication would not be satisfying, because the discussion would have no connection to the student's real life (the project would not be authentic). (Student on the German campus)

I have to agree that I do not like questions which are too personal like questions concerning my family and so on. But in order to make this thing work I, nevertheless, answer them vaguely and not that detailed. (Student on the German campus)

Don't you think that to ask for something like your relationship with your parents and how often you call them is too personal? I really got quite upset when I was supposed to answer this question. (Student on the German campus)

Moreover, the forum entries are not anonymous at all. This is the only thing I don't like. (Student on the German campus)

I don't want to answer personal questions and I don't see the point why someone should be interested in these answers. Moreover, I doubt that everybody's writing what he or she really thinks. Actually I dislike that everyone in my seminar knows now what I think about it (so I'd definitely prefer an anonymous forum). (Student on the German campus)

Obviously, these statements express some grave concerns and might, as some of the students quite adequately remark, jeopardize the entire project if its participants felt so uncomfortable about sharing personal information that they would rather not answer a particular question at all or even respond in a not (entirely) truthful way:

I also think it's strange that people are not writing what they feel in the forums. It's disappointing to think that some of the stuff you are reading may in fact just be completely made up, and it makes it harder to try to understand the people. (Student on the U.S. campus)

This statement captures the—apparently existing—danger of causing the exact opposite of what the project wants to achieve, that is, to undermine cultural understanding instead of promoting it. As mentioned above, 26 students on the German campus voiced their concerns regarding this issue, whereas 10 German students as well as 12 students on the U.S. campus stated clearly that they felt quite comfortable, both with regard to the online forum environment and the "personal" character of some of the questions:

> Personally I don't have a problem with the questions we had to answer so far. I think they were quite personal, but not too intimate. (Student on the German campus)

> I can't understand the students who felt uncomfortable about answering the questionnaires. Everybody was free what to write and nobody was forced to give away his/her most personal thoughts. (Student on the German campus)

> Personally, I don't see much differences between writing on the web, that is our forum, and contributing something to the class. (Student on the German campus)

> I definitely do not think that we should have been anonymous!! The internet is anonymous enough, I prefer to know at least the names of the people I share my thoughts with! I don't think that the questions were so private that we had to hide behind a nickname. (Student on the German campus)

> I don't have any problem writing about myself on the web in this forum, and would talk about almost anything. What people might consider too personal just depends on their level of comfort but it seems like most of the students are cool with writing about themselves. (Student on the U.S. campus)

> Most things are not too personal for me to divulge, especially over the internet where you have no face, you're just a bunch of abstract symbols. (Student on the U.S. campus)

> But generally I am honest about what I write, especially because on this forum I don't personally know any of the Germans, so why should I care who knows something about me? And it's not like my life is all that special that it's a big deal if people learn something about me. (Student on the U.S. campus)

> . . . it doesn't seem to bother us [i.e., the American students] as much. I can see what you're saying about personal questions about family and school life, but I guess that's why you can limit what you say. (Student on the U.S. campus){\ex}

Overall, the students on the U.S. campus seemed to be much more relaxed to share personal information and experiences in a non-anonymous format than the students on the German campus. Interestingly, this discussion *about* the project—that is, on a meta-cognitive level—revealed a cultural difference between Germans and Americans: "American openness" vs. "German reserve." Of course, to use this stereotype as a shorthand does not do justice to the complexities of reality, but it seems that this German-American difference did play a role in the specific context we are looking at. Furthermore, the German students' concerns about sharing "personal" information with all of their classmates and teachers bring to the fore a particular characteristic of the German educational system: Home-school connections, as stimulated by the ICE and the ABC's Model, are just not typical of schooling in Germany. For instance, when discussing this issue in one of our classes, some of our students did not like the idea of teachers coming into their homes for home visits at all; they considered it an intrusion into students' privacy.

As far as we can conclude from our students' feedback, the implementation of the ICE project did not accomplish a sufficiently comfortable or trustworthy environment for more than half of the German students. On the other hand, the American students as well as the remaining German students did not seem to see a problem here. Based on the data we obtained, it is very difficult to recognize any clear pattern, but in all likelihood, the question whether something is too personal to share in a project like this one is of an individual nature.

However, it would be wrong to simply disregard our students' concerns regarding anonymity, trust, and honesty; rather, it is necessary to think about the specific character of the online environment that we created for our project and how our students perceived it. We would like to discuss the following questions with an audience interested in this field:

- Is an online environment suitable for academic discussions only?
- To what extent is it meant for personal communication, getting to know and bonding with each other?
- Where does the "public" sphere end, and where does the "private" sphere start, and vice versa?
- How can we define the borderline between "public" and "private?"
- How do we deal with "public" and "private" issues in institutions that are clearly defined as "public?"

That we need to bear these questions in mind becomes clear when we consider the following: Even though none of the students on the U.S. campus seemed to be concerned with sharing personal information and experiences in a non-anonymous format, some of their statements quoted earlier as well as the actual level of detail they supplied in their responses (see Table 10.5 above) support the assumption that the ICE environment was not perfectly suited for truly personal communication. For instance, consider a student's statement like "over the Internet you have no face, you're just a bunch of abstract symbols," or a question like "on this forum

I don't personally know any of the Germans, so why should I care who knows something about me?" Forum postings like these illustrate how difficult it can be to build an online community that goes beyond a virtual meeting place for "academic" discussions, which may be adequate for a Cultura-style intercultural exchange but not a more personal, biographic approach such as the ABC's model. However, we would also like to mention that, despite these difficulties, some students did succeed in developing a deeper relationship with their transatlantic partners; these culminated in personal visits on both sides.

## The Form of Electronic Communication and Its Impact on How to Convey Personal Information

We would like to conclude with some suggestions on how we plan to tackle the problems outlined before. It turned out to be fortunate that some of the students in Santa Barbara and Kassel participated in two "rounds" of the ICE and were thus able to give us some specific feedback on the changes we had made in the setup of the project. Specifically, they commented on the different forms of electronic communication they had used and how this affected the way they felt about conveying personal information: While in the second ICE project the students were required to discuss the questionnaire responses by email, they used an online forum (or bulletin board) for this purpose in the third ICE.

There was unanimous agreement among the students that the online forum was more appropriate for discussing the issues raised in the questionnaires, in particular as far as the public side of the message was concerned, as the following comments illustrate exemplarily:

> I think that the online forum was a much better format for the discussions that the email partners last quarter. I was more interested in sticking to the subject of the questionnaires with this format. However, the email partners provided a better opportunity to get to know the other person individually, which brings a lot of insight into understanding other cultures. The email also allows for further private discussions.

> I also thought this board was better than the email exchange; well at least as far as for writing on the topics. The email had the advantage of being a little more personal and doing other things like sending e-cards. But as far as for doing the assignments, this was better.

> I have mixed feelings about the forum versus the e-mail partners thing. In some ways, there was more of a sense of immediacy and personal interaction with the e-mail partners system. On the other hand, the forum was more appropriate for discussing the topics, answers, etc.

At the same time, however, the students clearly emphasized the more personal nature of email in comparison to the forum. This raises the question whether our students would have been more willing to talk about more personal topics (see above) if they had been allowed to do this via email with one or two partners they had got to know a little better, that is, on a somewhat more individual level. Clearly, some of the German students seemed to categorically object to the idea of sharing "personal" information and opinions on the web, especially when they were asked to do this in a forum with their (real) names attached to their postings.

Apparently, there seem to be two diverging positions: Some students would like to build closer relationships with their partners overseas, which would provide them with a sufficiently "trustworthy" environment for more personal exchanges (as it could be done in an online ABC's); some other students, in contrast, would prefer to stay completely anonymous (e.g., by using nicknames) in order to feel "safe" when discussing topics at a personal level (granted that they would be willing to do so at all). Some suggestions on how we plan to tackle this challenge are outlined in the following conclusion of this chapter.

## SOME LESSONS WE HAVE LEARNED: GETTING READY FOR AN ONLINE ABC'S

At first glance, it seems obvious that a face-to-face environment is superior to an online environment in intercultural learning, especially when the focus is more on the private than on the public. While questions, as posed in Cultura, seem to be suitable and adequate to be answered and discussed online, more personal issues as raised in the ABC's are more difficult to deal with. However, particularly since the online environment allows for cooperation between people across the world—independent of time and space constraints—we strongly believe that we need to face the challenge of creating an adequate, interesting, and safe online environment for intercultural learning that serves the linguistic, cultural, and emotional needs of our learners. In order for this to happen we suggest the following for future research as well as practice:

- Students' participation in intercultural online projects must be voluntary; this means that planning must be made long beforehand, so that students can already make the decision for or against the project when they register for a class. In this way, the learners have a better feeling right from the beginning, as they are taken seriously, and the instructors can rely on motivated participants. Whenever a class is mandatory (such as most classes in secondary school settings), teachers need to find agreement with the class whether to start working on such a project (Finkbeiner, 1995).

- Phases of mutual feedback and meta-cognition have to be included that do not only focus on the content and subject matter, but also, on aspects such as feelings and anxieties.

- The issue of "private" vs. "public" must be explicitly dealt with in class. This relates to the linguistic, emotional, cultural, and subject-specific level.

- Topics need to be negotiated by the participants. They determine the topics they are interested in, which can make them feel safer within the online environment.

- Last, but not least, there needs to be constant technological support, as in the most crucial project phases, computer problems seem to occur. The instructors ought to cooperate closely with the web master; ideally, the instructors themselves, with the help of student assistants, can manage the online environment.

Despite all the problems and questions raised, we would like to encourage all readers to join the adventure of intercultural online exchanges together with people from all over the world. Cooperating and interacting online on a global scale is a big step toward world peace, and all of us are responsible for this, just as mentioned before: "We are the world."

### NOTES

1. The ICE projects were followed by two more online projects with our partners at UCSB. These projects were also aimed at refining the ABC's for use in an online environment (Knierim, Wade, & Wilden, 2004).

2. The authors of this chapter—each of whom (co-) taught two of the classes mentioned above—hereby wish to acknowledge the commitment and support of our colleagues Eva Wilden and Christine Koplin in conducting the ABC's and ICE projects.

3. We would like to thank Dr. Dorothy Chun, Evelyn Wade, and Patrick Rebuschat, all of whom have contributed at various stages to the ongoing development of the project; we hereby wish to acknowledge their cooperation and suggestions in this joint project.

4. It should be noted that, as is typical of teaching degrees in Germany, all of the Kassel students had one or two other subjects (besides English) for which they were seeking qualification.

5. Here we already have to face the problem that the term "education" stands for two terms in German: "Bildung" and "Erziehung." We decided for the first ("Bildung"; adjective: "gebildet") as it has a stronger connection to academic learning and the acquisition of knowledge, whereas "Erziehung" foregrounds the social process of raising one's children and imparting

societal norms with the goal of shaping a person's behavior (cf. the definitions in German encyclopedias/dictionaries such as *Brockhaus* and *Duden*, or the German version of *Encarta* at http://de.encarta.msn.com).

## REFERENCES

ACTFL (American Council on the Teaching of Foreign Languages). (2001). *Preliminary proficiency guidelines*. Writing (Revised 2001). Alexandria, VA: ACTFL. Retrieved February 15, 2005, from: http://www.actfl.org/files/public/writing-guidelines.pdf.

Belz, J. (2003). Linguistic perspectives on the development of intercultural competence in telecollaboration. *Language Learning & Technology, 7*(2), 68-117.

Clark, I. (1997). *Globalization and fragmentation. International relations in the twentieth century*. Oxford: Oxford University Press.

Fehling, S. (2005). *Language Awareness und bilingualer Unterricht: Eine komparative Studie*. Frankfurt: Lang.

Feyten, C.M., Macy, M.D., Ducher, J., Yoshii, M., Park, E., Calandra, B.D., & Meros, J. (2002). *Teaching ESL/EFL with the Internet: Catching the wave*. Upper Saddle River, NJ: Prentice Hall.

Finkbeiner, C. (1995). *Englischunterricht in europäischer Dimension: Zwischen Qualifikationserwartungen der Gesellschaft und Schülereinstellungen und Schülerinteressen. Berichte und Kontexte zweier empirischer Untersuchungen*. Bochum: Brockmeyer.

Finkbeiner, C. (2001). One and all in CALL? Learner—moderator—researcher. *Computer Assisted Language Learning, 14*(3-4), 339-361.

Finkbeiner, C. (2004). Cooperation and collaboration in a foreign language teacher training program: The LMR plus model. In E. Cohen, C. Brody, & M. Sapon-Shevin (Eds.), *Learning to teach with cooperative learning: Challenges in teacher education* (pp. 111-127). Albany: State University of New York Press.

Finkbeiner, C. (2005). *Interessen und Strategien beim fremdsprachlichen Lesen. Wie Schülerinnen und Schüler englische Texte lesen und verstehen*. Tübingen: Narr.

Finkbeiner, C., & Fehling, S. (2002). Bilingualer Unterricht: Aktueller Stand und Implementierungsmöglichkeiten im Studium. In C. Finkbeiner (Ed.), *Bilingualer Unterricht. Lehren und Lernen in zwei Sprachen* (pp. 9-22). Hannover: Schroedel.

Finkbeiner, C., & Koplin, C. (2000). Handlungsorientiert Fremdverstehen lernen und lehren. *Fremdsprachenunterricht, 44/53*(4), 254-261.

Finkbeiner, C., & Koplin, C. (2001). Fremdverstehensprozesse und interkulturelle Prozesse als Forschungsgegenstand. In A. Müller-Hartmann & M. Schocker-v. Ditfurth (Eds.), *Qualitative Forschung im Bereich Fremdsprachen lehren und lernen* (pp. 114-136). Tübingen: Narr.

Finkbeiner, C., & Koplin, C. (2002). A cooperative approach for facilitating intercultural education. *Reading Online, 6* (3). Retrieved February 15, 2005, from: http://www.readingonline.org/newliteracies/lit_index.asp?HREF=/newliteracies/finkbeiner.

Furstenberg, G., Levet, S., English, K., & Maillet, K. (2001). Giving a virtual voice to the silent language of culture: The Cultura project. *Language Learning & Technology, 5*(1), 55-102.

Hanna, B.E., & de Nooy, J. (2003). A funny thing happened on the way to the forum: Electronic discussion and foreign language learning. *Language Learning & Technology, 7*(1), 71-85.

Herring, S. (2001). Foreword. In C. Ess (Ed.), *Culture, technology, communication* (pp. vii-x). Albany: State University of New York Press.

Internet World Stats. (2005a). *Usage and population statistics: Oceania & South Pacific.* Retrieved February, 15, 2005, from: http://www.internetworldstats.com/pacific.htm.

Internet World Stats. (2005b). *Usage and population statistics: Africa.* Retrieved February, 15, 2005, from: http://www.internetworldstats.com/africa.htm.

James, C., & Garrett, P. (Eds.). (1991). *Language awareness in the classroom.* London: Longman.

Knierim, M. (2004). Chatten im Fremdsprachenunterricht—Making the most of it. *FMF Hessen, 18,* 47-59.

Knierim, M., Wade, E., & Wilden, E. (2004, September 1-4). *Intercultural learning online with the ABC's of intercultural understanding and communication.* Paper presented at the EUROCALL 2004 conference, Vienna, Austria.

Kramsch, C. (1993). *Context and culture in language teaching.* Oxford: Oxford University Press.

Menzel, U. (1998). *Globalisierung versus Fragmentierung.* Frankfurt: Suhrkamp.

O'Connor, P.E. (2000, May 26). *Language and culture—connections and disconnections.* Paper presented at the SIETAR Deutschland Kongress "Interkulturelles Lernen und interkulturelles Management," Ludwigshafen, Germany.

O'Dowd, R. (2000). Intercultural learning via videoconferencing: A pilot exchange project. *ReCALL, 12*(1), 49-61.

O'Dowd, R. (2002). Intercultural learning and the Internet: An overview. *TELL & CALL, 3,* 6-11.

Omaggio Hadley, A. (1993). *Teaching language in context* (2nd ed.). Boston, MA: Heinle & Heinle.

Schmidt, P.R. (1998). The ABC's of cultural understanding and communication. *Equity and Excellence in Education, 31*(2), 28-38.

Schmidt, P.R. (1999). Focus on research: Know thyself and understand others. *Language Arts, 76*(4), 332-340.

Schmidt, P.R. (2001). The power to empower: Creating home/school relationships with the ABC's of cultural understanding and communication. In P.R. Schmidt & P.B. Mosenthal (Eds.), *Reconceptualizing literacy in the new age of multiculturalism and pluralism* (pp. 389-433). Greenwich, CT: Information Age Publishing.

Smith, B. (1997). Virtual realia. *The Internet TESL Journal, 3*(7). Retrieved February 15, 2005, from: http://iteslj.org/Articles/Smith-Realia.html.

Sussex, R., & White, P. (1996). Electronic networking. *Annual Review of Applied Linguistics, 16,* 200-225.

Weaver, G. R. (1993). Understanding and coping with cross-cultural adjustment stress. In M. Paige (Ed.), *Education for the intercultural experience* (2nd ed., pp. 137-167). Yarmouth, ME: Intercultural Press.

CHAPTER 11

# USING THE ABC'S MODEL IN MANAGEMENT EDUCATION

**La Verne Hairston Higgins**

*Business students have to learn to speak other languages and
have to respect for other cultures.*
—Shalala (2002)[1]

*Cross-fertilization of ideas and issues seems a productive approach to take to the
development of theory and empirical research ...*
—De Cieri and Dowling (1999)

## ABSTRACT

Many colleges and schools of business or management have been responding to calls for increased emphasis on diversity and global issues and perspectives in their curricula. This has given rise to debate on how best to
infuse these issues into the curriculum as well as questions about which pedagogical approaches will be most effective mechanism for delivery. After
more than a decade, these debates remain largely unresolved. The questions assume an added saliency for small, mono-ethnic institutions. In
addressing these issues, the pedagogy of multicultural education, specifically Banks' (1993) typology of knowledge, is presented as a framework for

*ABC's of Cultural Understanding and Communication:
National and International Adaptations*, 245–264
Copyright © 2006 by Information Age Publishing

management education. Within this framework, issues of diversity and cross-national interaction become integral to the education of organizational learners. The *ABC of Cultural Understanding and Communication* (Schmidt, 1998a), a successful model used in the multicultural education of United States teachers, has been translated for the education of U.S. management students.

## INTRODUCTION

Issues of globalization and diversification emerged as salient concerns for businesses in the last two decades of the twentieth century. Johnston and Packer heralded the changing worldwide demographics in 1987; and businesses paid attention. Some firms had already begun to recognize the need for awareness of cultural, ethnic and national differences. For example, Hofstede's (1980a,b, 1983, 1984, 1991) work chronicling cultural dimensions at the national levels was given early assistance by IBM. By 2000, management scholars had created volumes of research and theory centered on issues of domestic diversity and globalization. AACSB,[2] the major accrediting agency for management and business[3] programs worldwide, had added diversity and globalization to its curriculum standards. While many of the practical issues that organizations face with regard to diversity and globalization have been addressed, an even larger gap exists concerning the pedagogy of diversity and globalization. Questions about how to improve the ability of management program graduates to function in multicultural, international environments requires such urgency that the Journal of International Management devoted a special issue in 2000 to the pedagogy and domain of international management.

Based on 2000 US Census data, Day and Jamieson (2003) reported significant variations in college enrollment by racioethnic[4] group. While Asian Americans had the highest enrollment rate for both traditional age (18-24 years) and older students, only one other group exceeded the average national enrollment rate—European Americans. Specifically, while approximately one third of the U.S. population 18 to 24 years of age was pursuing higher education in 2000, only 28% of all non-European American populations were doing so. This percentage drops below 24% when Asian Americans are excluded. Furthermore, only 14% of Hispanics of all racial groups were enrolled.

For faculty in those institutions populated by students from very homogeneous backgrounds, the question of how to enhance students' ability to interact in a multicultural, multiracial environment presents an added challenge. Even given the increased diversity on college campuses, U.S. higher education remains dominantly European American and middle class. On private as well as non-urban campuses the proportion of students from diverse ethnic, cultural and linguistic backgrounds is rarely found to attain 25% (Day & Jamieson, 2003). It is not surprising then that many management instructors are seeking pedagogically valid techniques for exposing management students to the issues of doing business in an extra-country environment.

## Why Cross-Cultural Education?

Findings similar to those of Hofstede (1980a,b, 1991) have resulted from the work of researchers such as Laurent (1983), Ronen and Shekar (1985) and more recently Trompenaars (1994), Trompenaars and Hampden-Turner (2004), and Trompenaars, Hampden-Turner, and Trompenaars (1998). The importance of cultural sensitivity for international management is today widely acknowledged (i.e., Adler, 1992, 2002; Adler & Ghadar, 1990a,b; Doz, Bartlett & Prahalad, 1981; Gladwin & Walter, 1980; Lincoln & Kalleberg, 1990; Punnett, 1994; Tung, 1995). While anthropological concepts such as ethnocentrism have now become part of the lexicon of international management (e.g., Adler, 2002, Gladwin & Walter, 1980; Harpaz, 1996), little attention has been paid to how best to disseminate this knowledge to students in a meaningful manner.

A parallel stream of theory and research has emerged in the diversity literature. Cox (1993), Gentile (1994), and Thomas (1996) have focused primarily on how to increase diversity awareness in organizations. Others like Bell and Nkomo (2001) and Thomas and Gabarro (1999) have chronicled the experiences of non-majority individuals in the U.S. workplace. In a variety of journals (e.g., Journal of Management Education) and books (e.g., Bucher, 2000; Cox & Beale, 1997; Gentile, 1996; Powell & Graves, 2003; Thomas, 2004), exercises and case studies have emerged as the main techniques for increasing diversity awareness in the workplace and to a lesser extent in the classroom. However, these techniques tend to be discrete in nature and do not result in long-term student engagement with diversity issues.

As business curricula have placed new emphasis on internationalization, teacher education programs in the United States have increased emphasis on diversity education. In recent years, the influx of culturally diverse populations from around the world has made it important for United States educators to promote an understanding and appreciation of diversity among their students (Kiefer & DeStefano, 1985). Also high rates of school dropouts have been linked to the alienation of students from non-majority ethnic and cultural backgrounds (Trueba, Jacobs, & Kirton, 1990). Potentially, educational institutions serve as sites where students may learn to examine and respect multiple perspectives and ways of life (Cummins, 1986; Delpit, 1995; Washburn, Brown, & Abbott, 1996). This additive view (Cummins, 1986) not only enriches and enlivens the classroom, but also encourages individuals from all groups to contribute to the mainstream in positive ways (Cummins, 1986; Nieto, 1995). Frequently, though, opportunities to share non-majority Western cultures are ignored. This is usually due to inadequate teacher preparation (Au, 1993; Banks, 1994), and the lack of teacher awareness of their own and other cultures (Paley, 1989; Pattnaik, 1997).

Consequently, diversity education, like international management, can trace its emergence in management curricula to the need to work effectively with diverse populations. Yet even as programs for international management and organizational diversity have recognized the need for curricular change, pedagogical advancement has not proceeded systematically (see Gallos & Ramsey, 1996).

Banks (1997) delineated approaches for integrating multicultural content into the curriculum. The first and easiest is "the contributions approach," in which discrete cultural elements are added to an existing curriculum. For the United States business curriculum, an example would be the identification of Buddhist holidays or the listing of Hindu deities during a discussion of religious discrimination in a human resource management course. "The additive approach" is the next level of curricula integration. In the additive approach, cultural concepts, perspectives, values and other cultural content are integral to a curriculum. An example of the "additive approach" is the inclusion of information about Confucianism in an organizational behavior course. These first two approaches are evident in many "international" text and courses used in business schools in the United States. The third and next step, "the transformation approach," necessitates changing curricula to fully integrate multi-cultural content. According to Banks (1997), this approach requires modifying a curriculum's basic assumptions by "the infusion of perspectives, frames of reference, and content from different groups that will extend students' understanding of the nature, development, and complexity of the ... world." How to accomplish this integration is the challenge facing educators. An understanding of the mechanisms for the construction and transmission of knowledge is the first step in developing strategies to achieve this level of cultural integration within curricula.

## Knowledge Construction

In response to changes within the populations of elementary and secondary education, Banks (1993) synthesized the pedagogy of diversity education. Banks outlined the four types of knowledge that blend to produce the body of knowledge that exists in the educational environment. These four types—personal/cultural, popular, mainstream academic and transformative academic—provide each individual in the educational setting with knowledge that affects how the facts, concepts and generalizations presented in the classroom are synthesized. Those facts, concepts and generalizations are termed "school knowledge" in Banks' typology. "Personal/cultural knowledge" is that which the student brings to the classroom from their family, past experiences and culture. Such knowledge guides their behavior, because it defines expectations and behavioral norms for individual learners. On the other hand, the institutionalized knowledge that is acquired through various mass media venues also influences the learning process within the classroom. Within Banks' typology this is termed "popular knowledge." "Personal/cultural knowledge" and "popular knowledge" provide the context within which learners interact with their teachers. Into the learning environment, teachers bring theories, practices and perspectives traditionally within the domain of social sciences. These are called "mainstream academic knowledge" and constitute the third class of knowledge in Banks' typology. Banks further defines this knowledge as "empirical knowledge, uninfluenced by human values and interests, constitut(ing) a body of objective truths … form(ing) the core of the … curriculum" (p. 8). Banks delineates this kind of academic truth from 'transformative academic knowledge' which is a body of concepts, theories and perspectives which challenges the universality of "mainstream academic knowledge" (Banks, 1993). Transformative academic knowledge is essential for the cultural integration of curricula (Banks, 1997).

Based on Banks' (1993) typology of knowledge, management education can be seen as "transformative academic knowledge" that enhances personal/cultural knowledge and mainstream academic knowledge, thus transforming school knowledge by providing the student with enhanced

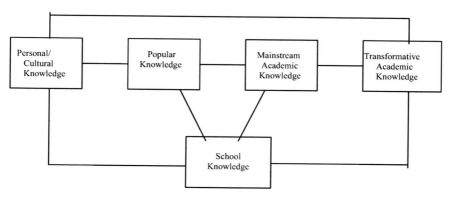

Figure 11.1.   The interrelationship of types of knowledge (Banks, 1993).

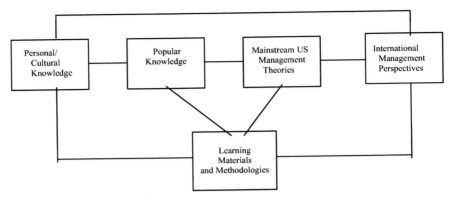

Figure 11.2.   A typology of business knowledge based on Banks (1993).

abilities to critically evaluate and assess their heuristics. The value of such a transformation centers on its use as a powerful tool in debunking the stereotypes and inaccuracies based in popular knowledge, which individuals bring into their learning and work environments.

The benefits of Banks' (1993) pedagogical approach for teaching international/multicultural issues and perspectives stem from the changes to the total environment, so that students understand how knowledge is constructed, which in turn allows them to investigate and determine cultures influence on those knowledge constructs. Thus, by first understanding their own cultural knowledge, which is the root of United States management perspectives (i.e., mainstream academic knowledge), the next step, the discovery of cultural roots of non-United States management perspectives ( i.e., transformative academic knowledge) is facilitated. After recasting Banks' typology in terms of management education, Figure 11.2 was derived to illustrate the role of international, diversity and multicultural management education of learners.

## APPROPRIATENESS OF THE ABC'S OF CULTURAL UNDERSTANDING AND COMMUNICATION© FOR MANAGEMENT CLASSROOMS

*The telling of personal stories appears to reduce the social distance between people with different social identities, while making the issues that confront the tell and the listener accessible to each other. When successful, educative encounters create the context for a sequence that in many cases propels itself from risk to reciprocity to respect.*

—Creed and Scully (2000)

One model for the incorporation of transformative academic knowledge is the ABC's of Cultural Understanding and Communication (Schmidt, 1998a,b, 1999, 2000, 2001). Schmidt's ABCs[5] Model uses students' personal knowledge to identify limitations of mainstream curriculum as well as barriers that impede acknowledgment of and conform with differences. Banks (1993) asserts that such an exercise develops in students the enhanced abilities to remain open to creative and non-heuristic ideas. By developing such abilities, students are able to "think outside the box" and to become lifelong or "continuous learners." The value of such abilities has been expounded widely by management scholars (e.g., Argyris, 1976, 1991; Inkpen, 1995; Pfeffer, 1994, Porter, 1990; Senge, 1990). Gentile (1996), for example, identifies the characteristics of organizational leaders for diversity as including "a commitment to learning: individuals who are energized by and drawn to new points of view, opportunities to enrich their view of their work, their world, and themselves ... are excited by the potential for innovation represented by different perspectives and styles of actions" (p. 477). Use of the *ABCs Model* in the education of teachers has been demonstrated to enhance receptiveness of students to insights into their own and others' personal/cultural knowledge (Schmidt, 1998a,b, 1999, 2000, 2001).

The homogeneous population of U.S. teachers encountered by Schmidt is analogous to U.S. management students. One management student stated "I'm an American; I don't have a culture." In fact, this characterization is typical for teachers in the United States, since 90.7% describe themselves as European American and from the middle socioeconomic levels (Florio-Ruane, 1994; Ladson-Billings 1994; Snyder, Hoffman & Geddes, 1997). Additionally, many teachers have not had sustained relationships with people from other ethnic and cultural groups, so their knowledge base has most likely been influenced by mass media, i.e., "popular knowledge" (Pattnaik, 1997). Consequently, these factors make it difficult for teachers to connect home and school for meaningful learning experiences (Heath, 1983; McCaleb, 1994; Schmidt, 1998a,b).

One twenty-year-old management student stated,

> I've just led such a sheltered life ... I was never, I never had any friends or people that I knew who were of a different race or anything. I had like a few Jewish friends and that was it. There were hardly any African Americans that lived in my town. There are no Asian Americans. Now there's more, but when I was a child there weren't any.

Like their education counterparts, management students require pedagogical approaches that prepare them to interact in the globally diverse workforces of modern business.

## Self-knowledge in Management Curriculum

One of the most traditional streams in management curricula is organizational behavior. This discipline grows out of various social sciences, with primary influences from psychology, sociology, anthropology, political science and economics. Many of the foundation scholars in management were trained in these fields. Consequently, the concept of self-knowledge arises in management education primarily in organizational behavior courses, often through discussion of leadership.

Anthropologists (e.g., Clifford, 1988; Enx, 1992; Geertz, 1973; Gergen, 1990) have noted the difficulties for those seeking to understand cultures other than their own. These theorists argue that awareness of one's attitudes, assumptions, beliefs and values is essential to understanding how one interprets the behaviors, customs, and values of others (Gergen, 1990). Self-knowledge, therefore, is an essential first step for the understanding of others. At the micro-level, Markus and Kitayama (1991) provided a detailed exploration of the psychological interplay between self-concept and culture. Manz and Sims (1987, 1991), Manz and Neck (2004) and O'Neil (1997) have married self-knowledge and business acumen in their work on leadership. However, the centrality of self-knowledge and self-leadership in management education for understanding issues of diversity and globalization trends has yet to be fully drawn. Recently, Lowney (2003) asserted "self-awareness is the prelude to fulfilled, committed engagement with the world," but did not specifically address national and cultural difference except within historical contexts. Earlier, Gallos and Ramsey (1996) chronicled the self-awareness journeys of several diversity educators in higher education business programs. Markus and Kitayama (1991) have highlighted the importance of culture to individuals' self-awareness. In their analysis of diversity training techniques, Bhawauk, Podsiadlowki, Graf, and Triandis (2002) discussed the role of understanding one's own culture for learning to how to work in diverse, multicultural situations. Nonetheless, the question of how to provide the transition from self-knowledge to openness to other cultures has not been pedagogically ameliorated.

Fortunately within the teacher preparation literature, descriptions of several promising research interventions (Cochran-Smith, 1995; Finkbeiner, 2004; Florio-Ruane, 1994; Noordhoff & Kleinfield, 1993; Spindler & Spindler, 1987; Tatum, 1992; Willis & Meacham, 1997) suggested new paths toward such preparation. All incorporate reading, writing, talking, and listening for gaining knowledge of self as an important step for understanding and bridging diverse backgrounds. From these studies and others, the model known as the *ABC's of Cultural Understanding and Com-*

*munication* (Schmidt, 1998a) was created and developed on the premise of knowing oneself and understanding others.

## ABC'S OF CULTURAL UNDERSTANDING AND COMMUNICATION

### Autobiography: Know Thyself

Research suggests that the first step in developing culturally sensitive pedagogy is to discover one's own cultural identity in order to appreciate the similarities and differences that exist between oneself and others (Gergen, 1990). Noordhoff and Kleinfeld (1993) concluded in their study of teachers preparing for multicultural classrooms that teachers increased their effectiveness in educating diverse student populations by examining their personal histories and educational biographies for clues to the ways their beliefs, images, and experiences.

The first step or "A" begins with one's own knowledge through thinking and writing about one's family histories that include memorable life events. This increases awareness of personal beliefs and attitudes that form the traditions and values of cultural autobiographies (Banks, 1994). Since it is well documented that writing is linked to the knowledge of self within a social context (Emig, 1971; Yinger, 1985), writing one's life story seems to construct connections with universal human tenets and serves to lessen negative ideas and stereotypes about different groups of people (Progoff, 1975). As a result, a new awareness of one's own perceptions regarding differences is acquired (Banks, 1994; Sjoberg & Kuhn, 1989). Finally, the process of writing an autobiography sets the stage for learning about another person's life story or "B," biography.

### Biographies: Interviewing and Discovering Others

Through the interview process, students can construct the biography of a culturally different person from key events in that person's life. Recently, research has demonstrated that interviewing people to write their life stories helped teachers as well as their students become more culturally sensitive (Schmidt, 1998a,b; Spindler & Spindler, 1987). After documenting a person's story, the discovery of similarities and differences permits interesting cross-cultural analysis. Furthermore, Crapanzano (1990) argues that such analyses lead to greater self-awareness.

### Cross-Cultural Analysis: Critiquing Similarities and Differences

Those who have interviewed people from others cultures and performed written, cross-cultural self-analyses or "C" to discover and discuss similarities and differences (Spindler & Spindler, 1987), acquired insights about others and began to sense their own ethnocentricity. Similarly, comparing similarities and contrasting differences forms the foundation for in-depth class discussions that lead to an understanding and appreciation of differences. Traditionally, similarities among people have been celebrated and differences have been ignored (Cummins, 1986; Gentile, 1994; Trueba et al., 1990). However, when differences are ignored, a disempowering process occurs as individuals' personal/cultural knowledge is subtracted from the learning community (Cummins, 1986). It is empowering when differences are recognized (Finkbeiner, 2004; Thomas, 1994).

## Communication: Building Bridges

Research suggests that when individuals meet with people who are different from themselves, the personal is accentuated and internalization of information is fostered (Enz, 1992; Erez & Earley, 1993; Gergen, 1990; Rogers, 1951). For teachers who have written an autobiography, cultural differences were subsequently examined in a positive manner and related to their own personal histories (Banks, 1994; Britzman, 1986; Ladson-Billings, 1994). The interview process can serve as a means for sharing life stories and learning about similarities and differences (Spindler & Spindler, 1987).

Those teachers who have experienced the *ABC's of Cultural Understanding and Communication* have noted specific differences in their classroom practice and communication with families and communities (Finkbeiner, 2004; Finkbeiner & Koplin, 2002; Schmidt, 1998a,b, 1999, 2000, 2001; Xu, 2000a,b). They report that since their experience with the process of careful examination in their autobiographies, they see others more clearly. Additionally, the biographies of others heightened awareness of their own problems and possibilities as well as increased an appreciation for others' lives. This, in turn, led them to create and successfully implement plans for greater understanding of similarities and differences in their work environments. Finally, they interact more frequently with diverse communities after their *ABC's* experience.

This key concept for the *ABC's Model* is a well-established psychological tenet (Crapanzano, 1990; Finkbeiner, 2004; Rogers, 1951). The idea that self-knowledge provides a firm foundation for the understanding of others is also central to recent trends in ethnographic research (see Brannen, 1996), as well as for international business research (e.g., Adler, 2002; Erez & Early, 1993).

## ABC'S OF CULTURAL UNDERSTANDING AND COMMUNICATION IN THE MANAGEMENT CLASSROOM

Given the parallel populations in education and management classrooms, and the similarities between multi/cross-cultural and international studies, the utilization of the *ABC's Model* among U.S. management students appeared to be a pedagogically appropriate adaptation. Therefore, over the last five years a number of management students have encountered this model as part of their classrooms.

In early 1999, a pilot application of multicultural education pedagogy to international management was initiated. Undergraduate management students were recruited to participate. The purpose of this pilot project was to explore the applicability of the *ABCs Model* for enhancing international management education. The pilot project was analyzed to identify modifications which might be necessary for the management student population. At the end of the pilot, no modifications of the *ABCs Model* were deemed necessary. Subsequently, the model was integrated into the curriculum of several management courses.

### Student Responses

The ABCs have been incorporated into courses enrolling students in their third year of undergraduate study as well as graduate students pursuing masters in business administration degrees. Reactions to the autobiography process were varied. One Latina from a large urban center characterized the process of writing an autobiography as painful, because it brought back memories that she had suppressed. "I thought of a lot of things that I had repressed." A European American male from a suburban community said writing his autobiography was fun, because he got to think about all the 'adventures' he'd had growing up. Through this exercise, a deep friendship developed between a European American female and an African American female when they discovered many parallels in their backgrounds, present lives and their values. This led one of them to state "it was really amazing … (that we had) so many things which were the same."

A European American male graduate student reported gaining new insights into the management style of his boss, who was from the same culture as the individual whose biography he wrote. The surprise expressed by an Asian male on discovering numerous similarities with an African American female was not uncommon. According to him, "our conversations were really different from what I had expected. She's not that different ... very unlike what the American movies (shown) back home (lead me to expect)."

Conversely, the differences were often dismissed as inconsequential or noted as cause of uneasiness. Two graduate students, an African male and a European American female, classified their differences as "almost non-existent," despite differences in economic and religious backgrounds. However, although an undergraduate European American female was very comfortable talking with a South Asian male, she did say "the way he explained things was very different for me."

One European American male undergraduate who interviewed an African male noted "When he was talking about growing up with his neighborhood friends, playing sports, playing soccer in particular ... (it) reminded me of playing ball at home with my friends." However a discussion of racial differences was a cause for concern because, it "made me uneasy, the only reason that I was real uneasy, was making him uncomfortable. That was my concern."

Some of the similarities and differences identified by the students during their interviews are detailed in the Table 11.1.

Each student was asked whether this project had any value for them as management students today and as future employees. All agreed that the project had been helpful for increasing their awareness of not only their own culture, but of cultural differences as well. Indeed, arguments were made for the inclusion of the *ABC's Model* into the management curriculum. Typical undergraduate student sentiments included "I wish I'd done this earlier. This should at the beginning (or one's management courses) ... I learned so much that was helpful."

Similar to the above expressions, one student seemed to summarize class reactions,

> If everyone could do just a little something that would make them think about exactly what kind of life they've lived and their differences between other people, I think it would be DEFINITELY beneficial ... being aware of my feelings and my thoughts, help me understand other people's feelings and other people's thoughts much, much better. And that would help anyone whether at work or at home, in social aspect, in being able to know other people, in understanding them. I think it would be very helpful. If people could just learn about themselves ... be aware of themselves, they'll be more aware of others.{\ex}

Graduate students generally attributed the benefits of the ABCs experience in terms of applicability to their workplace and community interactions. Their reflective statements centered primarily on gaining "new insights" for use with co-workers (at all levels) and customers whose nationalities, religions, and behavioral norms are "very strange" or differ-

**Table 11.1.   Similarities and Differences Identified by Students During Interviews**

| Similarities | Differences |
|---|---|
| • first name | • relationship with parents |
| • large families | • ability to cook |
| • earned associates degrees | • house vs. apartment |
| • Dean's list | • religion |
| • head lice in elementary school | • year in college |
| • baby sitting experience | • high school graduation |
| • vacation locales | • financial support from parents |
| • best friend who is like a brother | • parents' age |
| • softball | • playing a musical instrument |
| • dancing | • having a best friend |
| • dolls and collections | • ulcer |
| • disciplinarian parents | • living style |
| • lots of friends | • closeness of family |
| • teen-age work experience | • resources available |
| • high parental expectations | • government |
| • divorced parents | • public's reaction to infractions |
| • views on education | • athletic involvement |
| • community involvement | • minority/majority status experience |
| • socioeconomic status | • sex |
| • no experience with poverty | • residing in country during a revolution |
| • travel | • private schooling |
| • supportive family | • color, ethnicity or race |
| • parental expectations | • cosmopolitan |
| • national college entrance exams | • free higher education |
| • multi-ethnic home country | • first language |
| • career goals | • Sabbath and holidays observed |

ent. One graduate student, for example, expressed new interest in travel outside the United States; "If given the chance, I would like to visit Iran and enjoy the rich historical culture they have." Such statements illustrate the openness to diversity needed by the twenty-first century enterprises.

## DISCUSSION

This examination of the *ABCs Model* focuses on its use to develop in management students an understanding of their own and other cultures in order to promote successful communication with diverse business interests nationally and internationally. This inquiry explored the question, "Does writing one's autobiography and comparing and contrasting it with the life story of an individual from another culture assist in understanding and appreciating cultural differences?"

From the identified patterns, three emerging themes seem to inform the theory that the *ABC's Model* could be a useful approach for developing an appreciation of cultural and national differences. The first theme is that management students seemed to gain a knowledge that illuminated thinking about their own lives. They looked at the past and could see how it related to present and future thinking. Secondly, through the interview and analyses processes, they also learned about people who they thought were quite different from themselves. Even though they discovered many differences, they also found numerous commonalities. When they studied differences, they gained understandings which lead to an appreciation of differences. Finally, participants could see the usefulness of this model in terms of preparing them for the modern business community.

In short, while completing the assignments associated with the *ABCs Model*, management students gained insights and awareness of themselves and others. They discovered, in many instances, that an individual's life experiences could be related to culture. Furthermore, the activities that future business people performed during the process gave them opportunities for divergent thinking, thus allowing them to examine difference and become aware of their own attitudes, feelings and behaviors. All are necessary to gain a multicultural perspective (Adler, 1992; Banks, 1993; Wallach, 1995).

Similar to previous research, this exploration demonstrated that the process of self discovery and inquiry into others' lives is an effective means for helping people change attitudes and consider possibilities for their future involvement in the business community (Joyce & Weil, 1986). These changes in thinking are necessary if management students are to become effective leaders in the national and international arenas. Recent studies have examined the writing and discussion of cultural autobiographies, interview and cross-cultural analyses (Spindler & Spindler, 1987), but no research has combined autobiography, interview and cross-cultural analysis to assist management students in their understanding of cultural similarities and differences. Therefore, use of the *ABCs Model* can provide management students with a process for their own professional use through which they can learn to communicate and connect with diverse populations.

The nature of the students whose experiences are recounted here prohibits generalizations beyond its participants. All of the students were enrolled at a small, private U.S. college. It is anticipated that the use of the *ABC's Model* with other student bodies will lead to more generalizable support of its use in management programs. In any case, the potential for the *ABCs Model* within the pedagogy of management education is very promising. Discussions are currently underway with professors at two large, public management programs in the United States with regard to how the *ABCs Model* might be used.

The *ABCs Model* is a procedure that may promote the development of business community so necessary in today's and future global economic environments. Similarly, the *ABCs Model* reinforces the promotion and communication with diverse business interests at home and abroad. A variety of cultural and ethnic groups within the business communities may be empowered to share and achieve in such a positive environment (Cummins, 1986).

The *ABCs Model* serves as a means for business leaders to develop comfort levels and communication when attempting to understand others in diverse settings. Various modifications of autobiographies, interviews and cultural analyses appear to be useful in preparing students for their futures in the business world. For example, modifications would permit its utilization for the training of all personnel who work with persons from other cultures, including expatriates. Since the *ABCs Model* dealt with issues associated with family life, communication, education, religion, work and socioeconomic status, management students can identify ways to connect cultural topics with business problem solving issues.

Finally, Schmidt's *ABCs Model* helps management students gain a most important insight—the realization that many elements of diversity, perceived as great dividers, may actually be powerful enhancers of creation and joy (Lowney, 2003; Osborne, 1996; Stimac & Hughes, 1995).

## NOTES

1. In an interview with Sharon Shinn published in *BizEd*.
2. AACSB is the abbreviated name for "AACSB International—The Association to Advance Collegiate Schools of Business."
3. The term "management" will be used to refer to academic programs designated as either management or business, as well as to their students and curricula. The term "business" will be reserved for enterprises of all economic and legal structures.
4. "Racioethnic" was coined by Taylor Cox in his 1990 article "Problems with Research by Organizational Scholars on Issues of Race and Ethnicity," *The Journal of Applied Behavioral Science, 26*(1), 5-23. Dr. Cox defined racioethnic as "biologically and/or culturally distinct groups" and subsequently this term has grown in usage to refer to both racial and ethnic diversity.
5. ABCs refers to A(utobiography), B(iography), C(ross-cultural analyses)s of Cultural Understanding and Communication.

## REFERENCES

Adler, N.J. (2002). *International dimensions of organizational behavior* (4th ed.). Cincinnati, OH: South-Western.

Adler, N.J. (1992). Managing globally competent people. *Academy of Management Executive, 6*(3).

Adler, N.J., & Ghadar, F. (1990a). International strategy from the perspective of people and culture: The North American context. In *Research in global business management* (Vol. 1, pp. 179-205). Stamford, CT: JAI Press.

Adler, N.J., & Ghadar, F. (1990b). Strategic human resource management: A global perspective. In R. Pieper (Ed.), *Human resource management: An international comparison*. Berlin: Walter de Gruyter.

Argyris, C. (1991, May-June). Teaching smart people how to learn. *Harvard Business Review*.

Argyris, C. (1976). Single-loop and double-loop models in research on decision making. *Administrative Science Quarterly, 21*, 363-377.

Au, K.H. (1993). *Literacy instruction in multicultural settings*. New York: Harcourt Brace.

Banks, J.A. (1997). *Teaching strategies for ethnic studies* (6th ed.). Boston: Allyn and Bacon.

Banks, J.A. (1994). *An introduction to multicultural education*. Boston: Allyn and Bacon.

Banks, J.A. (1993). The canon debate, knowledge construction, and multicultural education. *Educational Research, 22*(2), 4-14.

Bell, E.L., & Nkomo, S.M. (2001). *Our separate ways: Black and white women and the search for professional identity*. Boston: Harvard Business School Press.

Bhawauk, D.P.S., Podsiadlowski, A., Graf, J., & Triandis, H.C. (2002). Corporate strategies for managing diversity in the global workplace. In G.R. Ferris, M. R. Buckley, & D.B. Fedor (Eds.), *Human resource management: Perspectives, context, functions, and outcomes* (4th ed.). Upper Saddle River, NJ: Prentice-Hall.

Brannen, M.Y. (1996). Ethnographic international management research. In B. J. Punnett & O. Shenkar (Eds.), *Handbook of international management research* (pp. 115-143). Cambridge, MA: Blackwell.

Britzman, D. (1986). Cultural myths in the making of a teacher: Biography and social structure in teacher education. *Harvard Educational Review, 56*, 442-456.

Bucher, R. D. (2000). *Diversity consciousness*. Upper Saddle River, NJ: Prentice-Hall.

Clifford, J. (1988). *The predicament of culture: Twentieth-century ethnography, literature, and art*. Cambridge, MA: Harvard University Press.

Cochran-Smith, M. (1995). Uncertain allies: Understanding the boundaries or race and teaching. *Harvard Educational Review, 65*(4), 541-570.

Cochran-Smith, M., & Lytle, S. (1992) Interrogating cultural diversity: Inquiry and action. *Journal of Teacher Education, 43*, 104-111.

Cox, T. Jr. (1993). *Cultural diversity in organizations*. San Francisco: Berrett-Koehler.

Cox, T. Jr. (1990). Problems with research by organizational scholars on issues of race and ethnicity. *The Journal of Applied Behavioral Science, 26*(1), 5-23.

Cox, T. Jr., & Beale, R.L. (1997). *Developing competency to manage diversity.* San Francisco: Berrett-Koehler.

Crapanzano, V. (1990). On self characterization. In J.W. Stigler, R.A. Shweder, & G. Herdt (Eds.), *Cultural psychology* (pp. 401-423). Cambridge: Cambridge University Press.

Creed, W.E.D., & Scully, M.A. (2000). Song of ourselves: Employees' deployment of social identity in workplace encounters. *Journal of Management Inquiry, 9*(4), 391-413.

Cummins, J. (1986). Empowering minority students: A framework for intervention. *Harvard Educational Review, 56,* 18-36.

Day, J.C., & Jamieson, A. (2003). *School enrollment 2000.* Retrieved December 10, 2004 from *http://www.census.gov/prod/2003pubs/c2kbr-26.pdf,* August.

De Cieri, H., & Dowling, P.J. (1999). Strategic human resource management in multinational enterprises. In P.N. Wright, L.D. Dyer, J.W. Boudreau, & G.T. Milkovich (Eds.), *Research in personnel and human resource management* (Suppl. 4, pp. 305-328). Stamford, CT: JAI Press.

Delpit, L. (1995). *Other people's children: Cultural conflict in the classroom.* New York: The New Press.

Doz, Y.L., Barlett, C.A., & Prahalad, C.K. (1981). Global competitive pressure vs. host country demands: Managing the tensions in MNCs. *California Management Review, 23,* 63-74.

Emig, J. (1971). Writing as a mode of learning. *College Composition and Communication, 28,* 122-128.

Enz, C A. (1992). The culture of social science research. In. P. Frost & R. Stablein (Eds.), *Doing exemplary research* (pp. 36-42). Newbury Park, CA: Sage.

Erez, M., & Earley, P.C. (1993). *Culture, self-identity, and work.* New York: Oxford.

Florio-Ruane, S. (1994). The future teachers' autobiography club: Preparing educators to support literacy learning in culturally diverse classrooms. *English Education, 26,* 52-66.

Finkbeiner, C., & Koplin, C. (2002). A cooperative approach for facilitating intercultural education. *Reading Online, 6*(3), New Literacies. http://www.readingonline.org/newliteracies/lit_index.asp?HREF=/newliteracies/finkbeiner    . Newark, DE: International Reading Association.

Finkbeiner, C. (2004). Cooperation and collaboration in a foreign language teacher training program: The LMR plus model. In E. Cohen, C. Brody, & M. Sapon-Shevin (Eds.), *Learning to teach with cooperative learning: Challenges in teacher education* (pp. 111-127). Albany: State University of New York Press.

Gallos, J.V., & Ramsey, V.J. (1996). *Teaching diversity: Listening to the soul, speaking from the heart.* San Francisco: Jossey-Bass.

Geertz, C. (1973). *The interpretation of cultures.* New York: Basic Books.

Gentile, M.C. (1996). *Managerial excellence through diversity.* Chicago: Irwin.

Gentile, M.C. (Ed.). (1994). *Differences that work.* Boston: Harvard Business Review Books.

Gergen, K.J. (1990). Social understanding and the inscription of self. In J.W. Stigler, R.A. Shweder, & G. Herdt (Eds.), *Cultural psychology* (pp. 569-606). Cambridge: Cambridge University Press.

Gladwin, T., & Walter, I. (1980, Summer). How multinationals can manage social and political forces. *Journal of Business Strategy*, pp. 54-68.

Harpaz, I. (1996). International management survey research. In B.J. Punnett & O. Shenkar (Eds.), *Handbook of international management research* (pp. 37-62). Cambridge, MA: Blackwell.

Heath, S.B. (1983). *Ways with words: Language life and work in communities and class-rooms.* Cambridge: Cambridge University Press.

Hofstede, G. (1991). *Cultures and organizations: Software of the mind.* London: McGraw-Hill.

Hofstede, G. (1984). The cultural relativity of the quality of life concept. *Academy of Management Review, 9*(3), 389-398.

Hofstede, G. (1983). The cultural relativity of organizational theories. *Journal of International Business Studies, 14*(2), 75-90.

Hofstede, G. (1980a). *Culture's consequences: International differences in work-related values.* London: Sage.

Hofstede, G. (1980b, Summer). Motivation, leadership, and organization: Do American theories apply abroad? *Organizational Dynamics*, pp. 42-63.

Inkpen, A. (1995) Organizational learning and international joint ventures. *Journal of International Management, 1*(2), 165-198.

Johnston, W.B., & Packer, A.E. (1987) *Workforce 2000: Work and workers for the twenty-first century.* Indianapolis, IN: Hudson Institute.

Joyce, B., & Weil, M. (1986). *Models of teaching* (3rd ed.). Engelwood Cliffs, NJ: Prentice-Hall.

Ladson-Billings, G. (1994). *The dreamkeepers: Successful teachers of African American children.* San Francisco: Jossey-Bass.

Laurent, A. (1983). The cultural diversity of Western conceptions of management. *International Studies of Management in Organization, 13*(2), 75-96.

Lincoln, J.R., & Kalleberg, A.L. (1990). *Culture, control, and commitment.* Cambridge: Cambridge University Press.

Lowney, C. (2003). *Heroic leadership.* Chicago: Loyola Press.

Manz, C.C., & Neck, C.P. (2004). *Mastering self-leadership* (3rd ed.). Upper Saddle River, NJ: Prentice-Hall.

Manz, C.C., & Sims, H.P., Jr. (1987). Leading workers to lead themselves: The external leadership of self-managing work teams. *Administrative Science Quarterly, 32*, 106-128.

Manz, C.C., & Sims, H.P., Jr. (1991). Superleadership: Beyond the myth of heroic leadership. *Organizational Dynamics, 19*(4).

Markus, H., & Kitayama, S. (1991). Culture and self: Implications for cognition, emotion and motivation. *Psychological Review, 98*, 224-253.

McCaleb, S.P. (1994). *Building communities of learners: A collaboration among teachers, students, families and community.* New York: St. Martin's Press.

Nieto, S. (1995). *Affirming diversity: The sociopolitical context of multicultural education* (2nd ed.). New York: Longman.

Noordhoff, K., & Kleinfeld, J. (1993). Preparing teachers for multicultural class-rooms. *Teaching and Teacher Education, 9*(1), 27-39.

O'Neil, J. (1997). *Leadership Aikido: 6 business practices to turn around your life.* New York: Harmony.

Osborne, A.B. (1996). Practice into theory into practice: Culturally relevant pedagogy for students we have marginalized and normalized. *Anthropology and Education Quarterly, 27*(3), 284-314.

Paley, V.G. (1989). *White teacher.* Cambridge, MA: Harvard University Press.

Pattnaik, J. (1997). Cultural stereotypes and preservice education: Moving beyond our biases. *Equity and Excellence in Education, 30*(3), 40-50.

Pfeffer, J. (1994). *Competitive advantage through people.* New York: McGraw-Hill.

Porter, M.E. (1990). *The competitive advantage of nations.* New York: Free Press.

Powell, G.M., & Graves, L.M. (2003). *Women and men in management* (3rd ed.). Thousand Oaks, CA: Sage.

Progoff, I. (1975). *At a journal workshop: The basic text and guide for using the intensive journal.* New York: Dialogue House Library.

Punnett, B.J. (1994). *Experiencing international business and management.* Belmont, CA: Wadsworth.

Ronen, S., & Shekar, O. (1985). Clustering countries on attitudinal dimensions: A Review and synthesis. *Academy of Management Review, 10*(3), 435-454.

Schein, E.H. (1994, Winter). How can organizations learn faster? The challenge of entering the green room. *Sloan Management Review.*

Schmidt, P.R. (1998a). The ABCs of cultural understanding and communication. *Equity and Excellence in Education, 31*(2), 28-38.

Schmidt, P.R. (1998b). The *ABC's Model*: Teachers connect home and school. In T. Shanahan & F.V. Rodriguez-Brown (Eds.), *National reading conference yearbook 47* (pp. 194-208). Chicago: National Reading Conference.

Schmidt, P.R. (1999). Know thyself and understand others. *Language Arts, 76*(4), 332-340.

Schmidt, P.R. (2000). Emphasizing differences to build cultural understandings. In V. Risko & K. Bromley (Eds.), *Collaboration for diverse learners: Viewpoints and practices.* Newark, DE: IRA.

Schmidt, P.R. (2001). The power to empower. In P. Ruggiano Schmidt & P.B. Mosenthal (Eds.), *Reconceptualizing literacy in the new age of multiculturalism and pluralism.* Greenwich, CT: Information Age Publishing.

Senge. P. (1990). *The fifth discipline.* New York: Bantam.

Shinn, S. (2002, July-August). At the top of her game. *BizEd*, pp. 18-21.

Sjoberg, G., & Kuhn, K. (1989). Autobiography and organizations: Theoretical and methodological issues. *Journal of Applied Behavioral Science, 25*(4), 309-326.

Snyder, T. D., Hoffman, C.M., & Geddes, C.M. (1997). *Digest of education statistics.* Washington, DC: National Center of Education Statistics, Officer of Educational Research and Improvement.

Spindler, G., & Spindler, L. (1987). *The interpretive ethnography of education: At home and abroad.* Hillsdale, NJ: Lawrence Erlbaum Associates.

Stimac, M., & Hughes, H.W. (1995). Student reflections on cultural autobiography: A promising curricular practice. *Multicultural Education*, pp. 18-20.

Tatum, B. (1992). Talking about race, learning about race: The application of racial identity development theory. *Harvard Educational Review, 62*(1), 1-24.

Thomas, D.A., & Gabarro, J.J. (1999). *Breaking through: The making of minority executives in corporate America.* Boston: Harvard Business School Press.

Thomas, K.M. (2004). *Diversity dynamics in the workplace*. Belmont, CA: Wadsworth.

Thomas, R.R., Jr. (1996). *Redefining diversity*. New York: AMACOM.

Thomas, R.R., Jr. (1994). From affirmative action to affirming diversity. In M.C. Gentile (Ed.), *Differences that work* (pp. 27-46). Boston: Harvard Business Review Books.

Trompenaars, A., Hampden-Turner, C., & Trompenaars, F. (1998). *Riding the Waves of culture: Understanding cultural diversity in global business* (2nd ed.). New York: Richard D. Irwin.

Trompenaars, F. (1994). *Riding the Waves of culture: Understanding diversity in global business*. New York: Richard D. Irwin.

Trompenaars, F., & Hampden-Turner, C. (2004). *Managing people across cultures*. Chichester: Capstone.

Trueba, H.T., Jacobs, L., & Kirton, E. (1990). *Cultural conflict and adaptation: The case of the Hmong children in American society*. New York: The Falmer Press.

Tung, R.L. (1995). Strategic human resource challenge: Managing diversity. *The International Journal of Human Resource Management, 6*(3), 482-493.

Vygotsky, L.S. (1978). *Mind in society: The development of higher mental process*. Cambridge, MA: Harvard University Press.

Wallach, K.M. (1995). Multicultural education: Social action vs. philosophical orientation. In C.A. Grant (Ed.), *National Association for Multicultural Education 1993 and 1994 Proceedings* (pp. 49-55). San Francisco: Caddo Gap Press.

Washburn, D.E., Brown, N.L., & Abbott, R.W. (1996). *Multicultural education in the United States*. Bloomsburg, PA: Inquiry International.

Willis, A.I., & Meacham, S.J. (1997). Break point: The challenges of teaching multicultural education courses. *Journal of the Assembly for Expanded Perspectives on Learning, 2*, 40-49.

Xu, H. (1998, December 2-5). *Preservice teachers and the ABC's*. Symposium paper presented at the Annual Meeting of the National Reading Conference, Chicago.

Yinger, R. (1985). Journal writing as a learning tool. *Volga Review, 87*(5), 21-33.

# AFTERWORD

## The Future of the ABC's

**Greta Nagel**

### INTRODUCTION

Use of the ABC's strategy has been effective in multiple contexts over time. As the authors before me, in this volume, have shown through their fine and varied research reports, it is a strong and useful tool for promoting communication about personal and cultural similarities and differences. These ten chapters stand upon almost a decade of scholarly publications and presentations, initially inspired by the work of Patricia Ruggiano Schmidt (1998a-c, 1999, 2000, 2001, 2005) and adapted in Europe by Claudia Finkbeiner (2004), Finkbeiner and Koplin (2001, 2002) and others in this volume. The adaptations presented in this volume remind readers that "it" works with students and teachers from elementary schools through universities, with groups as small as two individuals to large roomfuls, in face-to-face proximity and, now, in the electronic media. The process can create deep, personal commitments and those of us who have led it, participated in it, and witnessed it in

*ABC's of Cultural Understanding and Communication:*
*National and International Adaptations,* 265–271
Copyright © 2006 by Information Age Publishing

action, have also seen its magic. But, of course, as a human endeavor, it is not foolproof.

In producing these invited words to bring closure to this volume, I hope to call upon some reasonable insights about the ABC's future. I also hope you will consider this to be a bit of personal chat after reading the book. Although predicting the future, like predicting the weather, is a risky and imprecise business. I am delighted and honored to give it a try. I admit that I am predisposed to advocating the use of the model, but beyond my enthusiasm, I think the answers to three questions will help make my case and point to expanded use of the model in educational contexts and beyond. The questions: *Why is the ABC's process effective? How does it intersect with the predictions of futurists? How can it find a niche in the over-committed schedules of busy teachers and professors?*

## WHY IS THE PROCESS EFFECTIVE?

Certainly one reason the ABC's "work" is that its components mirror tried-and-true procedures for making friends. Although there is a rich literature on friendship (e.g., Meyer et al., 1998), I include here only very key elements.

First, is the phenomenon of self-disclosure. We find that the sharing of secrets is an indicator of trust, hence, of friendship. As individuals participate in the ABC's process, creating their autobiographies and responding to their partners, they are faced with decisions about what to reveal and how much to say about the event, relationship, preference, once it has been told.

Second, is the overt seeking of common traits. When strangers meet, even only briefly, they seek commonalities through "Do you know?" inquiries. When partners in the ABC's process meet, they find exquisite delight in discovering the many ways they are the same. Only two examples, from a volume of potential responses: "Oh, when I was child, I always spent hours listening to music too," and "No kidding! I had four sisters too!"

Third, virtually all advice about communication and the development of relationships incorporates knowing how to listen. Why? The satisfaction of being listened to promotes a loving attitude toward the other. But in addition to advocating listening, Dale Carnegie (1990/1937) seems to have said the rest. I think most of my fellow readers will recall his famous work, *How to Win Friends and Influence People.* It has been a bestseller in an ever-repeating publication since the 1930s. His language pulls no punches.

### Six Ways to Make People Like You (Carnegie, 1990/1937)

1. Become genuinely interested in other people.
2. Smile.
3. Remember that a person's name is to that person the sweetest and most important sound in any language.
4. Be a good listener. Encourage others to talk about themselves.
5. Talk in terms of the other person's interests.
6. Make the other person feel important—and do it sincerely.

Another way the process gets at friendship is the way it promotes visits into one another's culture. Learning one another's personal stories, living the daily life, experiencing the physical context is like being an exchange student in another nation, always said to be a life-changing experience. But seldom do we enter the homes of those truly different from us across the divide of our own socioeconomic and ethnic neighborhoods. The ABC's get us there. It helps us to pay these visits without the assistance of autos or airlines. Just as powerful, as neuroscientists tell us, is the process of visualization. A well-traveled member of the world wide Friendship Force organization once described her experiences this way, "We have slept in the luxurious beds of mansions and felt our feet dangle off the ends of beds in crowded city apartments, but we have all come to understand and care for each other." An ABC's participant can do it all, but a lot less expensively.

I also find that a group dynamics model for motivation can explain why individuals persist in any group relations. Surely we are all seeking ways to enter relationships wisely and sustain them in satisfactory ways. My own investigations (Nagel, 2001), along with those of at least eleven others, confirm that the key interacting sociopsychological components are knowledge, power, and affection (KPA), all of which are evident in the ABC's. Its activities acknowledge participants at their individualized levels of knowledge. Each person knows (K) his or her life well, and although early remembrances may always be strong, other recollections always come forth. A study of self is also quite engaging. Participants in the ABC's process also have individualized power (P) to decide whether to share (or not) the details of their lives and to frame the formats by which they will be shared. The third component, affection (A), is promoted by the process, because the ways in which participants listen to one another signify caring. The ways in which partners involve themselves with each other registers as something beyond mere tolerance. I have seen even "difficult" students rise to the expectations of the process.

## HOW DOES IT INTERSECT WITH THE PREDICTIONS OF FUTURISTS?

*Number One (my placement):*   We need to build adaptability to change.

Need for self-knowledge and flexible thinking is the lifeblood of situations in which people must live and work together. The importance of "EQ" over IQ, as described by Daniel Goleman (1995) in *Emotional Intelligence*, lets us know that many outcomes of the ABC's help prepare individuals to build their repertoire of change skills.

*Number Two (really big):*   We are experiencing the greatest change in technology.

As a matter of fact, it is a curve of exponential change! Since 1959, the capacity of a chip has doubled 29 times, actually meaning a multiplication by 400 million. In contrast, since the same era, support for research and work in human relations has actually dropped off, dramatically but not exponentially. We have all witnessed the expansion of communication through internet access, email, phoning and messaging, visual arts and gaming is the internet really the great equalizer? Well, we seem to be creating new collectives of friendship, and allowing every voice to lift and sing ... well, at least blog (to the tune of 15 million and growing).

Futurist Joel Garreau (2005), talks about genetics, robotics, information, nanotechnology and even gives us a mnemonic device, GRIN, to help us remember the explosion of work in these areas. Now, with technology, we can even replicate the strengths of superheroes through x-ray vision, telescopic sight, and suits that make us super strong. We can even alter our minds and memories in positive ways. In Radical Evolution, he takes us a step further through (fictional) use of internal wireless modems that download information directly into the brain. Still, despite our dynamism, we suffer the frailties of the human condition. Technology has amplified the human mind and body, but what about the spirit?

*Number Three (my favorite, for obvious reasons to those who know of my interests in Taoism):*   We struggle to provide the *yin* to the overwhelming *yang* of technological growth. Adding High touch to complement high tech is the current thinking, beyond *Megatrends*, of futurist John Naisbitt (2001). Efforts are underway and growing to make things simple to temper immense complexity, to slow down to offset the dizzying speed, to engage in reflection to soothe the intense activity, to find time for craftsmanship to offset the mode of "faster and cheaper," to cherish preservation to counter obliteration, to lessen needs in order to make irrelevant the desires of consumerism. Efforts to instill high touch coincide with the ABC's; it is not just a microtrend.

Principles of group dynamics also support the importance of the one-to-one, face-to-face meeting. The initiating episode from which the traditional ABC's process grows is an interpersonal connection between two individuals, no more. Efforts to recognize and understand difference are best achieved face-to-face, although electronic contacts between earnest and motivated individuals may achieve appropriate disclosure. Distance relationships always seem to yearn for proximity and touch. And it is from two-person kernel that further benefits grow for the larger groups involved.

## HOW CAN IT FIND AN APPROPRIATE NICHE IN THE OVER-COMMITTED SCHEDULES OF BUSY TEACHERS AND PROFESSORS?

Although cutting to pragmatics might be nice here, it is important for teachers and their administrators to examine their perceptions of the purposes of education. Teaching strategies flourish only when nested in the appropriate philosophical incubator. An ABC's advocate sees learning as preparation for life, not just preparing for the next grade (on a paper, on a report card, or the next level of education). Only then will the ABC's be seen as a desired technique to reach for positive interrelationships. It is important, therefore, that teachers try the model out and analyze the dynamics of their own contexts. A teacher's behaviors and instructional activities, along with the general school and classroom climate, can work together to enhance or deflate the effects of the ABC's. It may never get off the ground in the hands of the wrong person(s).

Next, out of political and (sometimes) personal attentiveness to standards, I suggest that is fortunate that there are districts and states that have labored over, and published, standards that embrace the workings of the ABC's, not by name (ABC's), but by outcome. The most likely arenas are Language Arts and History/Social Studies, and in addition to the ABC's having plenty of motivation and opportunity for speaking, listening, reading and writing, there are also many reasons for learners to set out on authentic sidebar quests to discover more about: When was that? Where was that? and Why was that? I have seen adult students poring over maps to see where in the world they both came from.

Fortunately, the ABC's is adaptable. Appropriate character education must include personalization, individualization to really make a difference, and that leads to extra expenditures of time on practices. Delivery of standard curriculum at a standard pace in order to ratchet up group test scores doesn't coincide with curricular "luxuries" like human relations and the arts. As with many processes involving humans, there are stops and starts and pitfalls, as long key traits of the process are kept, participants will reap the benefits. The multiple approaches and insights discussed in this volume should help fellow readers to augment and refine ideas for their own ABC's journeys. Finding time seems to come easily to committed individuals. We have the capacity to multitask, don't we?

And, last, as well as least (only because this one is short), it is memorable. What's not to like about ABC's? It is even easier to remember than KWL or SQ3R (or KPA, for that matter.) Teachers can relate.


## CLOSING


As more and more educators find ways to incorporate the ABC's Model in their learning environments, they will also come to appreciate its power. They will see that the strategy can be carried forward into other contexts within their lives as well. Development of self-knowledge, learning more about one another, and exercising flexible thinking should hardly be limited to academic settings. Coming to recognize and understand differences while forging positive relationships can be goals for families, businesses, religious groups, book clubs, social organizations, ... and political entities.

From personal settings in my own life, adaptations of the ABC's have, indeed, made a difference. At a large, intergenerational family reunion, individuals who had not seen each other for years—or perhaps never— had a chance to meet in person and found delight in their new relationships because of pair-share-compare memories activity based on the philosophy of the ABC's. Participation in a long-term ABC's by members of our book club, *Wine and Wisdom*, allowed me to know far more about my husband's youth than I'd ever known before, in more than thirty years of marriage, helping me to see several of his attributes in a fascinating, developmental, light. How treasured those written words became when he died not long afterward.

I believe that the *ABC's of Cultural Understanding and Communication* is ready for wider use in other parts of society, as well as in the broader world. Crossing cultures isn't limited to relationships between ethnic groups or nations. Building understandings across genders, ages, regionalisms, abilities, religions, sexual orientations, or careers can reveal understandings and unravel misunderstandings. I hope other readers of this book will agree that this strategy is certainly important to add to their repertoire of techniques for developing intercultural knowledge. As Mark Twain once wrote, "To a man with a hammer, everything looks like a nail." To possess many tools allows the user to develop broader and deeper perceptions of the world. And, after all, nobody can have too many tools.

# REFERENCES

Carnegie, D. (1990/1937). *How to win friends and influence people*. New York: Pocket.

Finkbeiner, C., & Koplin, C. (2001). Fremdverstehensprozesse und interkulturelle Prozesse als Forschungsgegenstand. In A. Müller-Hartmann & M. Schocker-v. Ditfurth (Eds.), *Qualitative Forschung im Bereich Fremdsprachen lehren und lernen* (pp. 114-136). Tübingen: Narr.

Finkbeiner, C., & Koplin, C. (2002). A cooperative approach for facilitating intercultural education. *Reading Online, 6*(3). Retrieved July 25, 2005, from http://www.readingonline.org/newliteracies/lit_index.asp?HREF=finkbeiner/index.html

Finkbeiner, C. (2004). Cooperation and collaboration in a foreign language teacher training program: The LMR plus model. In E. Cohen, C. Brody, & M. Sapon-Shevin (Eds.), *Learning to teach with cooperative learning: Challenges in teacher education* (pp. 111-127). Albany: State University of New York.

Garreau, J. (2005). *Radical evolution: The promise and peril of enhancing our minds, our bodies—and what it means to be human*. New York: Doubleday.

Goleman, D. (1995). *Emotional intelligence*. New York: Bantam.

Meyer, L.H. Meyer, Park, H.S. Park, Grenot-Scheyer, M., Schwartz, I., & Harry, B. (Eds.). (1998). *Making friends*. Baltimore, MD: Paul H. Brooks.

Nagel, G.K. (2001). *Effective grouping for literacy instruction*. Boston: Allyn & Bacon.

Naisbitt, J. (2001). *High tech/high touch: The co-evolution of technology and culture*. New York: Broadway Books.

Schmidt, P. R. (1998a/2002). *Cultural conflict and struggle: Literacy learning in a kindergarten program*. New York: Peter Lang.

Schmidt, P.R. (1998b). The ABC's of cultural understanding and communication. *Equity & Excellence in Education, 31*(20), 28-38.

Schmidt, P.R. (1998c). The ABC's model: Teachers connect home and school. In T. Shanahan & F.V. Rodriguez-Brown(Eds.), *National reading conference yearbook 47*. (pp. 194-208.) Chicago, IL: National Reading Conference.

Schmidt, P.R. (1999). Know thyself and understand others. *Language Arts, 76*,(4), 332-340.

Schmidt, P.R. (2000). Emphasizing differences to build cultural understandings. In V. Risko & K. Bromley (Eds.), *Collaboration for diverse learners: Viewpoints and practices*. Newark, DE: IRA.

Schmidt, P.R. (2001). The power to empower. In P.R. Schmidt & P.B. Mosenthal (Eds.), *Reconceptualizing literacy in the new age of multiculturalism and pluralism*. Greenwich,CT: Information Age Press.

Schmidt, P.R. (2005). *Preparing educators to communicate and connect with families and communities*. Greenwich, CT: Information Age Publishing.

# ABOUT THE AUTHORS

**Patricia A. Edwards** is a professor of literacy at Michigan State University, Lansing, Michigan, and is the 2006 president elect for the National Reading Conference. She is a world-renown scholar, as well as a recognized outstanding teacher, with numerous articles and chapters in the most prestigious volumes and journals. Her most recent book, *Children's Literacy Development: Making it Happen Through School, Family, and community Involvement* (2004), published by Allyn and Bacon has added significantly to the field of literacy learning and academic achievement in high poverty areas. Dr. Edwards inspires with her vast knowledge of literacy teaching and learning and great love for humanity.

**Sylvia Fehling** is a research assistant and teacher trainer at the University of Kassel, Germany (teaching English as a foreign language and foreign language research and intercultural communication). Additionally, she is a teacher at a grammar school in Kassel. Her research interests include Content and Language Integrated Learning (CLIL), language awareness, intercultural learning, evaluation. Dr. Fehling's dissertation, titled, *Language Awareness und bilingualer Unterricht: Eine komparative Studie*, was published by Peter Lang, Frankfurt in 2005. Dr. Fehling may be contacted by e-mail at sfhling@unikassel.de/ or http://www.uni-kassel.de/~sfehling/

**Claudia Finkbeiner** is a professor in the English department, School of Modern Languages, at the University of Kassel, Germany. Her field is applied linguistics with a strong emphasis on foreign language research and teaching English as a foreign, second, or other language. Her research and teaching concentrates on literacy, intercultural education, interest and motivation, learning strategies in reading, holistic learning, multiple intelligence activities, cooperative learning, content-based language learning, and computer-assisted language learning. She has conducted research on intercultural learning issues using qualitative and quantitative methods in the university setting since 1989. In 2001, Claudia won a Multicultural Issues Travel Award from the National Reading Conference and continues to serve as a world field officer for NRC. She can be reached by e-mail at cfink@uni-kassel.de ; http://www.uni-kassel.de/flul

**La Verne H. Higgins** is an associate professor in the Department of Industrial Relations and Human Resource Management at Le Moyne College, Syracuse, New York, where she also teaches in the undergraduate and graduate business programs. Her research interests include human resource management in highly competitive industries, strategic international human resource management, the impact of intercultural dynamics on human resource practices, and the pedagogy of international management education. Dr. Higgins received her BA and MBA from the University of Minnesota. After more than a decade as a manager, she continued her education at the University of Oregon where she completed a doctorate in human resource management and international management.

**Andrea Izzo** is an assistant professor at Gallaudet University, Washington, DC, where she teaches courses in literacy development and language arts methods as well as practicum and student teaching seminars. Before coming to Gallaudet, Dr. Izzo was an assistant professor at Le Moyne College, in Syracuse, New York. In that position, she was involved in field-based collaborative research on developing culturally relevant literacy lessons for diverse populations. Before earning her PhD in curriculum and instruction at the University of New Orleans, in New Orleans, Louisiana, she taught in elementary public and private schools. Her current research interests include classroom-based action research for literacy learning and peer evaluation by pre-service teachers. She enjoys long distance bicycle touring,, French fries and sushi (but not on the same plate), and sunshine.

**Markus Knierim** is a doctoral student and research assistant at the University of Kassel, Germany. His current research focuses on task-based language learning in blended learning environments, with a special emphasis on sociocultural factors and students' interaction. He has been involved in numerous e-learning and intercultural online exchange projects. Mr. Knierim may be contacted at the following email: mknierim@uni-kassel.de

**Stacey Leftwich**, an associate professor at Rowan University, Glassboro, New Jersey and a native of the southern part of the state. Dr. Leftwich began her career as an elementary classroom teacher. Currently, she teaches literacy courses to both undergraduate and graduate education students and also works closely with preservice and inservice classroom teachers as a Professional Development School liaison in the Glassboro school district. Dr. Leftwich is an active presenter at state, national, and international conferences. Her area of study includes using culturally diverse children's literature in the classroom to enhance literacy instruction.

**Midge Madden**, an associate professor at Rowan University, Glasboro, New Jersey, brings over thirty years of experience to the teaching of reading and writing. She currently teaches literacy courses to undergraduate and graduate teacher education students and works closely with elementary classroom teachers as literacy coach and staff developer in New Jersey, Virginia, and Maryland. Dr. Madden presents frequently at state, national, and international conferences. She has recently co-authored and published a book on writing entitled, *Teaching the Elements of Powerful Writing*, and is currently working with children in Guatemala on a visual literacy and "testimonio" writing project.

**Greta Nagel** is a professor in the Department of Teacher Education at California State University, Long Beach, where she teaches courses related to literacy and the historical, philosophical, and social foundations of education. She has been a classroom teacher, reading specialist, and school administrator. Nagel obtained her PhD from the Claremont Graduate University, jointly with San Diego State University, and her research interests are related to social contexts for literacy development, as well as to museums as learning centers. She is the author of *The Tao of Teaching, The Tao of Parenting* (both published by Penguin/Plume), and *Effective Grouping for Literacy Instruction* (Allyn & Bacon), and has published numerous articles in the field of education. Her current work in progress is *When Will We Ever Learn? The Story of the Great New Museum of Teaching and Learning*. During her career she has received a variety of awards, including the IRA Celebrate Literacy award, a Claremont dissertation grant for *Good Groups: The Search for Social Equity and Instructional Excellence Through First-Grade Literacy Groupings*, and the Outstanding Alumna, California State University Reading Program. Dr. Nagel may be contacted at (e-mail nagel@csulb.edu).

**Judith M. Osetek** is an English as a second language teacher for the Oswego City School District. In 1990, upon completing her undergraduate program at the State University of New York at Binghamton, Ms. Osetek worked in the children's services divisions in both Oswego and Rensselaer Counties before returning to school to complete her master of science in education: elementary, pre-K-6 at SUNY Oswego. She received her TESOL (Teaching English to Students of Other Languages) certification from Le Moyne College in 2003. Ms. Osetek is a strong proponent of the home and school communication for teachers, students, and families. Her interests are in early literacy intervention and connecting students' cultural backgrounds with their social and academic development to improve their educational experience. Furthermore, she actively promotes character education in the elementary school setting and is currently in the Master of Science in Education: Literacy Birth - Grade 6 program at SUNY Oswego.

**Jyotsna Pattnaik** is a professor of early childhood education at California State University, Long Beach. She was a teacher and teacher educator in India and has obtained her Doctorate in Education degree in the United States. Her research explores issues of equity for children, national language policies, early childhood education, and global child advocacy. She is the guest editor for the 2005 international focus issue of the journal, *Childhood Education* (Theme for the issue: Education of Aboriginal Children: Global Perspectives and Practices). She has authored/coauthored more than 20 publications (book chapters and journal articles). Her recent publications include: Childhood in South Asia: A Critical Look at Issues, Policies, and Programs (Editor: Jyotsna Pattnaik); A Critical Examination of India's "Language Policy" in Primary Education (Book: Contemporary Perspectives on Language Education and Language Policy in Early Childhood Education. Editors: Saracho & Spodek); Global Pets: Bonding with and Caring for Animals Across Cultures and Countries (Book: The World's Children and their Companion Animals: Developmental and Educational Implications of the Child/Pet Bond: Editor: Mary Renck Jalongo); Multicultural Belief: A Global or Domain-Specific Construct? An Analysis of Four Case Studies. (Book: Reconceptualizing multicultural literacy and pluralism for the 21st century. Editors: Schmidt & Mosenthal). Learning About the "Other:" Building A Case For Intercultural Understanding Among Minority Children (Journal: *Childhood Education*); Multicultural Literacy Starts From Home: Supporting Parental Involvement in Multicultural Education (Journal: *Childhood Education*); On Behalf of Their Animal Friends: Involving Children in Animal Advocacy (Journal: *Childhood Education*).

**Patricia Ruggiano Schmid**t is a professor of literacy at Le Moyne College, a Jesuit Institution in Syracuse, New York. After 20 years as a classroom teacher and reading specialist, Schmidt earned her doctorate from the Syracuse University Reading and Language Arts Department. Observing and interviewing elementary and secondary teachers who were interested in improving the teaching and learning of students in diverse school settings, inspired her to design the model known as the *ABC's of Cultural Understanding and Communication*. Her numerous articles, books, and book chapters concerning multicultural literacy and culturally relevant pedagogy explore and present research related to the ABC's Model. Recently, Dr. Schmidt, with the help of grants from New York State and the International Reading Association, has been preparing teachers with the ABC's Model in order to close the achievement gap in schools with ethnically, racially, and linguistically diverse populations. Her latest edited book, *Preparing Teachers to Communicate and Connect With Families and Communities*, serves as a powerful resource for in-service programs in rural and urban high poverty schools. Dr. Schmidt may be contacted by email: Schmidt@lemoyne.edu

**Eva Wilden** is a doctoral student and research assistant at the University of Kassel, Germany. She holds a degree in teaching history and English as a foreign language from the University of Duisburg-Essen, Germany. Eva Wilden has ben involved in various projects using computers and the Internet for learning and teaching. Her current research focuses on intercultural learning in online exchange projects. She may be contacted at eva.wilden@uni-kassel.de or www.evawilden.de

**Shelley Hong Xu** is an associate professor of teacher education at the California State University, Long Beach. She earned her doctorate at the University of Nevada, Las Vegas and her research includes preparing teachers for diversity and integrating multimedia texts into literacy curriculum. Her numerous book chapters and articles appear in literacy volumes and journals. Her most recent works *Teaching Early Literacy* (2005), with Barone and Mallette, published by Guilford Press, and *Trading Cards to Comic Strips: Popular Culture Texts and Literacy Learning in Grades K-8* (2005), published by the International Reading Association add to the body of research on successful literacy learning and development. Dr. Xu has the distinct honor of being the Essay Book Review Editor for *Reading Research Quarterly*, one of the premier literacy journals in the world.

# INDEX

Printed in the United States
53096LVS00001B/19-63